The Forms of Youth

Stephen Burt

The Forms

of Youth

TWENTIETH-CENTURY POETRY

AND ADOLESCENCE

Columbia
University
Press
New York

Columbia University Press
Publishers Since 1893
New York   Chichester, West Sussex
Copyright © 2007 Columbia University Press

Library of Congress Cataloging-in-Publication Data
   Burt, Stephen, 1971–
     The Forms of youth : twentieth-century poetry and adolescence / Stephen Burt.
        p. c.m
     Includes bibliographical references (p.   ).
     ISBN 978–231–14142–0 (acid-free paper) — ISBN 978–0–231–51202–2 (e-book)
     1. English poetry—20th century—History and criticism.   2. American poetry—20th
 century—History and criticism.   3. Adolescence in literature.   4. English-speaking
   countries—Intellectual life—20th century.   I. Title.

   PR605.A33B87   2007
   821′.909354—dc22

                                                                        2007003447

∞

Columbia University Press books are printed on permanent
and durable acid-free paper.

This book is printed on paper with recycled content.

Designed by Lisa Hamm

Printed in the United States of America
c 10 9 8 7 6 5 4 3 2 1

To Nathan Bennett Burt

Contents

The Forms of Youth

Introduction

W HAT WAS THE most important new word of the
twentieth century? In December 1999, one authority
on the English language picked "teenager" (Cornwell, "The Words of the Decade," ii).[1] Forty years earlier, the controversial
historian Philippe Ariès called "adolescence ... the privileged age ... of the
twentieth" century, as childhood was the privileged age of the nineteenth
(32).[2] Teenagers are adolescents of a particular era, of a particular kind;
other kinds appear in other eras. The *Oxford English Dictionary* defines adolescence simply as the "period between childhood and manhood or womanhood." While earlier thinkers such as G. Stanley Hall and Erik Erikson
considered it a human universal, historians and social scientists now recognize our concept of adolescence—with its quasi-autonomous tastes, lingo,
peer groups, and youth subcultures—as distinctively modern.[3] Some argue
that adolescence was "invented" or "discovered" in the late nineteenth or
early twentieth century; all agree that the category became more important, organized more experience in more ways, in America after about 1900
and in Britain decades after that.[4]

Twentieth-century poetry in English built twentieth-century adolescence, its changing meanings and its cultural powers, into its succession of
projects. William Carlos Williams, Marianne Moore, W.H. Auden, Philip
Larkin, Thom Gunn, Gwendolyn Brooks, George Oppen, Robert Lowell,
Paul Muldoon, and Jorie Graham—among others—made ideas of and
about adolescence inseparable from their aesthetic goals, for part or all of
their careers. Changes in the meanings of adolescence also lend interest to
poets less well known, either because they now seem outmoded or "minor"

or because their careers are still underway. The poets covered here, I hope to show, repay rereading in the light of adolescence, of what adolescence meant to them and to their readers, where and when they wrote their poems.

John Ashbery's "Soonest Mended" (1968) has as good a claim as any to representative, even canonical status in contemporary American verse: often and rightly discussed as an *ars poetica*, the poem also offers incontrovertible evidence that the poetic art it displays can identify itself with adolescence. The poem begins with poets, or would-be poets, "living on the margin," hoping "to be small and clear and free," and ends in nostalgia for youthful origins, "always coming back / To the mooring of starting out, that day so long ago" (Ashbery, *Selected* 86, 89). Its climactic passages imagine fluidity, incompletion, "this not being sure, this careless / Preparing," as the best state of mind: "fence-sitting / Raised to the level of an aesthetic ideal" (88–89). "From this standpoint," Ashbery continues, "None of us ever graduates from college, / For time is an emulsion, and probably thinking not to grow up / Is the brightest kind of maturity for us, right now at any rate" (88). The place in the life course that the poem describes—neither innocent nor adult, slippery and unfixed—resembles the place in the American language that Ashbery's slippery syntax seeks. And the self or speaker whom Ashbery imagines—so different, as his critics note, both from the autobiographical self of confessional poetry and from the impersonal authority of some modernists—is immature, promising, uncertain, and even indefinitely undergraduate: a trope or an instance of modern adolescence.[5]

Poets quite unlike Ashbery share his occasional identification of adolescence as a source of poetry, a trope for contemporary culture, and a model for the poet's state of mind. In Amy Clampitt's "Gooseberry Fool" (1985), the poet promises to cook for a friend the eponymous dessert; she describes at length its chief ingredient, a "thorny and tart" berry whose taste is like

> having turned thirteen.
> The acerbity of all things green
> and adolescent lingers in
> it—the arrogant, shrinking
> prickling-in-every direction thorn-
> iness that loves no company except its,
> or anyway that's what it gets.
>
> (COLLECTED POEMS, 133)

The adolescent, like the berry and like the poet, resists, and shrinks from, "company," except for that of its peers. Liminal between nature (the bush) and culture (the dessert, the "fool"), a "not quite articulated thing" which tastes "unripe" even when it is ready for use, the gooseberry also stands for Clampitt's own poem, and for her "thorny," hyperelaborate style, which gives her a way to negotiate the demands of the wider world. So the poem concludes:

> I've wondered what not quite articulated thing
> could render magical
> the green globe of an unripe berry.
> I think now it was simply
> the great globe itself's too much to carry.
>
> (133-34)

An undergraduate, for Ashbery, is someone who entertains many ways of being, many ideas, but has committed himself to none; a girl who is turning thirteen for Clampitt is already immersed in a state that can "linger" (in a plucked gooseberry, or in a grown-up poet) unless and until it is treated in the right way—and that right way (as with the makings of a "fool" for dessert) permits much of its sour flavor to remain. The gooseberry thus becomes the girl and the poet and the poem (which must be treated, interpreted, by its reader). Both Ashbery and Clampitt liken their poetry to adolescence as a state of being or becoming, as an attitude toward experience, a state of mind: one describes "turning thirteen," the other an endlessly deferred graduation from college—the lower and upper limits, respectively, of adolescence as many of us now define it.

Together Clampitt's and Ashbery's poems reflect the twentieth-century heritage that this book hopes to describe. That heritage extends from William Carlos Williams and Marianne Moore (Moore being one source for Clampitt's style), through the early Auden (one source for Ashbery's), to contemporary poets whose disidentification with maturity and authority, whose identification with youth and its subcultures, goes much further than Ashbery's or Clampitt's. Poems from every decade in the last hundred years attend to the distinctive powers, the even more distinctive language, and the unfinished, uncertain, or unstable attitudes that characterize adolescence, as adults continue to imagine it, in much of the English-speaking world.

What do we mean by adolescence, and how do we know what we mean? The educational researcher Gerard LeTendre writes that Americans (and many Western Europeans) "assume . . . that the normal course of human development will involve a period of adolescence in which the person will undergo puberty, attend school, and develop a somewhat adultlike sense of identity." Yet "Americans did not make these assumptions 150 years ago, before the term *adolescence* had been popularized, and many people did not go to school at all" (*Learning to Be Adolescent*, xviii).[6] Though the word "adolescence" is attested in English in 1440, it "did not acquire widespread usage," writes the historian Steven Mintz, nor did it carry "associations with puberty, generational conflict, identity formation and psychological volatility until" the twentieth century (*Huck's Raft*, 3, 196). For all their argument over earlier analogues, historians agree that modern adolescence depends (in Aaron Esman's words) on "peer groups . . . defined, at least in part, by their antagonism to 'adult' values" (*Adolescence in Culture*, 4). Especially after G. Stanley Hall's *Adolescence* (1904), psychologists and social thinkers ascribed great importance to this state, which they observed in the peer groups created by cities, movies, telephones, motorcars, colleges, and high schools; some writers identified this state not just with sexuality, conflict and energy, but with creativity itself.

Modern adolescence thus comprises a cluster of sometimes hard-to-reconcile ideas:

- Both boys and girls experience a distinctive period of life, starting in the early teens and ending in the teens or twenties, before socially recognized maturity and distinct from dependent, presexual childhood.
- This period is either new in modern life, or newly important; today's youth differ from their elders more than previous generations did.
- This period is characterized by special psychological phenomena, among them heightened sexuality; rebellion against authority; group-mindedness or conformism; a focus on the inner life or the authentic self; emotional volatility; unstable or rapidly changing beliefs and commitments; and freedom from adult mores and norms. Though incompatible with some adult responsibilities, these phenomena may constitute virtues.
- Those virtues may resemble the virtues sought in a particular kind or genre of art (such as modernist writing, lyric poetry, or rock music).
- Modern youth acquire norms from one another rather than inheriting them from their elders or from long-extant institutions; they have created peer cultures, or subcultures, of their own, with new styles of speech and costume, and even new art forms.

Together these propositions form the definition of adolescence that the rest of this book will use. I arrange them above from least to most new (that is, from most to least evident in pre-twentieth-century writings); only the last seems unique to the twentieth century, though the popularization (not invention) of the term "adolescence" signaled a rise of interest in them all. Only in the twentieth century did the idea of adolescence as a valuable state of consciousness (perhaps even a state preferable to adulthood) acquire the widely recognized importance that could make it the explicit subject of many English-language lyric poems and the foundation for some strong poets' styles. Not all the poets I discuss accept the premises above; some set out to challenge them directly. In doing so they respond to other writers and to a culture that took them seriously indeed.

Poets do not, as a rule, react to cultural changes by striving to represent them fairly and comprehensively. Rather, poets react to the changes that move them, to what they see in their locales and in their social strata (often, urban, educated elites), or else to popular impressions of a changing culture: those impressions can include moral panics, uncritical celebrations, unrepresentative samples, and tenacious beliefs undercut by later research. Modern and contemporary poetry—reaching far fewer people than does prose fiction, film, or television—would make a poor base for a study that aimed to describe a whole culture's attitude toward adolescence (or toward anything else). Rather, I use what we already know about attitudes toward adolescence, what cultural historians, psychologists, social critics, and poets themselves have said and shown about modern youth, to draw conclusions about poets, poetry, and poems.

In showing explicitly that adolescence matters, that some major poets and some gifted minor ones derive both subjects and forms from it, I hope also to hint at patterns in the history of literary ideas and modes. One pattern involves pastoral and its sometime opposite, radical or revolutionary advocacy. Poets who associate youth with pastoral—with a self-enclosed, artificial, or innocent other world—suggest that youth does not change from cohort to cohort, that young people will grow up as they always have. Poets who view a particular generation, or a particular adolescent, as something new imply otherwise. The tension between youth as pastoral and youth as rebellious or revolutionary novelty emerges in the development of teen cultures through the twentieth century and in poetic reactions to them. In recent decades, both youth as pastoral and youth as revolution have often come to seem untenable as literary or cultural ideals: contemporary poets have sought alternatives. Some create modes of protest and inquiry specific to girls' and women's experience. Other contemporary poets (Ashbery in "Soonest Mended" among them) eschew narrative and conventional closure in forms that emphasize adolescence as uncertainty, as a persistent failure (or refusal) to settle on any one self-definition or goal.

A great deal of modern fiction—as both Patricia Meyer Spacks and John Neubauer have shown at length—depends on ideas about youth.[7] "Since puberty has traditionally involved self-discovery," Spacks writes, "the subject of adolescence lent itself readily to concentration on selfhood" (*The Adolescent Idea*, 16). In *The Adolescent Idea* (without which my own study could scarcely exist), Spacks describes in modern novels a "literature of antidevelopment" in which "the young stand for the authority of the personal" and narrators grow, from one question to the next, more and more congenial to youth (290–91).[8] Admittedly, many people's actual experience of adolescence—especially if we limit it to high school—involves repressive conformism or simple misery. Yet the idea of adolescence in literature has meant, above all else, inwardness and self-creation. "Adolescence, most commentators would agree, is the period during which a young person learns who he or she is and what he or she really feels"—so wrote the historian John Springhall in 1986 (*Coming of Age*, 3). Nor are these ideas confined to academics: a *New York Times Magazine* feature called "Being 13" claimed in 1998 that "only when children approach adolescence" do they "start to develop private, inaccessible selves" (McGrath, 30).

If innerness, selfhood, privacy, and individuality are now the province of adolescence, they are also the province of the lyric poem. Allen Grossman writes that with the rise of liberalism "poetry became lyric overwhelmingly, because lyric was the social form of the unknowable singularity of the liberal individual" (*The Sighted Singer*, 247). No wonder, then, that so many modern writers—poets, critics, journalists, novelists—equate adolescents with poems. Clampitt's "Gooseberry Fool" is, among other things, such an equation: there are other such figures, such equations, in the work of almost every poet this book views at length. For now, one additional recent example will do: in Paul Naylor's poem "The Adolescent"—one in a series based on the I Ching—the relevant hexagram is "mountain resting on water": "always the unstable I / appears for the first time" (46).

The adolescent also resembles the modern poem in that she must become the same and yet not the same as her precursors, must both enter and alter their lineage and social space. Walter Jackson Bate in 1970 deemed the task supposedly facing post-Romantic poets uniquely difficult: "In no other case are you enjoined to admire and at the same time to try, at all costs, *not* to follow closely what you admire. . . . The arts [thus] mirror the greatest single cultural problem we face . . . how to use a heritage . . . how to grow by means of it, how to acquire our own 'identities,' how to be ourselves" (*Burden of the Past*, 133–34). The originality that Bate says we expect of the lyric "I" is—far from being unique to poetry—the individuation that modern people, especially Americans, expect or demand of the young. Thus, the philosopher Charles Taylor writes,

> we can talk without paradox of an American 'tradition' of leaving home. The young person learns the independent stance, but this stance is also something expected of him or her. . . . Each young person may take up a stance which is authentically his or her own; but the very possibility of this is enframed in a social understanding of great temporal depth, in fact, in a 'tradition'.
>
> (*SOURCES OF THE SELF*, 9)

Poems in their uniqueness stand for people in theirs: poems, like adolescents, have to learn from their parents and then leave in order to become themselves. The tension in modern and contemporary poetry between a drive to create new forms, on the one hand, and a sense of participation in a tradition (even one as broad or vague as "lyric" or "voice"), on the other, is like—indeed, for Ashbery in "Soonest Mended," just is—the conflict between accounts of adolescence as something each generation undergoes and accounts of the next generation as something new.

The story of English-language poets' searches for language and for forms adequate to the youth of their times—a youth conceived sometimes as revolution, sometimes as a source of sexual energy, sometimes as a figure for contemporary indeterminacy—takes in some of the century's strongest poems: Williams's *Spring and All*, Auden's *Orators*, Bunting's *Briggflatts*, George Oppen's *Of Being Numerous*, Gwendolyn Brooks's *In the Mecca*, Robert Lowell's *Notebook*, and some of the highest lyric achievements of (among others) Larkin, Muldoon, and Graham. Any attempt to consider every relevant poem on a topic as broad as adolescence would make telling that story a fool's errand. My story will not answer—perhaps no critic could answer—the question, "What can poetry in general tell us about adolescence?" (It is like asking "What can poetry say about life?") Clearer questions—questions I do hope to answer—are "What can individual modern poets tell us about adolescence, as they saw it, as it appeared in their time?" and—more important for a book of literary criticism—"What can modern ideas of adolescence tell us about modern poets, about why they wrote as they did?" The twentieth century, this book argues, makes available particular concepts of adolescence that my poets adopt. Yet these poets do not simply write poems about teenagers or student protesters, as they might write about pears, pavement, or peregrine falcons. Rather, these poets alter or reinvent verse forms, literary modes, and verbal resources, trying to make new kinds of poems in order to match the new kinds of young people they see.

❖ ❖ ❖ ❖ ❖

Narrative works about youth and coming-of-age, about what the nineteenth century called *Bildung*, date back (depending on how one interprets the term) to Homer's Telemachus, to *Romeo and Juliet*, to Henry Fielding's *Tom Jones*, to Goethe's *Werther*, or to Jane Austen. Lyric poems about what we now call adolescence have a far thinner pre-modernist heritage. Yet some idea of youth in verse—especially in pastoral poetry—is far older than the English language: when Milton writes of "young Lycidas," "dead ere his prime," and recalls the early mornings of youth, he calls on Greek and Latin precedents (*Poetical Works*, 447). Pastoral is, Spenser's "E.K." explains, a "kind of writing" that "the best and most auncient Poetes" set for young poets "at the first to trye theyr habilities"; Spenser's Colin Clout (the poet within the *Shepheardes Calendar*) is an "unstayed yougth," "a shepheards boy" who likens "hys youthe to the spring time, when he was fresh and free from loues folly" (*Complete Poetical Works*, 9, 52).⁹

Harry Berger explains how critiques and celebrations of youth in the *Calendar* fit together in one view of the life course, which Spenser conceives as a kind of dynamic equilibrium. "Since the elders bemoan their lost youth and try to project it into the next generation," Berger writes, Spenser's "youthful and aged speakers hold the same values in spite of their apparent antipathy"—that antipathy becomes "the tradition, which is handed down from one generation to the next" (*Revisionary Play*, 416). Youth is, in Berger's sense, a "Green World," which "appears first as exemplary or appealing. . . . But when it has fulfilled its moral, esthetic, social, cognitive or experimental functions, it becomes inadequate," and those who remain there "are . . . in some way deficient" (*Second World*, 36). Indeed, youth is the pattern for such Green Worlds in early modern narrative and dramatic works, most of all in Shakespeare's *As You Like It* (Garber). Yet freestanding lyric poems from the Elizabethan era are at least as likely to deprecate immaturity as to praise it.¹⁰

The modern adolescent is not the green youth of early modern writing; nor is he (much less she) the Romantic child. "Before the Romantic" period, claimed William Empson, "the possiblities of not growing up had never been exploited so far as to become a subject for popular anxiety" (*Seven Types of Ambiguity*, 21). The idea that immaturity might be preferable to maturity per se, that incompletion of any sort might be better than completion, that remaining outside society indefinitely might be better than joining it, that irrational, instinctive, excessive, emotion-driven speech and behavior might have more value than rational, considered action and thought—these are all, of course, Romantic ideas; they inform, but predate, modern adolescence, which acts them out and represents them often.[11] The Romantic child, with his or her absolute opposition to the adult world, and the Romantic fragment, with its appreciation of potential and of the incomplete, are necessary but not sufficient conditions for the realization in poetry of modern adolescence; we can trace those conditions through major Romantic poems.[12] Wordsworth in the *Prelude* describes

> That twilight when we first begin to see
> This dawning earth, to recognize, expect
> And, in the long probation that ensues
> (The time of trial, ere we learn to live
> In reconcilement with our stinted powers)
> To endure this state of meagre vassalage,
> Unwilling to forego, confess, submit,
> Uneasy and unsettled—yoke-fellows
> To custom, mettlesome, and not-yet tamed
> And humbled down.
>
> (1805: 5:540-46)

This twilight (the twilight of childhood, as infancy is its morn) resembles our modern adolescence but is not, for Wordsworth, a state out of which—or even about which—freestanding poems can be written. Rather, his narrative and discursive poem depicts it as a state to be overcome, as love of nature (recollected from an earlier state called childhood) leads him back to love of humankind.

As for Continental analogues, Rousseau described in himself, and Goethe depicted in Werther, a stormy inwardness something like modern adolescence: Harold Bloom even claims that "Rousseau had invented that interesting transition, since," in Bloom's view, "literature affords no trace of it before him" ("Introduction," 3). But neither Rousseau nor Werther finds, for that transition, new verse forms (much less new forms that respond to a peer culture): Rousseau is not a poet, and Werther is a character in a novel (though one much imitated by real young men).[13] Nor is Keats a modern adolescent. Rather than celebrate his own immaturity, or hold it up as any sort of ideal, Keats apologized for his youth, and for the unhealthy senti-

ments that (his medical training perhaps suggested) came with it. His preface to *Endymion* explains:

> The imagination of a boy is healthy, and the mature imagination of a man is
> healthy; but there is a space of life between, in which the soul is in a ferment,
> the character undecided, the way of life uncertain, the ambition thick-sighted:
> thence proceeds mawkishness, and all the thousand bitters which those men I
> speak of must necessarily taste in going over the following pages.
>
> (*MAJOR WORKS*, 60)

Keats warns his readers to go easy on the poems—even to expect failures—
because they describe his immaturity, which is anything but an asset. Christopher Ricks calls this passage "a sigh, and not . . . a statement that should
be altogether believed"; Ricks continues, "what truths about life is the adolescent better stationed to see than either the boy or the man?" (*Keats*, 10–
11) It is, perhaps, modern even to ask that question: we may ask it about
Keats, but Keats does not ask it about himself. Nor does he ask it about the
"happy, happy" young men and girls on the Grecian urn, pure examples of
an undying Green World (*Major Works*, 288).

Matthew Arnold's updated Wordsworthianism differs from its master
partly in its pessimism about recompense and partly in Arnold's location of
a superior innocent state not in preverbal childhood, not always in nonhu-
man nature, but in an idea of male youth drawn partly from classical pastoral, partly from Oxford University. Arnold's Scholar-Gipsy, who "wander'd
from the studious walls / To learn strange arts, and join a gipsy tribe," thus
stays closer to his life at Oxford than any of the ordinary students who
took exams, graduated, and joined the adult world; in that world, the poem
adds, "mortal men . . . exhaust" their "energy," "numb the elastic powers,"
and succumb to "this strange disease of modern life" (*Poetical Works*. 259).
Arnold's lyric poems invoke "youth's . . . thwarting currents of desire," its
"step so firm, its eye so bright" (37, 21). His poems set a precedent for Auden
and for other moderns with a particular interest in colleges and schools.[14]
Robert Lowell once remarked, though, that "there's no childhood or adolescence in Arnold," and in an important sense he was right: Arnold's poetry does not present young rebels (of either gender) whose tastes and language bind them together to discomfit the adult world (quoted in Vendler,
"Lowell in the Classroom" 28). And never does Arnold seek, in his ideal of
youth, a model for incomplete, uncertain, or newly energetic poetic form.

For such a model we could look to Byron.[15] Yet Childe Harold is either
alone or stuck amid adults: there is no peer culture, for him, worth describ-

ing in literary terms. "None did love him" (*Major Works*, 25). There is, however, an energetic instability in much of Byron's verse—in its motions as well as its sentiments—that we might associate with the phase of life both *Childe Harold* and *Don Juan* invoke. Byron likes to say that he himself has grown old too soon, that he has outlived himself despite his few years.[16] "There's not a joy the world can give like that it takes away, / When the glow of early thought declines in feeling's dull decay"; "Alas! our young affections run to waste, / Or water but the desert" (259, 182). With his rapidity, his stormy exclamations, his unstable transitions from tone to tone, Byron is the only considerable poet in English before literary modernism for whom ideas of youth are not ideas of pastoral and for whom they contribute to inventions of form.

❖ ❖ ❖ ❖ ❖

The ingredients of modern adolescence evolve from Byron and from Arnold forward to the twentieth century, but they do not appear together often in poems. The authors in John O'Sullivan's *Democratic Review*—a group soon known as "Young America"—pursued in the late 1830s and 1840s, as Ted Widmer writes, a "rhetoric [of] youth and newness"; O'Sullivan's "persistent obsession with novelty and youth" led to eulogies on America as a young country, and on the promise and force of its young men (*Young America*, 3, 43). But this ideology produced no poems of lasting consequence, and it faded from literary history fast: by the time Whitman—a contributor to *Democratic Review*—began *Leaves of Grass*, he had left Young America's point of view behind. Indeed, Whitman said as much, asking in 1855: "Where is the huge composite of other nations, cast in a fresher and brawnier mode, passing adolescence, and needed this day, live and arrogant, to lead the marches of the world?" ("Walt Whitman and His Poems," 30)

Postbellum America instead seemed preoccupied with innocent boyhood. Tony Tanner, Kenneth Kidd, and Steven Mintz have all described this theme in novels and in Gilded Age popular culture; we can find it also in American poems.[17] In Henry Wadsworth Longfellow's "My Lost Youth" (1855)—part of the schoolroom canon after the war—school time and innocent boyhood are one phase of life, identified with Longfellow's Maine: "the native air is pure and sweet, / And the trees that o'ershadow each well-known street / . . . Are sighing and whispering still: / 'A boy's will is the wind's will, / And the thoughts of youth are long, long thoughts'" (*Poems*,

339). Despite the "gleams and glooms that dart[ed] / Across the school-boy's brain," Longfellow presents his hometown as a focus for pure and pu-rifying nostalgia, without sexuality and without change, as uncomplicated as his clear syntax and end-stopped line (339).

"My Lost Youth" thus represents (and many other poems could do the job) a nineteenth-century poetics of childhood that the modern poetics of adolescence would displace. Angela Sorby (whose own poetry I will examine in chapter 4) has shown how in late-nineteenth-century America—with its schools named for Longfellow and Whittier, its popular acclaim for James Whitcomb Riley and Eugene Field—"the popular experience of poetry came to be defined as juvenile" (*Schoolroom Poets*, xiv). With "poets framed as children, children seen as poets, children posited as readers" in and outside schools, "children recruited as performers, and adults wishing themselves back into childhood," Sorby writes, postbellum American poetry seemed "dominated by children": consider the popular success of Whittier's "Bare-foot Boy," Field's "Little Boy Blue," and even the early (posthumous, but pre–World War I) reception of Emily Dickinson, who was taken, or mistaken, as a winsome poet for girls (xvii). American modernists reacted both against the idealized childhood of Longfellow and his peers (whose poetry they did not want to rewrite) and against a prosaic, utilitarian modernity (which seemed to hold no place for poetry at all) by associating *their* poetry with the new, much-publicized, third term of adolescence.

Robert Frost—the title for whose first book quotes "My Lost Youth"—may be the last important American poet whose lyric poems describe an apparently ahistorical, purely "pastoral" youth, as A. E. Housman is the last such poet in England.[18] Housman's "chaps from the town and the field and the till and the cart" are not modern adolescents because they have no dis-tinctive and new peer culture (much less a new language with which to ex-press them) (*Collected Poems*, 38). Housman's poems do not only argue the case for an unchanging aspect to the feelings of youth; one hundred and ten years after the first of them appeared in print, they provide strong evi-dence for it. "Youth's a stuff will not endure" sounds like Housman, but it is Shakespeare (*Twelfth Night* 2.3.53). And yet, as with most pastoral, the po-ems make more sense if set against the civilization that read them, the civi-lization out of which their author's powers come: the ideal of village youth and village courtship, not to mention local athletic games, was already ob-solescent in late-Victorian Britain, as lads like Housman's either extended their educations, or migrated to urban jobs.

The closest nineteenth-century predecessor for the modern English-language poetry of adolescence was written in French. A book much like mine, with a few of the same examples, might be entitled *Rimbaud in English* or *Rimbaud and Contemporary Poetics* (perhaps surprisingly, no such book exists). Composed in the 1870s, Rimbaud's poetry seemed to him and to its later readers rebellious, uncontrollable, immature, unstable, hostile to received authority, radiant with sexual energy, sensitive to urban social change (i.e., the Paris Commune), and in search of an extraordinary new language. Not coincidentally, Rimbaud was himself in his teens. In "Roman" ("Novel" or "Romance") Rimbaud reminds himself—or reminds us, or asserts in the hope that we will deny it—"No one's serious at seventeen" (*Rimbaud Complete*, 30). One of his most famous letters begins: "These are the months of love; I'm seventeen, the time of hope and chimeras, as they say" (363). Fredric Jameson even discovers in Rimbaud "the production of the adolescent body" as something new ("the emergence of the New") in Western literature ("Rimbaud and the Spatial Text," 67, 87).

And yet Rimbaud's poetry reflects the social formations of his own time, not of the succeeding century that read and reinterpreted him: it is almost, but not quite, a poetry of modern adolescence. Consider the boys and girls in "First Communions," who anticipate not high school, dates, or universities but cafés, compulsory military service, and an adult culture of gender segregation:

> The girls always go to church, glad
> To hear the boys call them sluts, standing
> On ceremony after mass or sung vespers.
> Boys destined for life in the garrisons
> Who'll sit in cafés and jeer at the better born,
> Wearing new shirts, shouting scandalous songs.
>
> (RIMBAUD COMPLETE, 73)

> Le filles vont toujours à l'église, contentes
> De s'entendre appeler garces par les garçons
> Qui font du genre après messe ou vêpres chantantes.
> Eux qui sont destinés au chic des garnisons
> Ils narguent au café les maisons importantes
> Blousés neuf, et gueulant d'effroyables chansons.
>
> (418)

Rimbaud's experiments before *Saison en enfer* catch him midway between a post-Keatsian paradigm in which youth means unripeness, hesitancy, and unreadiness and a twentieth-century paradigm in which the energy of doing and saying already belongs to those who are not adult. The prologue to the unfinished prose piece "Deserts of Love" begins, as Wyatt Mason renders it: "What follows is the work of a young—very young—*man*, whose life came together by hook and by crook [d'un jeune, tout jeune *homme*, dont la vie s'est developpée n'importe où]" (183, 481). Yet the young man's "strange suffering holds an uncomfortable authority [bizarre souffrance possédant une autorité inquiétante]" (183, 481).[19]

Rimbaud does demonstrate a phenomenon frequent in twentieth-century poetry of adolescence (one that Spacks also finds in *The Mill on the Floss*): absolute resistance to *Bildung*, to any and all attempts to mold, from a youthful life, an adult life course or a career. Instead, as Kristin Ross writes, Rimbaud "proposes the impossible: a narrative which consists of pure transformational energy, pure transition or *suradolescence*," "a voice which speaks from the place of youth rather than ventriloquizes it, and the impossible notion that youth might not have to come to an end" ("Resistance," 198). Ross calls this notion an "attack on identity," a resistance at once to plot, to sequential time, and to goals such as marriage or a profession: the poetry stakes out, instead, a "liminal zone of adolescence" that can and should lead nowhere (*Emergence of Social Space*, 14, 44). That notion of youth as goal seems paradoxical in Rimbaud, which is one reason he surrounds it with other sorts of self-contradiction and paradox. The same notion becomes almost a cultural commonplace in certain parts of 1990s America, with its Generation X and Yers, indie rockers, perpetual students, and "kidults"; we will see them, and the poets who find language for them, at the end of this book.

That we like to read Rimbaud as an archetypal adolescent, in other words, says no more about him than it does about us. Paul Verlaine's edition of *Illuminations* appeared in 1886, the first *Collected Poems* in 1891, and the first book of Rimbaud's letters not until 1931, which is to say that Rimbaud's work entered Anglo-American consciousness during, and not before, the rise of "adolescence" as we know it now. Sustained English and American attention to Rimbaud began in the late 1910s, with the first book about him in English (Edgell Rickword's *Rimbaud, The Boy and the Poet*) appearing only in 1924 ("Etiemble," *Le mythe*, 370). Wallace Fowlie's melodramatic *Rimbaud: The Myth of Childhood* (1946) explained that "in forcing the secret of childhood, Rimbaud discovered revolt; in forcing the secret of adolescence, he discovered poetry" (16). Robert Lowell translated Rimbaud's "Poets at Seven Years Old"; John Tranter made his running quarrel with Rimbaud the subject of one of his longest poems. Other poets I examine, though, do not seem interested in Rimbaud at all, or do not regard him as a poet of adolescence.[20] The sense that youth had evolved its own tastes and language; the later sense that the young might take over (or tear down) American, British, or Australian social institutions; and the sense afterward that the young had failed to do so are consequences of twentieth-century cultural, economic, and even demographic history, anticipated in Rimbaud only by retrospective analogies.[21]

What most sets Rimbaud apart from all of the poets discussed in the rest of this book is a quality that also, paradoxically, gives him some of the appeal he has had for actual adolescent readers: his sense that he is one of a kind, a new creation, alone. "I'm an inventor unique among my predecessors" (*Rimbaud Complete*, 231). "If only I had one predecessor in French history! But no, none" (196). He speaks from a phase not child and not adult, but he also speaks from an impulse to prophecy, as a (failed) metaphysical revolutionary, the first and only of his kind. There is, in Rimbaud's imagination, *no group of people like him*, unless one counts the already dispersed (and not especially youthful) Communards.

By contrast, all the poems in English in this book depend on the idea not of one specially endowed (much less miraculously gifted) youth, but of a whole class of people called adolescents, who have and share with one another new habits, words, and tastes. Such people, in their joys and in their griefs, inspire, influence, and *are like* poems, even though the people who write those poems are, by and large, adults. Those poems see adolescents paradoxically as people defined by a peer group but also as incarnations of individuality (whose inner lives prompt lyric poems), as inheritors of pastoral conventions (hence proper subjects for poetry), and as rebels whose force requires new forms.

❖ ❖ ❖ ❖ ❖

My first chapter looks at the first generation of poets to make sustained use of adolescence as an idea and as a word. Exciting, sexually potent, given to innovation, full of potential, necessarily incomplete, modern adolescents were like modernist poems, and modernist poets pursued the analogy. No one did so with more success than William Carlos Williams, whose sequences of poems and poetic prose liken their own deliberately unfinished structures and surfaces to the lives of the adolescents they sometimes depict. Marianne Moore answered this idealization of adolescent bodies by portraying another kind of admirable youth: the careful students in some of her finest poems, and the idealized college education in others, reflect her temperament, her ethics, and her undergraduate years at Bryn Mawr.

A modern idea of adolescence arrived in British poetry amid the early work of W.H. Auden, with whom my second chapter begins. Critics often take his early poems as attacks on the closed, elaborate, homoerotic culture of British public schools (that is, elite private boarding schools). Yet those schools' privileged codes and small groups form the basis of his early style; sometimes, they are all the poems admire. Fascinated by the public school boys who he would never be, and by the girls (in school and outside it) whom he would never meet, Philip Larkin in his own youth and in middle age found ways to make art from that fascination. Thom Gunn, who moved to America just as the idea of youth culture took root in Britain, made the subcultures he saw—bikers, hippies, and, later on, gay club kids—the models for his own admiring poems. Basil Bunting's long poem *Briggflatts*, devoted to a transhistorical adolescence, could not have come into being without the subcultures of the British 1960s, to which it also pays homage.

My third and longest chapter looks at ideas about youth in American poetry from the Second World War through the 1970s, beginning with scattered poems by many hands and ending with three poets whose major late works react to 1960s youth. After a war noted for its young soldiers, new affluence and new national media made possible the dawn of the teenager. Formally conventional poets—most of all the talented and now nearly forgotten Phyllis McGinley—reacted to this new kind of American. Stereotypes about juvenile delinquents affected how Beat poets were received. George Oppen's optimistic ambivalence about student movements suffused his best-known 1960s poems. Gwendolyn Brooks overhauled her style and wrote some of her finest verse by taking cues from militant black youth. Incorporating failed struggles and continual frustrations, the sonnets of Robert Lowell's *Notebook* build into their line-by-line style Lowell's pessimism about the promise of youth, even as they review his own life course.

My last three chapters trace developments in poets' representations of adolescence since the 1960s. Despite the examples of Moore and Plath, a feminist poetics of adolescence—a set of strategies by which poems could encompass the experience of young women and girls *as* young women and girls—came about only in the last thirty-odd years. My fourth chapter shows how those modes took shape, concentrating on the achievements of Laura Kasischke and of Jorie Graham. These poets regard female adolescence not only as a time of self-making but also as a locus of danger: for them, girls' emergence into the social world also means emergence into sexual visibility, into the "compulsory heterosexuality" that Adrienne Rich has denounced (*Blood, Bread, and Poetry*, 23).

During the 1960s, youthful rebels who claimed to speak for their generation—if not for youth as such—promised to establish a Green World on Earth. In retrospect, they do not seem to have done so, and many recent poems of adolescence respond to the vacancy that the failure of those utopian projects has left. We will see those responses in Ireland and in Australia, whose key poets of adolescence—Paul Muldoon and John Tranter, respectively—make that phase of life stand neither for pastoral remove nor for social power but rather for a continuing uncertainty. Another prominent Australian poet, Les Murray, rejects adolescence and all it represents—in doing so he rejects modernity too.

We will then see more American responses, differentiated by generation: Baby Boomers—especially male ones, such as Larry Levis—write of adolescent promise nostalgically, as something that has already failed, in language, in society, in their own lives. More recent American poets, among them Ange Mlinko, Thomas Sayers Ellis, and Liz Waldner, speak not so much *about* adolescence, its idioms and its subcultures, but *as though from within* them. For these twenty-first-century writers, adolescence is not so much a stand-in for poems in general but a name for the attitude—hence the poetry—of their generation, and an appropriate synecdoche for the life of our culture now.

I have made my book international, as the idea of adolescence is now international, even if this book is not, could not be, truly global. Some of the most original poems of adolescence come from poets who think transnationally, such as W.H. Auden, Thom Gunn, and the American-inspired "Generation of '68" in Australia. My first chapter begins in America, because a modern understanding of adolescence (as most cultural historians have it) began in America too. It ends in America in part because I live here and in part because American poets of the last decade seem to have gone further and done more to frame the oddities and the energies of youth subcultures fruitfully in literary poetry. Given world enough and time, there might be another chapter on youth subcultures in contemporary British verse—on John James, Iain Sinclair, and punk rock; on the New Lad in the poetry of Simon Armitage, Paul Farley, and John Stammers; on the bleak models of growing up, or failing to grow up, in the poetry of Lavinia Greenlaw.

This is a book about poems *about* adolescence, not (except coincidentally, as with Rimbaud and Plath) about poems *by* adolescent writers, nor a book about what poems young readers read.[22] Fine individual poems by eminent poets (James Merrill's "Days of 1941 and '44," for example, and Audre Lorde's "Hanging Fire") are not discussed, either simply for reasons of space or because adolescence never became central to those poets' oeuvres. Other eminent poets (such as Elizabeth Bishop) do not appear in this book because adolescence makes little appearance in their poems; that the topic is broadly and deeply of interest for twentieth-century poetry does not make it omnipresent. Almost every colleague and acquaintance who has seen this book in progress has suggested additional poets or poems that I might include. I hope that readers will judge this study for what it says about the writings it does consider, rather than taking umbrage at its failure to bring in all possible relevant works.

This book about immaturity has perhaps itself taken too long to mature; if so, all blame accrues to me. Credit alone accrues to Jennifer Crewe, Bonnie Costello, James Dawes, Langdon Hammer, Jenny Ludwig, Stuart McDougal, Helen Vendler, and two extraordinarily attentive anonymous readers for Columbia University Press, who read part or all of the manuscript and responded with encouragement and advice. Another sort of credit, of course, belongs to Jessica Bennett, and to our son Nathan, years away from his own adolescence. Many people, and several colleges and universities, have given hearings to my ideas. I thank, especially, Langdon Hammer and Yale University; the University of Connecticut; Mark Ford and University College–London; Ben Friedlander and the University of Maine; Robert von Hallberg and the University of Chicago; Matthew Hofer and the University of New Mexico; Eric Weisbard and the Experience Music Project in Seattle. Parts of some chapters have seen print in earlier versions elsewhere: in *Something We Have That They Don't* (University of Iowa), edited by Mark Ford and Steve Clark; in *Jorie Graham: Essays on the Poetry* (University of Wisconsin), edited by Thomas Gardner; in *Paul Muldoon: Critical Essays* (University of Liverpool), edited by Tim Kendall and Peter McDonald; in *This Is Pop* (Harvard University), edited by Eric Weisbard; in *Wallace Stevens Journal*, edited by John Serio; and in *Boston Review*, then edited by Timothy Donnelly, Mary Jo Bang, and Josh Cohen. My thanks to all these editors, readers and presses; my thanks, as well, to the students at Macalester College—too many to name—whose queries, arguments, writings, and comments have, I hope, taught me enough to make a book.

1

Modernist Poetics of Adolescence

IN 1981 THE Los Angeles punk band Rhino 39 made its third appearance on record, on the compilation LP *American Youth Report*; Rhino 39's anthemic "J. Alfred" took all its words from T. S. Eliot's "Love Song of J. Alfred Prufrock," snarling and yelping through Eliot's "Let us go then, you and I"; "I have heard the mermaids singing"; and other lines (though not the whole poem). For these punk rockers, Eliot's poem of hesitant anxiety—identified by John Berryman as the site at which "modern poetry begins"—became a fit emblem for the energies, anxieties, uncertainties, and aggressions of modern adolescence (Berryman, *Freedom*, 270). Rhino 39 got their scholarship partly wrong: Eliot's backward-looking Prufrock, who sees himself proleptically as middle-aged, belongs not to modern adolescence, with its unchaperoned dates and peer-group slang, but to a pattern of Gilded Age social life in which courtship involved "calling on" young women at adult-sponsored social events or at home (Bailey, *From Front Porch to Back Seat*). Though he began the poem at Harvard, Eliot was living in France and England during the years when the newer American system of dates, public entertainments, and self-consciously youthful taste cultures came into its own.

Yet Rhino 39 got something right. Not only does American modernist poetry, in retrospect, permit contemporary adolescents to see versions of themselves, but some American modernists (though not Eliot, with his "strenuous insistence on his own maturity") took a sustained and self-conscious interest in adolescence, in the kinds of experience and the new kinds of persons associated with young men and women in their teens and early twenties (Rosen, "Lost Youth," 487). Poets' responses to the new

American adolescents—in high schools, in colleges, in cars, and on city streets—make up a neglected side of American modernism. Little magazines and their editors echoed the celebratory views of adolescence they found in social and psychological thought. During the late 1910s and 1920s, William Carlos Williams embraced, but complicated, his peers' devotion to the new American youth. Marianne Moore, however, rejected the types (and stereotypes) of youth that her peers embraced; she drew forms and ideas instead from her own experience at a women's college, where students found more freedom and more respect than the adult world would give.

❖ ❖ ❖ ❖ ❖

Adolescent peer groups emerged in America simultaneously as a cultural idea and as demographic, economic, and institutional fact. Between 1890 and 1920, total (public and private) high school "enrollment approximately doubled every decade"; between 1900 and 1929, "a new high school opened every day" (Macleod, *Age of the Child*, 149; Mintz, *Huck's Raft*, 175). Howard Chudacoff explains that "the growth of junior high schools, high schools, and, especially, colleges after the turn of the century . . . provided environments in which adolescents and young adults could increasingly insulate themselves."[1] "The public high school," Joseph Kett writes, "enabled "the mass reclassification of young people in school as adolescents," even if many working-class young people did not or could not attend (*Rites of Passage*, 235, 243).[2] Parallel changes took place on evenings and weekends, as public entertainments (arcades, movie theaters, dance halls) and streetcars let urban young people gather in groups, or on dates. "As never before," Kevin White adds, "the period of youth began to be comprehended as a distinctive time of life with its own patterns of norms, mores and values," such as dating and "petting" (*The First Sexual Revolution*, 17–18).[3]

This visible social change inspired new theories of youth, foremost among them the psychologist G. Stanley Hall's two-volume *Adolescence* (1904).[4] Hall addressed his work "only to those still adolescent in soul" and wrote that "the best definition of genius is intensified and prolonged adolescence" (1:viii, 2:90–91). Deploying a raft of sometimes contradictory qualities and superlatives, from malleability to determination, from sexual energy to religious faith, Hall opined (echoing Wordsworth's description of infants) that adolescents' "trailing clouds of glory usher in a new inner dawn . . . that only poetry can ever describe, which it has not yet adequately done, but which I believe it is its very highest function to do" (2:302). Hall's book sold 25,000 copies in a year, and marked—if it did not help cause—a great change in how Americans viewed the life course (Ross, *G. Stanley Hall*, 336). Writing in 1950, the poet and critic Louise Bogan included Hall's *Adolescence* in her short list of books important to modernist poets (*Achievement*, 30). Gerald LeTendre writes that Hall's "'discovery' of adolescence . . . set off an explosion of studies . . . that have become part of the general educational culture and the broader culture as well" (*Learning*, 175). Examples stretch from Jane Addams's *Spirit of Youth and the City Streets* (1909) to William D. Lewis's *Democracy's High School* (1914) (with a preface by Theodore Roosevelt), to novels such as Booth Tarkington's bestselling *Seventeen* (1915), F. Scott's Fitzgerald's *This Side of Paradise* (1920), and the racy and controversial *Flaming Youth* (1923) by "Warner Fabian" (Samuel Hopkins Adams).

Adults of the 1920s, Beth Bailey explains, grew "fascinated with 'youth'—young men and women who defined themselves, as *youth*, partly through public sexuality" (*From Front Porch to Back Seat*, 78). East Coast intellectuals' interest crystallized earlier, thanks in part to the New York critic Randolph Bourne (1886–1918). A regular writer for *The Dial* and *The Seven Arts*, Bourne achieved prominence with *Youth and Life* (1913), which combined a call to radical activism, a generational manifesto, and a rhapsody (equal parts Hall, Emerson, and William James) on the meaning of youth. Himself twenty-five and a junior at Columbia (having entered college late), Bourne spoke for the rising generation with confidence: "it is the young," he explained, "who have all the really valuable experience" (12).[5] "Their vision is always the truest, and their interpretation always the justest" (15). Older adults and young people, Bourne added, now "misunderstand each other as they never did before"; he attributed the gap in part to "the four years' period of high-school life" (35).[6] Bourne—and Bourne's peers—applied his findings to the arts. Like Hall, and like Addams, Bourne saw in modern adolescence a new and unrealized vocation for poetry: "In this scientific age there is a call for youth to soar and paint a new spiritual sky. . . . If the old poetry is dead, youth must feel and write the new poetry" (179).[7]

The first American poet widely received, in her time, as a voice of adolescence is rarely considered an innovator now. Edna St. Vincent Millay, then in her teens, won a national award for "Renascence" (1912); her first book appeared in 1917, before she left Vassar but after she had entered the protomodernist New York and Provincetown literary circles around Edmund Wilson and Floyd Dell. "Renascence" had passion and religiose sincerity, but none of the social facts, nor the new sense of freedom, associated with youth. Millay's lyrics and epigrams of the late 1910s, however, made that new, sometimes scandalous freedom their subject. "Recuerdo" (1920) celebrates as innocent merriment an urban adventure that would have shocked the generation before—Millay and her friends have traveled in an urban public conveyance, unsupervised, till dawn: "We were very tired, we were very merry— / We had gone back and forth all night upon the ferry" (*Collected*, 128) Millay's "Figs"—epigrams in the carpe diem tradition—celebrate ephemerality and immediacy, rejecting plans, prudence, responsibilities, adult virtues of all kinds: "Safe upon the solid rock the ugly houses stand: / Come and see my shining palace built upon the sand!" (127) Middlebrow journals and modernist little magazines concurred in celebrating Millay's adolescent qualities: energy, bold eroticism, "pride of youth . . . discovering a new world" (Van Doren, "Youth and Wings," 122–23). "The artless and passionate artistry of this rhapsody of girlish mysticism," *The Double Dealer* asserted in 1923, "makes Miss Millay one of our ranking American poets" (Nethercot, "Sophisticated Innocents," 205). Gorham Munson remembered the vogue for Millay as "the symbol of the 'flaming youth mood'" (*The Awakening Twenties*, 3); the editor John Hutchens later described her as "the lyric voice of the newly liberated and uninhibited young" (*The American Twenties*, 19).

Ideas about generational difference had even more influence in the self-conscious American vers libre of the little magazines than over the relatively popular, and formally conventional, Millay. The *Dial* began to publish poems in 1918: one issue led off with James Oppenheim's poem "The Young World." Six pages and twenty Whitman-inspired sections long, it reads in part:

> O the pride
> Of the young world
> These youngsters are aliens and exiles among their parents
> Where they go
> Goes rebellion,
> It could not be otherwise.
>
> (175)

Oppenheim's 1919 memorial poem for Bourne remembered his "great love / Of the spirit of youth" ("Randolph Bourne," 7). *Youth: Poetry of Today*, a journal published in Cambridge, Mass., from 1918 to 1919 and devoted to "youth, the symbol of growth," included in its six issues poems by Conrad Aiken, Malcolm Cowley, Witter Bynner, Amy Lowell, and Arthur (Yvor) Winters. In Bynner's "Youth Sings to the Sea," a personified "Youth . . . Sweeps his hand with a stroke of fire / And calls to the mountain, to the sea, / To make him the god that he should be" (10).[8] "Poets today, like modern young folks, *know*" *The Double Dealer* agreed (Nethercot, "Sophisticated Innocents," 202; emphasis his).

Margaret Anderson's *Little Review* grew especially strident in associating modernism with youth. Anderson announced in her first issue (1914), "we take a certain joyous pride in confessing our youth" ("Announcement," 2). In the next, she mused, "someone accused us of being 'juvenile.' What hideous stigma was thereby put upon us?" ("The Germ," 2). (The facing page ran a poem entitled "Rebellion.") Anderson's own Whitmanesque poem "Reveals" asks, "What do you call this fantastic place where age that is weak rules youth that is strong? / Where parents prescribe life for children they cannot understand[?]" (2) Other contributors shared her interest: "Sophomoric Epigrams" (1915) by "A.E.D." claims, "There is no wisdom but youth. . . . Man loses his Ego at thirty and becomes conceited. . . . There is no beauty but youth" (37–38). Florence Frank's essay on Freud linked the modern interest in adolescence to the coming vogue for psychoanalysis: "The priest of the future will be the Inspired Physician. . . . To the adolescent the value of the Inspired Physician can scarcely be overstated" ("Psycho-Analysis," 15). Ben Hecht, later a celebrated screenwriter, contributed an essay, "The American Family," in which a daughter's "awakened mental curiosity" and "spirit of revolt" represents American artists' resistance to philistinism (2).[9]

The words "adolescent" and "adolescence" also enjoyed an American modernist vogue. *The Double Dealer* ran a poem called "Florizel Adolescent."[10] E.E. Cummings, who called the moon "a song of adolescent ivory," noticed adolescent social life as well: "spring omnipotent goddess . . . thou stuffest / the parks with overgrown pimply / cavaliers and gumchewing giggly / girls" (*Collected*, 214, 61). One of Cummings's most famous poems, "in Just-" epitomizes the point in the life course where heterosexual desire overtakes childhood's homosocial play. "Eddieandbill come / running from marbles," "bettyandisbel come dancing // from hop-scotch and jump-rope" at the whistle of "the / goat-footed // balloonMan" (*Collected*, 24). This call from Pan, this version of adolescence, stresses its continuities with older kinds of carpe diem lyric (Robert Herrick's, say), as other American modernist versions would not.

After her move to America in 1916, Mina Loy used the words "adolescent" and "adolescence" in poem after poem. "Perlun" (1921) describes "the whipper snapper child of the sun," who "puts the world / to the test of intuition":

> His head
> > an adolescent oval
> > ostrich egg
> The victorious   silly   beauty of his face
> awakens to his instincts.
>
> (141)

"Songs to Joannes" (1917) declaimed: "I am the jealous store house of the candle-ends / That lit your adolescent leaving" (6). In 1920 Loy gave the term an almost worshipful cast:

> Goddesses and Young Gods
> Carress [sic] the sanctity of Adolescence
> In the shaft of the sun . . .[11]
>
> ("O HELL," 7)

American literature could be deprecated as well as praised for its seeming adolescence. Amy Lowell's "Miss Columbia: An Old-Fashioned Girl," which appeared in the *Little Review* in 1914, explained that "Miss Columbia" "is in her artistic teens, and is as unimaginatively conventional as is the human animal at the same age" (37). Van Wyck Brooks in 1918 complained that American "life is, on all its levels, in a state of arrested development," adding in 1921 that "the chronic state of our literature is that of a youthful promise which is never redeemed" (*America's Coming of Age*, 97, 164). Calls for maturity, for an adult mindset, would later become a New Critical signature: T. S. Eliot in 1926 complained that the modern "literature of disillusionment is the literature of immaturity" (*Varieties*, 128). John Crowe Ransom—whose elegant early-1920s lyrics (such as "Blue Girls") treat youth as pure premodern pastoral—in 1929 decried American "men in a state of arrested adolescence" (*My Stand*, 5). A decade later, Ransom protested that "the kind of poetry which interests us is not the act of a child, or of that eternal youth which is in some women, but the act of an adult mind" (*World's Body*, viii) These critics reacted against the very experiment and enthusiasm—and the desire to find, for a new generation, new forms—which "little magazines" of the teens and twenties sought.

Such magazines invoked youth, with only occasional anxiety, as subject, metaphor, and positive model. None did so more often than *Others*, coedited by William Carlos Williams. Its first issue (1915) opened with Mary Carolyn Davis's "Song of a Girl," which asked what it meant "Just to be young / Young enough to laugh when one should weep" (4). In Skipwith Cannell's "Ikons" (1916), "We young men come up from our beginning crying / 'Way! Make way for us!'" (156, 158). If *Others* poets pursued youth as an ideal; they also observed particular young men and women; some wrote amorous verses to alarmingly young girls.[12] Douglas Golding's "High-browettes" (subtitled "Merveilleuses de nos jours") describes the "rows of young women" at a poetry reading, who "smoke a great deal, bathe little, and wear no stays" (131). The American modernist interest in adolescence included both praise for young men's vigor and attention to girlish allure: indeed, one sign of the new thinking about adolescence was that these two qualities were sometimes conflated, or treated similarly, as "youth." In such treatments, the adolescent—like the modernist poem—is disturbing, full of potential, incomplete, sometimes baffling, and no longer innocent; he (and, as with Millay, she) does not pretend to ignorance of the wide world.

Not all modernists shared in the vogue for youth: one who had mixed feelings was Wallace Stevens, whose undergraduate sonnets pursued the idea obsessively but whose first published poems (such as "Le Monocle de Mon Oncle") often concerned middle age.[13] Stevens's 1917 play "Bowl, Cat, and Broomstick" (whose title names its speaking parts) made fun of the French "poetess" or poetaster "Claire Dupray." The character Bowl praises Dupray's photograph: "She cannot be more than twenty-two," which, Bowl explains, "is an age when red becomes tawny, when blue becomes aerial— and when a girl, at least, when a girl like Claire Dupray, becomes a poetess" (*Collected*, 622–23). Bowl, Cat, and Broomstick also read Dupray's poems aloud (in English prose): "Does not such a poem, so young, so communicative, warrant the definition of the poetess made by her portrait? How new she is!" (630). Dupray seems to caricature Millay, who would have been famous already in 1917; Millay had acted in the Provincetown Players, who performed Stevens's previous work for the stage.

Others's most sustained look at adolescence arrived with the poet Emanuel Carnevali, a manic charmer who appeared first (aged twenty-one) in Harriet Monroe's journal *Poetry* in 1918; he met the *Others* circle in New York through her (Parisi and Young, *Dear Editor*, 235–36). Carnevali's essay "Arthur Rimbaud" ran in *Others* in 1919. Much of it applies the optimistic ideas in Hall and Bourne to Rimbaud's poetry (and by implication to Carnevali's own verse): "Rimbaud is the Advent of Youth. Almost everything else in the world is unbelief in Youth. . . . Almost everything else in the world, beside the poets, who have all believed in Youth, is a construction of the error that life is from Youth up: it is from Youth down" ("Rimbaud," 20). Rimbaud (Carnevali continued) represents "certainties of the age of seventeen and eighteen, certainties born of a perfect harmony of Youth's life and being, certainties of God." "As for me I know Youth in love, I know Youth encountering the first men. . . . For this I believe in Arthur Rimbaud" ("Rimbaud," 20, 23). In Lola Ridge's salon in 1919, Carnevali accused New York modernists (Williams among them) of having "forgotten your youth"; he would soon found "a little club" in New York devoted to "youth, sheer youth" as a principle, apparently, of literary interpretation (Carnevali, *Autobiography*, 147, 124). As late as 1925, Ernest Walsh in *This Quarter* found Carnevali "more important than Keats," since Carnevali marked "the beginning of the *Republic of Youth*"; he was, Walsh continued, "a major poet and primarily the poet who has given us the life of the youth of this age. Perhaps that is the only life that matters" ("A Young Living Genius," 324, 328).

Though Rimbaud's poems were not unknown in America, Carnevali seems to have prompted fresh attention to them. *The Dial* in 1920 ran excerpts from *Illuminations* and *Une Saison en enfer*, as well as W.G. Blum's "Remarks on Rimbaud as Magician." "Disgust," as expressed in *Une Saison en enfer*, Blum explains, "is not the peculiar adjunct of genius, but an emotion perfectly familiar to no end of adolescents" (727). According to Munson, it was through these articles that Hart Crane discovered Rimbaud (*The Awakening Twenties*, 204). Though the first poem in Crane's first book hailed "all those who step / The legend of their youth into the noon" (*Complete Poems*, 3) Crane's later published poems rarely emphasize either his own youth or youth as a principle in the way that the poems of Carnevali— and Millay—did. Modernist attention to adolescence did, however, shape ways in which Crane was received: his status as *the* archetypal young poet, the youth of promise (succeeding several failed candidates for that post, such as Millay, Carnevali, and John Rodker), let his contemporaries demand from him either a definitive realization of youth (a contradiction in terms) or else a "mature" long poem, both finished and promising, of a sort which nobody could have produced.[14]

European Futurists, to be sure, also invoked youth. Blaise Cendrars's "Transiberian Prose" (1913) begins, "En ce temps-là j'étais en mon adolescence [In those times I was in my adolescence]" (19, 20). Repeating its opening line, Cendras's poem emphasizes youthful ardor to the point of disorientation: "mon adolescence était alors si ardente et si folle / Qui mon coeur . . . brûlait comme le temple d'Éphèse ou comme la Place Rouge de Moscou / Quand le soleil se couche" [My adolescence was so ardent and so foolish/ That my heart . . . blazed like the temple of Ephesus or like Red

Square in Moscow / At sunset] (*Poésies complétes*, 20). F.T. Marinetti boasted in 1910 "the oldest of us is thirty"; Giovanni Papini in 1912 described himself a "man of twenty," to whom "even sunsets seem to show the delicate white spangles of lingering sunrises" (Apollonio, *Futurist Manifestos*, 23; 95). Loy knew both Papini and Marinetti from her years in Florence; Carnevali modeled both his verse and his personality on their examples.[15] Yet these writers' "futurist moment" (Marjorie Perloff's term) entered poetry in English largely through the Vorticism of Wyndham Lewis and Ezra Pound, London-based writers relatively uninterested in the new cohort of American boys and girls.[16] As late as 1929, Ezra Pound asked George and Mary Oppen (both twenty years old, and newly arrived from the United States) "What do 'girlfriend,' 'boyfriend' mean?" (Mary Oppen, *Meaning a Life*, 132). Other American modernists—and even Loy, in her poems of New York—located their evocations of adolescence in America, representing America's new youth.

Carnevali's 1919 essay provoked Williams to think through his own relation to adolescence as an American phenomenon and to youth as a literary ideal. An editorial in the last number of *Others* (for which Williams served as sole editor) construes Carnevali's emphasis on youthful energy as the reductio ad absurdum of *Others* aesthetics: Carnevali's

> poems are bad, full of nonsense . . . because he is young . . . But he is wide. Wide, WIDE open. He is out of doors. He does not look through a window.
>
> We older can compose, we seek the seclusion of a style, of a technique. . . . And THAT is *Others*. The garbage proved we were alive once, it cannot prove us dead now. But THAT is *Others* now, that is its lie.
>
> ("GLORIA!" 3)

(The next page of this final *Others* contained Moore's poem "Poetry.") That issue concludes with a much longer essay, unsigned but clearly by Williams, that asks in what sense, if any, modern writers had to be young: "Perhaps a man does get a bellyache at 19, perhaps he does run to verse for aid . . . but I deny this has anything to do with the question as between excellence and modernity" ("Belly Music," 26). Williams goes on to deplore the vogue for startlingly young poets, naming the Idahoan H.L. Davis (born in 1896), deriding H.L. Mencken's then-recent quip that "every poet" should be "killed at 26," and taking the occasion to explain his own aesthetic goals:

> Say I cannot write as well as Davis, I have not the locale, the stability, of anything—the youth. My youth we'll say was crass, steeped in a mad ignorance.

Yet I am not forbidden from singing. It is damnable nonsense to think to anchor a poet on his Byronic adolescence of body and mind. . . . There IS a way to come through the loss of youth or first youth and the loss of love. . . . It is art. . . . It is the NEW! not one more youthful singer, one more lovely poem. The NEW, the everlasting NEW, the everlasting defiance.

(26, 28)

For Williams, modernist newness is like adolescence but not the same as "adolescence of body and mind"; those who confuse them take the sign for the thing. The then thirty-six-year-old doctor goes on to distinguish artistic from biophysical youth:

It is the youth, I have seen written somewhere, that won the war; it is to the youth then that we must look for the energy that will carry us—etc., etc. The devil with youth! What does youth care or what do I care for it? . . . It is a lie that there is any significance in youth because the brain is young. The new is not in any way related to the work of a BEGINNER but to that of a MASTER. He is young. He is the unborn. . . . What is the difference between 17 and 70? I see none save a certain hardening and weakening of the flesh. There are far more important differences between individuals of the same age than that.

(32)

If modernism connotes youth, immaturity, newness, Williams argues, it must do so figuratively, in its language, not simply due to the age, in years, of the writers. Williams's prose of 1919 thus echoes Stevens's play of 1917, whose character Broomstick disabuses Cat and Bowl of their admiration for "Dupray," refuting the assumed link between the poet's youth and the "newness" of her expressions: "She is young. Therefore she is new. Or her poetry is young. That is one of the most persistent of all fallacies. Her poetry is young if her spirit is young—or whatever it is that poetry springs from. Not otherwise" (*Collected*, 631–32). Dupray, Broomstick shows, is in fact fifty-three years old (634).

❖ ❖ ❖ ❖ ❖

Despite his critique of the cult of youth in *Others*, Williams found in adolescents and their peer culture after the First World War important analogues for the newness, demotic speech, and sexual energy he sought in his own New World verse. Biographically oriented critics (among them Paul Mariani and Mike Weaver) have noticed Williams's accurate sense of himself as a late bloomer. Readers have been slower to see how Williams's ideas about physical, psychological, and sexual development, as they inform his verse, draw on ideas about youth. Williams compared his poems to young people's actions almost as soon as he embraced a modernist idiom. "January Morning" (1917) likens the poet's attitude to that of the girls he observes:

> Well, you know how
> the young girls run giggling
> on Park Avenue after dark
> when they ought to be home in bed?
> Well,
> that's the way it is with me somehow.
>
> (*CPW* 104)

Williams's individual, spontaneous, repeated rule-breaking activity in writing poetry resembles the girls' spontaneous, repeated, and inherently social rule breaking in staying out after their curfew. He identified poetic energies with groups of girls again in "The Lonely Street" (1921), one of several poems he chose to publish in the Rutherford High School magazine:

> School is over. It is too hot
> to walk at ease. At ease
> in light frocks they walk the streets
> to while the time away.
> They have grown tall. They hold
> pink flames in their right hands.
> In white from head to foot,
> with sidelong, idle look—
> in yellow, floating stuff,
> black sash and stockings—
> touching their avid mouths
> with pink sugar on a stick—
> like a carnation each holds in her hand—
> they mount the lonely street.
>
> (*CPW* 174, 499)

Attractive, lyrical, symbolically defiant, sociable (arranged in groups), immature, deliberately demotic, and at home on the street, these colorful "pinkish" girls prefigure the strong and promising, "reddish, purplish" weeds of "By the road to the contagious hospital," weeds that Williams's critics often understand as figures for his own art. Carl Eby writes that in "The Lonely Street" "the male observer becomes 'one of the girls'" ("'The Ogre'").[17]

Williams staged further debates about the literary uses of adolescence in the periodical *Contact* (1920–23). Its third issue includes Kenneth Burke's essay about Jules Laforgue: "Of course, Laforgue was an adolescent. The metaphysical interest, when it is emotional rather than intellectual, is quite the common thing with adolescence" (9). *Contact*'s version of modern writing would identify adolescence not with Laforguean languour but with youthful, American strength. Such was the burden of Williams's own essay "Yours, O Youth," also from *Contact* 3: "The American critical attitude! it is that we are seeking to establish. It is young. It is not necessarily inexpert . . . but it is necessarily young" (15). That is (remembering Williams's earlier demurral to Carnevali), the writers need not *be* youthful, nonadult, immature, but their "critical atittude" must let them sound as if they were. The "Critical Note" that concludes *Contact* 5 (appended to Williams's poem "New England" and almost certainly his work) praises in choppy syntax the vitality to be found in West African woodcraft, dance, and nudity, and among the young people (boys and girls) "at the High School play" (n.p.).

Williams explored the new American youth culture—with its high schools, social groups, insistent sexuality, cars, and dates—most thoroughly in his experimental verse and prose sequences of the late 1910s and 1920s. *Kora in Hell* (1917) associated beauty and poetry almost shamefacedly with nubility, youth, and spring: one Kora (Persephone) figure prompts Williams's exclamation "It is no part of the eternal truth to wear white canvas shoes and a pink coat. It is a damnable lie to be fourteen. The curse of God is on her head!" (*I* 68) All Williams's readers find images of birth in the first poem of *Spring and All*, where young weeds "enter the new world naked." We might also find, in that poem's later verbs of sexual discovery, individuation, and self-definition, a botanical trope for adolescence:

> One by one objects are defined—
> It quickens: clarity, outline of leaf
>
> But now the stark dignity of
> entrance—Still, the profound change
>
> has come upon them: rooted they
> grip down and begin to awaken
> (*I* 95-96)

No one would claim that *Spring and All* describes, *primarily*, American adolescents, nor that all its sections of poems and prose reported on the American high school.[18] Yet the farther we move into *Spring and All*, the more it looks in part like a report on the new world of American youth. In Williams's American-Petrarchan love poem (no. 4) a lover brings his beloved into the new, big city, with its terrestrial "lights" and then offers "a crown for her head with / castles upon it, skyscrapers / filled with nut-chocolates—" (*I* 99). What could this candied crown represent except an inexpensive, innocent night out in Manhattan—in other words, a date? Couples on dates, of course, attended movie houses, whose "phenomenal / growth" made them the new "cathedrals" of poem 15, and whose films helped standardize the erotic, "thrilling" kiss (*I* 127; Kevin White, *The First Sexual Revolution*, 158).

Since *Spring and All* identifies American virtues with American adolescents, its complaints about American inequality begin with a girl who has missed out on adolescence for reasons of geography and social class. "Sent out at fifteen to work in/ some hard-pressed/ house in the suburbs," Elsie in poem XVIII (later titled "To Elsie") reveals "the truth about us"—about the more fortunate citizens of Williams' America—because the country and its institutions will not let her realize her own adolescent potential, the potential Williams in other moods ascribes to America as a whole (*CPW* 218). She can neither "witness" the folly of adults (because she is already its victim), nor redirect it ("drive the car").

If these readings seem unduly speculative, poem XIX makes its adolescent contexts unmistakable:

> This is the time of year
> when boys fifteen and seventeen
> wear two horned lilac blossoms
> in their caps—or over one ear.
>
> (*I* 135)

Spring, in other words, announces itself through new plant life and through (certain working-class) teenage boys' habits: flowers and boys stand for each other, as Williams's new art can stand for both. Resembling and holding "Lilacs" (the word gets a line all its own), these boys

> stand in the doorways
> on the business streets with a sneer
> on their faces

adorned with blossoms
Out of their sweet heads
dark kisses—rough faces

(*I* 136)

Williams's new art in *Spring and All* identifies him at once with such boys and with the girls they mean to, or try to, kiss.

At this point we can see modernist adolescence in Williams not just as a topic but as a component of style: it means not only sexualized energy but unfinished surfaces, refusals of inherited norms and of inherited ideas of mastery. We can also see in the flower-bearing tough boys an attempt to synthesize youth as pastoral (present in every generation) and youth as something rebelliously new (and American, too), an attempt that the newly visible peer culture both represents and permits. Williams may be the first poet to attempt that synthesis in a lyric poem.

He attempted it, too, in experimental prose. *The Great American Novel* (1923) spends even more time than *Spring and All* in the new world of consumption-driven youth, which it both mocks and enjoys. Here Williams's new words, and the naïveté they connote, look so much like high school crush notes that the resemblance makes the poet cringe: "Liberate the words. You tie them. Poetic sweet-heart. Ugh. Poetic sweetheart. My dear Miss Word let me hold your W. I love you. Of all the girls in school you alone are the one—" (*I* 167). Blocking agents attempt to repress new words just as adult educators attempted to mold and control new boys and girls: "Save the words. Save the words from themselves. They are like children. Young Men's Hebrew Association. Save them while they're still young. Words must not be allowed to say, to do—Geld them" (*I* 172). Identifying sexual and artistic potency, Williams identifies both with the newly visible sexuality of youth, which the YMCA, YMHA, and similar adult-run groups tried to restrain (Kett, *Rites of Passage*; Kidd, *Making American Boys*).

Williams's interest in youth culture may never remain fully separate from the erotic interest in much younger women, or girls, described in some of his writings (such as "The Ogre"). Yet Williams's work of the 1920s also reveals a time when (in Beth Bailey's words) "young people thought the divisions between men and women were less important than the division between young and old" (*Front Porch to Back Seat*, 78). However unlikely it seems in retrospect, Williams and his contemporaries identified adolescent refusals of authority, and a drastic lessening of gender inequality, with high school. Bourne wrote in 1913 that high schools present "a youthful society where there is perfectly free intercourse, an unforced social life of equals," with the "result . . . that the boy's and the girl's attitude toward life, their spiritual outlook, has come to be the same" (*Youth and Life*, 35). Indeed, "during the 1910s [boys'] premarital sexual experiences and those of girls grew increasingly similar" (Mintz, *Huck's Raft*, 229). As a physician with both an obstetric and a pediatric practice, Williams would have seen evidence for these changes, which took place long after his own teens.

The Great American Novel thus identifies high school students as New World explorers: "Now they lay half covered in the leaves and enjoying the warmth looked out on the new world. And he was passing and saw them. And wondered if it were too late to be Eric. What a new world they had made" (*I* 182). "The boys kick the ball up into the wind and the wind hurriedly writes a love note upon it: Meet me tonight. Say you are going to the Library and I will have my car at the corner of Fern Street. I have something to tell you. There is one word you must hear: YOU" (*I* 179–80). The wind here is another American youth who drives his—or her—car and arranges a secretive date. So is the automobile itself, the supposed heroine of Williams's antinovel: "Oh, to be a woman, thought the speeding mechanism. For they had wrapped something or other in a piece of newspaper and placed it under the seat and there were pictures there of girls—or grown women it might be, in very short skirts" (*I* 190). American novelty, as this car—and Williams's text—understand it, has everything to do with a "new look," a new way of being, in which "grown women" look more than ever like "girls," boasting "very short skirts" and (one page later) "Greenwich Village honkie-tonk bobbed hair" (*I* 191). Just such a fast young woman becomes the heroine of *Flaming Youth*, a book that Williams goes out of his way to praise, incorporating or parodying its disapproving newspaper reviews (*I* 201). Youthful "flamboyance" and "creative energy," Williams writes twice in these passages, mark "at least the beginning of art" (*I* 200–201).[19]

Williams's views of American adolescence as it developed in the 1910s and 1920s thus gave him models and metaphors for his own deliberately unfinished, always-beginning-again works of art. Spacks writes that "adolescence *means* possibility: so writers in all centuries have felt. Not until [the twentieth] century," however, "have novelists sustained a fantasy of preserving its values and its indeterminacy" (*The Adolescent Idea*, 250). We might read *The Great American Novel*, with its insistence on the "new" and its almost spasmodic avoidance of plots and conclusion, as just such a fantasy—though it might be better to call it a *project*: we might, in fact, see the similar projects of specifically adolescent energy and indeterminacy throughout Williams's book-length works of the 1920s, all of which (excepting his conventional novel, *A Voyage to Pagany*) feature repeated beginnings without clear conclusions and almost all of which (except *Pagany* and *In the American Grain*) include at least one segment devoted to the new 1920s youth.

A final instance of adolescence in Williams also stands among the most condensed and most powerful. Cars and dates and athletes and schools, boys and girl, turn up again in *The Descent of Winter* (1928), whose "11/1" segment constitutes a *multum in parvo* of 1920s youth. Williams's hopes of artistic rejuvenation (which *The Descent of Winter* as a whole takes up) here rests on his ability to incorporate young people's culture into his own poems:

> I won't have to powder my nose tonight 'cause Billie's gonna take me
> home in his car—
>
> The moon, the dried weeds
> and the Pleiades—
> Seven feet tall
> the dark, dried weedstalks
> make a part of the night
> a red lace
> on the blue milky sky
>
> Write—
> by a small lamp
> the Pleiades are almost
> nameless
> and the moon is tilted
> and halfgone
>
> And in runningpants and
> with ecstastic, aesthetic faces
> on the illumined
> signboard are leaping
> over printed hurdles and
> "1/4 of their energy comes
> from bread"
>
> two
> gigantic highschool boys
> ten feet tall
>
> (*I* 248)

"11/1" starts with something a girl on a date might say and ends by depicting the boys she might admire: the poem becomes the place where girls and boys, night and morning, written text and heard or seen young people meet. The lyrical aspect of youth here appears eternal (it harks back to Sappho's poem about the Pleiades), but its energies also seem—like running pants and billboards—historically new. A rejuvenated American poetry such as Williams hopes to write must (this poem suggests) include all these phenomena: Pleiades, nameless weeds, nameless athletes, dates, hurdlers, moon. The athletes and dates continue a tradition in which old love poems (now rewritten) can also take part; just as the hurdlers leap over their "printed" hurdles, the lines about hurdlers vault over their line breaks, showing off the enjambments that Stephen Cushman has plausibly read as the prime source of Williams's formal innovations. Only if such new young characters (on billboards and in person) fit into Williams's 1920s style can he accomplish the poetic rejuvenation that *Descent* (like Williams's earlier sequences) seeks, in which "a young dog / jumped out / of the old barrel" (*I* 238).

❖ ❖ ❖ ❖ ❖

If *Spring and All* found one symbol for its aesthetic objectives in the new youth of American suburbs and towns, it found another in the writings of Marianne Moore, who (Williams wrote) "is of all American writers most constantly a poet" (*CPW* 230). Bonnie Costello writes that Moore "became the heroine of Williams' *Spring and All*, where he praised her for precisely the qualities he was trying to achieve" (*Marianne Moore*, 11).[20] They were not the qualities she was trying to achieve. Williams lauded the young for their sexualized, very much extracurricular energy. Moore also used adolescence—tastes, habits, and attitudes proper to modern young people after childhood and before adulthood—as model and metaphor for her own poems. Yet Moore—with her notes and notebooks, her enthusiasm for quotations, and her fastidious attributions—identified her poetic methods with the procedures of a responsible student. Dissenting from models of youth as praiseworthy rebellion, Moore's writing (in verse and prose) about youth and young people defends the virtues of mind engendered by well-run educational institutions. Her early poems announce their collegiate roots, which contribute to their distinctive tones. Few of her later poems depict students or adolescents at length, but those which do include several of her most admired works. Drawing both on her reading about education and on her experience of it, Moore found not only precepts to embody the qualities *she* sought in American youth but a style that gave those precepts their due.

We can see those precepts in the prose she contributed to the *Dial* during her editorship (1925–1929). Moore devoted three pages to an exhibit of art by "children from eight to thirteen years of age," praising its "unstrained-for *esprit*" (and remembering that "at the age of thirteen one feels older than one can ever really be"). Moore also reminds us that students produced all these artworks with and for teachers, in school: "these diverse designs" offer "proof that imagination gains rather than loses by guidance, and one is assured that the creating of beauty is, like the appreciating of beauty, in part the result of instruction" (*Complete Prose*, 153). In Moore's prose (if not in many people's experience), middle school, high school, and college appear as continuous parts of one potentially virtuous instructional process. Where her contemporaries found a generation gap, Moore emphasized the continuity of instruction and of student life from medieval times to her own. "Gabriel Harvey's report of intellectual assumptiveness at [late-sixteenth-century] Cambridge applies equally to our [collegiate] halls of residence," Moore wrote in 1927; in 1929 she deplored "the dreary way in which some 'keep speaking of "adults" and "adolescents"'" (*Complete Prose*, 190, 217). Three years earlier, she commented: "Our most presentable young people seem to share in the attitude of haste, and are accused of irreverence, ingratitude and flippancy. We are, however, encouraged to suspect beneath the mannerism of quick self-sufficiency, a root of seriousness" (quoted in Taffy Martin, *Marianne Moore*, 55). Moore dissents here both from the journalists who celebrated flappers and "petting parties" and from the social critics who excoriated them. She finds in modern youth something else to admire.[21]

Biographically inclined readers have made perhaps too much of Moore's years of teaching at the Carlisle Indian School (1911–1914), which seem to have left her overworked, unhappy, and in conflict with its management. By contrast, as Charles Molesworth notes, "her college education" at Bryn Mawr "was one of the transforming experiences of her life"; she later "toyed with . . . writing an appreciation of college education in America" (*Marianne Moore*, xii). Moore expected to like Bryn Mawr before she got there, and she did like it very much, writing during her first year, "I am wandering through the enchanted land as I had pictured to myself" (*Complete Prose*, 571; *Selected Letters*, 15). Her rebuff by the English Department did little to dim her loyalty to the college: she wrote to Bryher in 1921, "my experience there gave me security in my determination to have what I want" (*Selected*

Letters, 178). While full of appreciation for individuals, Moore's letters do not describe her adult workplaces in anything like such devoted terms. A 1929 letter describes Moore's attendance at "a luncheon . . . in the interest of endowment for women's colleges & I feel the need a very great one" (*Selected Letters*, 247).[22] Cristanne Miller (citing Carroll Smith-Rosenberg) has discussed Moore's place among the "college-educated women coming to professional maturity in the United States between 1890 and 1920," a group shaped by "the proliferation of women's colleges" (*Marianne Moore*, 97). Miller sees Moore as "determined to establish in her writing a communally focused authority that avoided egocentric and essentialist assertions . . . while also avoiding . . . self-erasure" (vii). Such a communal authority resembles, and may derive from, an idealized college or scholarly community—or so Moore's poems about students suggest.

Those poems consider schools, colleges, and students in three separable ways. First, poems in *Observations* (some written *at* college) situate the book partly in a collegiate context. Second, Moore's style, with its quotations, borrowings, notes, gestures of deferred or refused authority, and scholarly trappings, invites readers to see certain poems as analogous to students' library-based research. Finally, poems of her middle period articulate Moore's dissent from popular versions of adolescence, likening her own approach to poetry to her less flashy ideals for American youth.[23]

Moore chose to open *Observations* with "To an Intra-Mural Rat"; its title puns on the Moore family's animal nicknames and on the titular adjective, denoting either a rodent between walls or an underhanded undergraduate (*Becoming Marianne Moore*, 51).[24] The poem, which might describe a collegiate rivalry, invites readers to view the whole book as a collection of student writings, "a parenthesis of wit." To say, as "Rat" does, "You make me think of many men" to an "intra-mural" rival at Bryn Mawr places both poet and target as women in men's roles; it also presents the book as an extension of Bryn Mawr (whose students, Moore included, sometimes took masculine pronouns). Moore follows "To an Intra-mural Rat" with "Reticence and Volubility," a poem in which Merlin speaks and a "student" answers (*Becoming Marianne Moore*, 52). Of the next few poems in *Observations*, one appears as thanks for a gift ("a yellow rose") of the sort Moore's classmates sent and received; the next, "Fear Is Hope," takes the form, but not the content, of undergraduate social verse, being an invitation to a "holiday" "for us two spirits"—the poet, and the sun (*Becoming Marianne Moore*, 56–57).

To open *Observations* as if it were an undergraduate endeavor, to present its contents as responses to student life, has implications both protective (the book should not quite be judged by adult standards) and empowering (it extends an environment in which women can sound scholarly, in which they may assume male roles). Sherrie Innes notes that "discourses surrounding college women" in the early twentieth century "taught them that rebellious behavior should be limited to the college years" (*Intimate Communities*, 8). Moore's interest in thinking—and in reading—like a student turned those teachings to advantage. Some of Moore's first male readers took the hint: T. S. Eliot in 1923 described Moore's "peculiar and brilliant and rather satirical use of . . . the curious jargon produced in America by universal university education" ("Moore," 49). (By "universal" Eliot meant perhaps "open to women," perhaps "held up to all as a goal.") Ezra Pound in 1918 wrote of Loy and Moore: "The arid clarity, not without its beauty, of *le temperament de l'Americaine* is in the poems of these, I think, graduates or post-graduates. If they have not received B.A.s or M.A.s or B.Scs. they do not need them" ("Others," 58).

Moore's major poems of the early 1930s also suggest the proclivities of a diligent student, busily learning and copying down (in Margaret Holley's words) "factual information on the habits and characteristics of creatures, procedures for cultivation and production, historical events, symbolic conventions, terminologies" (*Poetry*, 95). Such a student would cite her sources. Moore's "Note on the Notes" (first published in 1941, and carried through into her 1967 *Complete Poems*) admits: "I have not yet been able to *outgrow* this hybrid method of composition" (*PMM* 375; emphasis added). Moore is perhaps remembering Eliot's remark about "the way . . . a poet borrows," his claim that "immature poets imitate; mature poets steal" (*Selected Prose*, 153); as Miller put it, Moore "represents her poetic act as a borrowing of ideas" (*Marianne Moore*, 189).[25]

Three of Moore's major poems consider youth and education in more direct ways. "Novices" (1923) begins with a clear attack on vices associated with (male) adolescence. "Novices" (Moore explains) rush foolishly into all they do or say: they solicit others' judgments before they know enough to form their own "the little assumptions of the scared ego confusing the issue" (*PMM* 152). Such novices (who may be as old as "thirty") "write the sort of thing that would in their judgment interest a lady."[26] They seek not truth but social approval. Against such callow sociability, "the good and alive young men demonstrate the assertion / that it is not necessary to be associated with that which has annoyed one" (*PMM* 153). Even these "young men," however, find themselves "bored by . . . the stuffy remarks of the Hebrews," that is, the Hebrew prophets, whom Moore herself revered.

The poem thus rebuts the reverence for rude youth that Williams (and Moore's other modernist acquaintances) espoused. "The spontaneous unforced passion of the Hebrew language" demonstrates the right kind of unpremeditated energy (the novices having demonstrated the wrong kind); so does the ocean, with its "reverberations and tempestuous energy."[27] In Williams such unselfconscious force seemed the root of all originality, visible in the boys and girls the poet observed, whose ways his style sometimes emulated. When contemporary people in Moore try to imitate unselfconscious force, they fail; they barge in like novices, or flatten others' sensibilities like steamrollers. Contemporary people ought to study that force (in nature as in literature) rather than setting up as its rivals. A poetry of studiousness, Moore suggests (in the next poem she finished after "Novices") will imitate "Chinese lacquer-carving," showing that "we are precisionists" (*PMM* 154). Though "precisionism" also denoted a school of modern painting, Moore here associates "precision" with formal education or (more precisely) with the sort of young people whom formal education helped to create.

Such a young person arrives, by name, in "The Steeple-Jack" (1932).[28] That poem includes three sorts of admirable characters: the steeple-jack himself (realigning the "star, which on a steeple / stands for hope"); "presidents who have repaid / sin-driven // senators by not thinking about them" (Moore probably meant Herbert Hoover); and a "college student / named Ambrose" whom Moore invites us explicitly to admire (*PMM* 183–84, 416; *Selected Letters*, 298). Ambrose

> sits on the hill-side
> with his not-native books and hat
> and sees boats
>
> at sea progress white and rigid as if in
> a groove. Liking an elegance of which
> the source is not bravado, he knows by heart the antique
> sugar-bowl shaped summer-house of
> interlacing slats.

(*PMM* 416).

It may be overreading to see in Ambrose's "not-native books" a riposte to Williams's and *Contact*'s campaign for American locality. It seems unavoidably right, however, to see in Ambrose a figure for Moore: their "likings," at least, are the same (they even like hats), and the "college student," combining "not-native" books with close observation, engages in just the activities that produced Moore's descriptive poems.[29]

If Ambrose so little resembles the "flaming youth" of Williams or Fitzgerald or Millay, in what sense is Ambrose adolescent? He is not adult: he comes to study, observe, and draw his own conclusions, and he is a product of a college. He is Moore's answer to the football players in Williams (for example) and to the racy couples in Millay, and he means more if we keep his rivals in mind. The long unruly lines in "Novices" imagine, first, the mess the novices make and then the ocean's admirable force. The syllabic stanzas of "The Steeple-Jack," by contrast, advertise an unemphatic order. Though Moore leads with the town's least attractive features—"stranded whales"—the town will by the end display unostentatious symmetries that offer both "a reason for living" there and a reason for living in general, for thinking well of life. Shaileen Beyer has suggested that the poem instantiates an argument from design: its natural features resemble its manmade ones, offering similar instances of reliable (yet sometimes dangerous) order (the steeple would fall without someone to repair it; the sea sometimes kills its whales) (Beyer, private communication). Named for the patron saint of schoolchildren and students, Ambrose becomes the only character in a position to see this order and affirm that argument.[30]

If "The Steeple-jack" invites both poet and readers to emulate a "student," who reads books, "sees . . . progress," and looks at life with generosity and reserve, "The Student" makes that invitation explicit. The poem's initial incarnation (as part 2 in "Part of a Novel, Part of a Poem, Part of a Play"), buries what would become the finished poem amid a debate about French and American education. In it, college looks like a type of Eden, with its "pair of fruit-trees"—"tree-of-knowledge— / tree of life—each with a label like that of the other college"; "these apple-trees should be for everyone" (*PMM* 417–18). Even college athletics (the subject, then as now, of vigorous debate) seems to Moore a source of moral strength:

> The football huddle in the vacant lot
>
> is impersonating calculus and physics and military
> books; and is gathering the data for genetics. If
> > scholarship would profit by it, sixteen
> > > foot men should be grown; it's for the football men to say. . . .
>
> Boasting provokes jibes, and in this country we've no cause to boast; we
> > are
> as a nation perhaps, undergraduates not students.

But anyone who studies will advance.

Are we to grow up or not? They are not all college boys in France.

(PMM 417–18)'

Perhaps remembering Eliot's remark about "universal university educa-tion," Moore defends the late-nineteenth-century educational model by which many high schools aspired (however unrealistically) to prepare every one of their students for college: facing rapidly rising enrollments (and noxious theories of sexual or ethnic difference), "progressive" educators in Moore's own college years had challenged just that goal.[31]

Moore (or Eliot) kept "The Student" out of her 1935 *Selected* but returned the poem to her oeuvre in 1941. If the original version shows Moore's im-mersion in debates about American undergraduate education, the later one gives the poem the precision it lauds: college degrees for all Americans stand not for decadence but for integrity:

> With us, a
> school—like the singing tree of which
> the leaves were mouths that sang in concert—
>   is both a tree of knowledge
> and of liberty.

Moore joins the "tree of knowledge" (now without fruit, since its fruit is the collegians themselves) to a patriotic image, the liberty tree. Moore then distinguishes her patriotism from nationalistic arrogance by catching Americans ("we") in a comic mistake:

>   It may be that we
> have not knowledge, just opinions, that we
>   are undergraduates,
> not students; we know
>   we have been told with smiles, by expatriates
>
> of whom we had asked "When will
> your experiment be finished?" "Science
> is never finished."

(PMM 185)

Education, for Moore, is never finished either: the habits of Bryn Mawr students—their curiosity, their energy, their distance from adult power, their purity of motive—ought to inform adult life. Moore represents the new youth of democratic higher education, and the new subject of modern poetry, as Moore optimistically wishes to see them:

> the student studies
>   voluntarily, refusing to be less
>
> than individual. He
> "gives his opinion and then rests upon it";
> he renders service when there is
> no reward, and is too reclusive for
>   some things to seem to touch
> him, not because he
>   has no feeling but because he has so much.
>
> (PMM 186)

With his intellectual armor and his "reclusive" inclination to study, this student becomes another of Moore's moral emblems: he resembles not only the poet and Ambrose (and Saint Ambrose) but also the abstract composite figure who concludes Moore's 1932 triptych, the figure "you may know / as the hero," whose earnest attention distinguishes him from mere tourists:

>   He's not out
>   seeing a sight but the rock
>   crystal thing to see—the startling El Greco
>   brimming with inner light—that
> covets nothing that it has let go.
>
> (PMM 420)

All three figures (Ambrose, "student," "hero"; "part of a novel, part of a poem, part of a play") represent the right kind of "observation"—selfless, careful, in search of moral exempla. All three represent Moore's poetic and moral goals in part by evoking formal education as a shaper of youth; all three hence recall Moore's own college experience. Collegiate life and an idealized student ethos gave Moore a way to mediate between youth as pastoral (self-enclosed, the same in each generation) and her own novelty of modernist form. As they had for Williams in *Spring and All*, as they did for so many of Moore's less accomplished coevals, the characteristics of modern adolescence—among them enthusiasm, "inner light," and a close relation to schooling—became for Moore not only a topic but a determinant (one among many) of style, even though Moore selected, from among these characteristics, some that Williams would not choose.

Modernist poems of adolescence—Williams's, Moore's, those of the little magazines—consider adolescence as both an extension of pastoral tradition—an enclosed, aestheticized space insulated from practical pressures and identified with poetry itself—and as a new kind of experience whose energies might transform the rest of the world. Both of these versions of adolescence remain available for later poets. Many would draw on them in a handful of poems, and a few would make them the basis for a style. Some poets with strong interests in adolescence (such as Robert Lowell) would ally themselves politically with youth movements, then use their poetry to reconsider that alliance. Others (such as Thom Gunn) would find subjects in the adolescent subcultures, the badges of rebellious taste in music or in clothing, which became distinctive features of teen life both in Britain and in America by the end of the 1950s. Still other poets (such as Jorie Graham and Laura Kasischke, Larry Levis and Liz Waldner) would ground poems in later models of youthful experience, some of them peculiar to one gender or to one generation. Yet these poets—and the others whom we will see in the rest of this book—all share something with those we have already seen: all find in the modern adolescent a focus for their own concerns and a figure for the distinctively modern poem.

2

From Schools to Subcultures

B RITISH ADOLESCENCE HAS a history of its own; so do the poems that describe it. "In England," the historian John Gillis writes, "the invention of adolescence was the unintended product of the reform of the public schools"—that is, elite private boarding schools such as Eton (*Youth and History*, 105).[1] Elite single-sex boarding schools—for girls and for boys—inspired much popular fiction and some poetry (by Rudyard Kipling and by W. E. Henley, among others) before 1900 (Springhall, *Coming of Age*, 132–33). Only in the twentieth century, however, could the life of the schools be juxtaposed with the psychological models that ascribed special importance to adolescence. After the Second World War, literary interest in schools receded, as postwar teenagers, mods, rockers, and hippies attracted vast publicity.

W. H. Auden built his early style from an idea of adolescence inseparable from the special conditions of schools. That idea would inform not only Auden's contemporaries but his legatees overseas. From his titillating undergraduate novellas to the title poem of *High Windows*, Philip Larkin's views of adolescence helped to shape his outlook and his oeuvre, much of it defined by his own felt distance from youth. Thom Gunn's early poems about motorcycle gangs and Elvis Presley reflect a measured identification with the youth subcultures through which Gunn would mark his Anglo-American career. Both poets' late work sets adolescence as pastoral against a sense that youth had become something historically new. For Basil Bunting, both apparently timeless and historically specific 1960s ideas about youth proved needed ingredients for his poetic monument, *Briggflatts*.

❖ ❖ ❖ ❖ ❖

Auden lived and worked in schools and colleges, as a student or as a teacher, in all but one of the years between 1915 and 1935. He became not only, in Edward Mendelson's words, "the first poet writing in English who felt at home in the twentieth century," but also the first important poet to experience in his formative years *both* the post-Freudian medical and literary models of adolescence *and* the social life of the English public school (Auden, *Selected Poems*, ix). Auden's early poems describe not a generalized immaturity but a particular kind of adolescence, enabled and mediated by all-male boarding schools. The poems, as Richard Bozorth suggests, both prefigure and instantiate Cyril Connolly's "Theory of Permanent Adolescence": Connolly argued in 1939 that "the experiences undergone by boys at the great public schools, their glories and disappointments, are so intense as to dominate their lives, and to arrest their development" (Bozorth, *Auden's Games*, 324–25).[2] Auden's homosocial, and sometimes homosexual, groups and teams find nothing worth developing into or toward, and they refuse the clearer rules of adulthood for the obscurities of in-groups and codes.[3]

"In Auden's poetry until 1932," writes Edward Mendelson, "the schoolboy was the measure of all things" (*Early*, 128). Yet most critics (Mendelson included) see schools and youth as standing for something else: for psychoanalytic models, for the nation-state, or for homosexuality generally. This chapter argues otherwise. Schools and youth in general—and elite boarding schools in particular—are why the poems sound as they do, and what they are about. Taken together the poems put forward a pattern: the group life created by and for "boys" in a school is for those boys both formative and insufficient. Graduating, becoming adult, means treason to groups defined by adolescence (and sometimes by homosexuality as well); not growing up, on the other hand, amounts to stagnation and death. To see Auden's early poetry first through his interest in schools and schooling might show how thoroughly that interest informs the poetry and how the poems' style fits the milieu they describe.

That interest appeared before the style did. Auden and Day-Lewis' preface to *Oxford Poetry, 1927* shrugged off readers' interest in youth qua youth: "Those who believe that there is anything valuable in our youth as such we have neither the patience to consider nor the power to condone" *(PTB 4–5)*. Yet the young Auden embraced youth as a subject. He wrote to Isherwood that in his poem "Thomas Prologizes" (1926), "The idea of course is an adolescent, who feels that all his old ideas are breaking up and have taught little but lyric and lechery. Then he thinks 'lets get on to something new'" (*sic*; quoted in John Fuller, *Auden*, 40). "I chose this lean country" (summer 1927) ends by invoking the "mildewed dormitory" to which the poet's readers ("this people") would return (Auden, *Juvenilia*, 211). A nine-section poem called "The Megalopsych" depicts fugitive schoolboys along with useless, failed "men": "The last boy vanishes, / A blazer half-on, through the rigid trees" (*Juvenilia*, 199). "Narcissus" (1927) asks: "But where are Basley who won the Ten, / Dickon so tarted by the House, / Thomas who kept a sparrowhawk?" (*Juvenilia*, 186). These lines adapt Villon's *ubi sunt* to the world of the public school. They would find their way into *Paid on Both Sides*, and may be the first bit of *Paid* Auden composed (*Juvenilia*, 241; *EA* 15).

Auden's poetry through 1933 often seems to dramatize not his own prep school, public school, or university life so much as that of his friends, especially Gabriel Carritt and Christopher Isherwood. Carritt's sporting exploits infiltrate several of Auden's works (among them *The Orators*), while Isherwood and Edward Upward's visions of school life as covert war predate Auden's similar models. Isherwood's *Lions and Shadows* recalls Isherwood and Upward ("Chalmers" in the novel) "swearing never to betray each other, never to forget the existence of 'the two sides' and their eternal, necessary state of war" (24). At Cambridge, the pair maintain a constant "conversation . . . hardly intelligible to anyone who had happened to overhear it: it was a rigmarole of private slang, deliberate misquotations, bad puns, bits of parody and preparatory school smut" (65).

By late 1927 Auden's poetry incorporated all those characteristics: it was evolving toward *Paid on Both Sides*, in which school and nation, real wars and school games, mingle inextricably. "Because sap fell away" takes place in school:

> Upon our failure come
> Down to the lower changing-room,
> Honours on pegs, cast humours, we sit lax,
> In close ungenerous intimacy,
> Remember
> Falling in slush, shaking hands
> With a snub-nosed winner;
> Open a random locker, sniff with distaste
> At a mouldy passion.
>
> (*JUVENILIA*, 227)

The locker contains "mouldy passion" both because boys' lockers smell of stale sweat and clothes and because the "changing-room" (now scene of a loss and prey to "lethal factors") holds motives and stages of development "we" should (but do not) outgrow. Katherine Bucknell links this poem to a rugby match Auden watched "between Oxford and Cambridge Old Sedberghians," in which Carritt led the Oxford side (*Juvenilia*, 228).[4] Auden's early poems equate geological change, the turning of the seasons, and graduation, each of which will destroy what is valuable in summer or in youth. So they warn their undergraduate hearers:

> But loving now, let none
> Think of divided days
> When we shall choose from ways,
> All of them evil, one.
>
> Look on with stricter brows
> The sacked and burning town,
> The ice-sheet moving down,
> The fall of an old house.
>
> (*JUVENILIA*, 242-43)

"Ways, / All of them evil" are not only geographic paths but means of employment. "The average private school child," Auden and T. C. Worsley wrote in 1937, "has a fuller and a more exciting life at school than he has at home, or, in many cases, than he is likely to have in his work" (*PTB* 397). "The fall of an old house" suggests architectural collapse and genealogical decay (as in "The Fall of the House of Usher") but also the end of a "house" in a public school ("Dickon so tarted by the House"), and perhaps the Oxford usage (still current) by which Christ Church students call their college "the House."

About *Paid* itself my argument scarcely needs to be made. John Fuller notes "particular references in [*Paid*] to sporting customs at Sedbergh School," and place-names near both Sedbergh and Gresham's (*Auden*, 23, 33). "The school saga world" of the play, Isherwood suggested, was "founded upon our preparatory school lives": "It is impossible to say whether the characters are really epic heroes or only members of a school OTC" (*Lions*, 192–93; *Exhumations*, 19). The Old Gang of *Paid* cannot envision any rules but those of school competitions:

> **w.** Did you ever see Warner? No, he'd be before your time. You remember him don't you Trudy?
> **T.** He was killed in the fight at Colefangs, wasn't he?
> **w.** You are muddling him up with Hunter. He was the best three-quarter I have ever seen. His sprinting was marvelous to watch.
>
> (*EA* 7, 4)

For Bozorth, *Paid* "amounts to a critique of the Auden group's own psychosexual arrested development, implicated as it is in a culturally conservative homosociality" (*Auden's Games*, 97). Yet the "critique" is only half the story: outside of *Paid*, the poems can admire school life, especially as it pertains to sex. Of Auden's many 1930s writings about teachers and schools, the best known is his 1934 memoir of Gresham's, with its often misinterpreted line "at school I lived in a Fascist state" (*PTB* 59). The passage describes not public schools generally (despite their emphasis on loyalty and team spirit) but an unusual feature of Gresham's, the "Honour System," which required the boys to inform on one another (*PTB* 58–59). This Honour System apparently prevented much of the semicovert homosexual life of other public schools, about which Auden at Oxford proved curious, even envious, at one time "planning to compile a three-volume study of preparatory school, public school, and university 'confessions'" (Carpenter, *Auden*, 78).[5] Auden could thus research the sort of desirable homosocial (if not overtly homosexual) gossip and ritual that (in his view) the Honour System of Gresham's ruled out.[6] He wrote in 1929 that in Berlin "I am having the sort of friendships I ought to have had at 16 and didn't" (quoted in Mendelson, *Early*, 59). Isherwood even told Humphrey Carpenter that during the months in which he and Auden had sex, "the value of the sex making was that it kept an adolescent quality in our relationship alive— almost as if we could go back together into the past" (*Auden*, 64).

Poems written after *Paid* return to dilemmas about growing up (or not growing up); they also return to belated erotic attachments, which Auden describes in terms drawn from school. "Pairing off in twos and two," "knowing what to do / But of no use," Auden's boys or young men seem destined for a life they cannot welcome, and they display nostalgia for an erotic life that they have outgrown:

> Never stronger
> But younger and younger
> Saying goodbye but coming back, for fear
> Is over there
> And the centre of anger
> Is out of danger.
>
> (*EA* 27)

The boys keep "coming back" to their previous lives just as the half-rhymes keep "coming back," one per stanza, with "stronger" distorted into "anger" and "danger."

Redemptive moments in these poems have not only homoerotic qualities but further qualities of rehearsal or sport: "Calling of each other by
name / Smiling, taking a willing arm / Has the companionship of a game"
(*EA* 32). Failures, conversely, are attempts to leave school. In "Consider this
and in our time," the "Financier" loses a game played "on the lawns / Of
College Quad or of Cathedral Close"; "Amid rustle of frocks and stamping
feet," the poem continues, "They gave the prizes to the ruined boys,"
a graduation gone wrong (*EA* 47). Auden's 1930 poem in the meter of
"Locksley Hall" depicts an England where male adolescents receive a glit-
tering homoerotic present but a subordinate, useless future: "Boon companions" have "betrayed us," "Taught us at the annual camps arranged by
the big business men / 'Sunbathe, pretty, till you're twenty. You shall be our
servants then'" (*EA* 48). Perhaps missing the irony, Naomi Mitchison
praised "the whole poem's young, strong rebellious he-quality," linking it to
"the modern youth movement in Germany" (in Haffenden, *Critical Heritage*, 82).[7]

The pattern of blocked development, of schoolboys with no destination
outside school, which drives the most serious poems of 1928 through 1932
generates broad comedy in Auden and Isherwood's plays. In *The Enemies of
a Bishop* (1929), a master named Augustus runs a strict reformatory: "Whatever you make of yourself here," he declares, "you'll make by discipline and
self control" (*Plays*, 45). One of Augustus's charges makes a mockery of his
rules by seducing him. When the permissive bishop arrives to save the day,
he and his campy "Flying Squad" reform the wayward adults by turning
them into schoolboys, via athletics, classroom punishments, and psycho-
analysis: "You will do the Cautley Spout run every afternoon for two
months. You will be timed. . . . Also, every Saturday morning, before lunch,
you will bring me five thousand lines. The motto for this week will be
'Mummy's been dead quite a long time now'" (*Plays*, 76).

Does the play, then, invite its audience to reenter adolescence? Not quite:
its epilogue distinguishes audience members (ordinary citizens who are
"going to have friends, to bring up children," "to be like this forever all the
time") from the characters in the play, who do not participate in "life's cir-
cular career":

We saw all this, but what have we to do
With the felicities of natural growth?
What reference theirs to ours, where shame
Invasive daily into deeper tissues
Has all convicted? Remain we here

Sitting too late among the lights and music,
Without hope waiting for a soothing hush.

(*PLAYS*, 78)

The actors in this epilogue suggest both schoolboys (stuck in their limited theater) and gay men, unlikely to "bring up children" or enter into the "profuse production" of "natural growth" *(Plays*, 78–79). *Enemies* evolved into *The Dog Beneath the Skin* (1935), losing many of its school elements in the process. An intermediate play, *The Chase* (1934), retains from *Enemies* the reformatory, the wrongheaded master, and the schoolboy who seduces him in drag. These plays and these poems imply, or describe, one pattern: a small group at school, speaking a language distinctively theirs and distinctively adolescent, creates a valuable homoerotic community whose members feel they must but cannot grow up.

The same pattern permeates *The Orators*. Auden told "boys and girls and their parents" in "Writing" that Homer produced "a kind of writing called epic—long stories in verse about the exploits of a small group of young warriors under a leader" (*PTB* 24). Auden perhaps defined "epic" as involving youth ("young warriors") partly because had just finished creating an anti-, semi- or parodic epic of adolescence. Yet if *The Orators* has a unifying conceit or form, it is less epic than dramatic miscellany. Public schools, and fiction about them, featured such miscellanies: Kipling's *Stalky & Co.* has a school pantomime whose script "had been rewritten and filled with local allusions"; its heroes "invented . . . catch-words that swept through the house" (47, 139–40). *The Orators* is just such a series of sketches, speeches, and recitations, into which almost any short lyric, dramatic, or narrative work, and almost any private reference, fits, as long as it has to do with the life of the school.[8]

Though critics tend to read *The Orators* as an attack on protofascist idealizations of adolescence, schools, and small groups, it would be truer to say that as a miscellany, it contains almost every conceivable view of such groups, from admiration to appalled mockery; what it does not contain is hope for adult (or heterosexual) satisfaction. The sixteen-line prologue to *The Orators* describes its boy's progress away from, and then back toward, a mother figure who cannot forgive him for growing up (*EA* 61). In 1945 Auden retitled the poem "Adolescence" (*Collected Poems*, 23).[9] This idealtypical adolescent also makes maps, inscribing "All the family names on the familiar places." These maps become the first of many failed guides in *The Orators*; another is the "scheme or plan" promised by the prize-day speaker

(*EA* 62). One may read the whole of *The Orators*, in fact, as a disintegrated or failed "map" of the progress from adolescence to adulthood. The young man "following his love" in Auden's sestina nearly completes that progress after he escapes the mentors who have drawn his "map of the country"; he turns the endless childhood they promise ("we shall watch your future") into his own "consummation," a vague independence (*EA* 77).

The rest of the people in *The Orators* may leave home, but they fail once they leave school. "Have a good look at the people you know," the poem warns, "at the boy sitting next to you at this moment, at that chum of yours in the Lower School. . . . Pray God, boys, you may not have to see them as they will be not so very long from now. 'What have you been up to?' you'd think; 'What did you ask for to be given that?'" (*EA* 63). Auden's mysteriously overspecified petitionary prayer includes all manner of English men and women, boys and girls, but especially schoolboys: "For those who cannot go to bed; for those in dormitories; for those in pairs; for those who sleep alone" (*EA* 67). Its blithe assignment of talents and fates recalls Auden's Christ Church habit of assigning destinies to his friends: "One is a lightning calculator; he is a young one. One is clumsy but amazes by his knowledge of time-tables" (*EA* 70).[10]

The often-remarked difficulty *The Orators* gives in telling readers how seriously to take it, or which parts of it are satire (and of what), stems partly from the work's roots in school culture (which nobody outside a given school can quite know how to read) and partly from its ideas about development: it cannot decide if the adolescence it models solicits envy or disdain. Most critics connect *The Orators* to school, not to university, but in Auden's imagination these are continuous: some "private associations" in the Airman's journal are reminiscences of Christ Church, with "an economics Don called Harrod / (Now Junior Censor)," "Bill [who] came from the same school but not till a year later," and "a lot about the Essay Club and Stephen" (*EA* 78, 88). The Airman's "enemy," as all commentators notice, incarnates adult (institutional, masculine, heterosexual) authority, which Auden sometimes mocks or impersonates and sometimes attacks with tones as blunt as Wilfred Owen's: "His collar was spotless; he talked very well, / He spoke of our homes and duty and we fell" (*EA* 81).

No surprise, then (especially after Auden's Third at Oxford) that the war with the enemy includes an exam: "At 6 p.m. passages of unprepared translation from dead dialects are set to all non-combatants. The papers are collected at 6.10. All who fail to obtain 99% make the supreme sacrifice. Candidates must write on three sides of the paper" (*EA* 92). The postexam revolutionary counterattack involves school disruptions: "Form-masters find crude graffiti on their blackboards; the boys, out of control, imbibe Vimto through India-rubber tubing, openly pee into the ink pots" (*EA* 92). The doomed student revolt here—a consciously inadequate metaphor for political revolution—recalls the war in Lindsay Anderson's film *If...* (1968). Here, as there, it becomes hard to know whether school stands for society or vice versa; part of the point of both works is our inability to think of one in terms uninflected by the other.

No wonder, then, that their revolution fails: Auden's young rebels achieve only "resistance," in James Kincaid's sense. "Resistance," Kincaid generalizes, "is so convinced of the primacy of power that it only wants to act against power, not independently of it. Resistance thus confirms power [through] an endless series of mildly subversive acts of protest or denial." In this sense, Kincaid explains, "resistance is the ultimate acquiescence. . . . It likes where it is, since that location provides the only identity it can know" ("Resist Me," 1329). For "location," read "school." "The defect in traditional education," Auden wrote in 1943, "was not that it failed to arouse passion, but that this, in too many cases, was the passion of rebellion, and rebellion is not a vocation . . . being only the mirror image of that against which it rebels" (*Prose*, 2:179).

Acknowledged sources for *The Orators* include the late essays and rants of D.H. Lawrence and the psychological theories of Homer Lane.[11] Like Auden's father, Lane took an interest in juvenile delinquents, whom Lane rehabilitated at his school, the Little Commonwealth (a model for A.S. Neill's Summerhill). Carritt recalled that in "talking about Homer Lane," Auden "made [Carritt] want to study adolescent deviance"; Carritt moved to New York in order to do so (Spender, *Auden: Tribute*, 57). Lane's *Talks to Parents and Teachers* (1928) called adolescence "the age which stamps the spirit with the seal of loyalty"; "the boy or girl who does not take an interest in games," Lane wrote, "has not become adolescent in the psychic sense," since he or she is not "one of a group" (104, 106). Auden would echo these views; he and Worsley wrote in 1937

> that many of the theories and practices which [fascism] prescribes for adults may be well adequated to the needs of adolescents. The emphasis on physical adventure and physical toughness, the segregation of the sexes, the distrust of intellectualism, the love of ritual, the gang and leader organization, all apply to many boys and girls from 11 to 16.
>
> (*PTB* 418)

Auden and his circle also read about adolescence in *Les Faux-Monnayeurs* (*The Counterfeiters*), by André Gide, whose English translation appeared in 1927; Isherwood records his own and his friends' enthusiasm for it (*Lions*, 167). Spender in 1930 "discovered a great passage in [*Les Faux-Monnayeurs*] which is rather like my life with my friends" (*Letters to Christopher*, 37).[12] Gide's "schoolboys" (in Cyril Connolly's laudatory précis) "when not engaged in bringing out a literary manifesto, are discovered organizing a brothel, stealing books, blackmailing their parents . . . and finally hounding the weakest to death by means of an extensive suicide pact" (*Condemned*, 20).

Almost all these actions take place in *The Orators*, whose concluding odes recapitulate the Airman's—and *The Counterfeiters*'s—school-centered model of youth. As in Gide, boys celebrate their own games in elaborate language marked as theirs alone. The second ode lauds Carritt's victorious rugby side, echoing both "The Wreck of the *Deutschland*," by Hopkins, and Housman's "To an Athlete Dying Young": "shoulder them high, who won by their pluck and their dare" (*EA* 96). This ode obeys Pindaric conventions in avoiding normal word order and in praising the athletes' families and towns of origin (*EA* 97). Mendelson calls *The Orators* "an account of everything a group ought not to be" (*Early*, 95, 93). But neither Auden's attachment to Carritt nor Carritt's commitment to his rugby side were satirical.[13] Auden taught rugby at Larchfield and seemed not to mind (Davenport-Hines, *Auden*, 119). Auden wrote in 1932, to the school-aged poet John Cornford, "everything your headmaster says about the team spirit . . . is absolutely right"; "it is the tone of his voice which makes it such a lie" (quoted in Davenport-Hines, *Auden*, 127).

The trouble with the school as small or idealized group is that group members are supposed to outgrow it. They can, however, return to groups as schoolmasters, in the manner not only of Auden but of Edward Upward, to whom Auden dedicates the third ode. Its incantatory concluding stanzas suggest that the schoolmasters made the best of a bad lot:

This life is to last, when we leave we leave all,
Though vows have no virtue, though voice is in vain,
    We live like ghouls
    On posts from girls
    What the spirit utters
    In formal letters.

(*EA* 100).

Here the component of parody has vanished; the ode covers (and its diminishing stanza form imitates) "the slight despair" of a life by choice confined (at least temporarily) to a school.

Not only Auden but most of his circle taught, just after graduating from Oxford or Cambridge, either in prepatory or in public schools: "For budding authors it's become the rule" (*PTB* 334). John Lehmann in 1936 pointed out that "Auden, Day-Lewis, Warner, Upward, are, or have at one time been schoolmasters" (he might have added Spender and *New Country* editor Michael Roberts) (in Haffenden, *Critical Heritage*, 179). "Schoolmastering suits me; I thoroughly enjoy it," Auden told his older brother in 1930 (quoted in Carpenter, *Auden*, 111). Auden contributed to school magazines; a former pupil, John Duguid, recalled that "he would be one of the gang and attend meals with us" (Carpenter, 159, 174; Izzo, "The Student," 30, 33).[14] Schoolteaching informed Auden's poetry after *The Orators*; in "Now from my window-sill I watch the night," the famous "Lords of Limit" appear in school as "Oldest of masters, whom the schoolboy fears" (*EA* 115). Auden then describes his own young charges, "Favel, Holland, sprightly Alexis" and their age-mates:

> At the end of my corridor are boys who dream
> Of a new bicycle or winning team;
> On their behalf guard all the more
> This late-maturing Northern shore
> Who to their serious season may shortly come.
>
> (*EA* 116)

These boys, in other words, will soon encounter the problems Auden's poetry has faced.[15]

If Auden's early poems described an adolescence particular to public schools, they were received—by the graduates of those same schools—as the voice of the nation's youth. "It would be hard," John Mortimer wrote, "to overestimate the effect Auden had on me and my generation of middle-class schoolboys. He wrote about *what we understood*: juvenile jokes about housemasters, homosexual longings, the Clever Boy, the Form Entertainer and the Show Off" (quoted in Firchow, *Contexts*, 27).[16] Michael Roberts wrote in 1932: "To condemn Mr. Auden's very frequent use of public school and O.T.C. imagery is . . . unreasonable, for in addressing the public-schoolboy he is attacking . . . English decadence at the crucial point" (in Haffenden, *Critical Heritage*, 109). The Auden number of *New Verse* (1937) reprised such comments: MacNeice's open letter to Auden indicated that "the taunt of being a schoolboy . . . is itself a compliment because it implies that you expect the world and yourself to develop," missing the poems' implications that Auden did not expect any such end (in Haffenden, *Critical Heritage*, 255–56). Charles Madge, who had once written "Yes England I was at school with you," later complained that Auden's "immature quality, once an attraction, becomes an embarrassment" (quoted in Hynes, *Auden Generation*, 112; in Haffenden, *Critical Heritage*, 272). As late as 1940, James Southworth—apparently the first American critic to write about Auden's homosexuality—called Auden's early poetry a description "particularly . . . of youth" (*Sowing*, 132).

Auden described it instead as an exorcism. "The work of a young writer," Auden explained, "is sometimes a therapeutic act. He finds himself obsessed by certain ways of feeling and thinking of which his instinct tells him he must be rid before he can discover his authentic interests." And yet "what he wrote in order to exorcise certain feelings is enthusiastically welcomed by his contemporaries, because it expresses just what they feel" (*Dyer's*, 18–19). One might think such prose described "Spain," or other political writings that Auden repudiated. Yet Auden wrote in 1966, in a new preface to *The Orators*, that his "unconscious motive in writing it was therapeutic, to exorcise certain tendencies in myself by allowing them to run riot in phantasy" (8). *The Age of Anxiety* (1947) offered an account—Auden's last—of the rebellion and solidarity specific to youth: the character Emble explains that "To be young means . . . to be held waiting in / A packed lounge for a Personal Call / From Long Distance," a call that "Defines one's future" (*Collected Poems*, 474). As in *The Orators*, such a call may never come.[17]

Auden's early preoccupations with adolescence became part of his legacy not only to later English writers, such as Keith Douglas (see his "On Leaving School") but also to midcentury North American poets; Daryl Hine, Randall Jarrell, and Karl Shapiro, among others, wrote dramatically and deliberately Audenesque poems about high school, college, and youth. "An Adolescent," by Hine, with its evasive Sapphic stanzas and anonymous chorus, makes one striking example (we will see others in chapter three) (Hollander, *Moment*, 135). Perhaps more surprising, Auden's ideas of adolescence entered the inventions of John Ashbery. Ashbery wrote his Harvard thesis on Auden and later told Aidan Wasley that among his influences, "Auden was the most important because he came first"; he sets *The Orators* among his favorite poems (Wasley, "Apprentice," 667, 681). Ashbery's debut volume, *Some Trees* (1956), which Auden picked for the Yale Younger Poets prize, adopted the conspiratorial tone of Auden's earliest lyrics, along with their shifting pronouns; in "Popular Songs," "All are aware, some carry a secret /

Better" (Ashbery, *Selected* 4). Those shifters, with their hint of private references, make one source for Ashbery's famously slippery style. "Of who we and all they are / You all now know," "The Grapevine" begins; "But after they began to find us out we grew" (*Selected*, 9). "They" in this poem resemble parents or schoolmasters, while "we" are their charges or students, still going through "These changes we think we are. We don't care / Though, so tall up there/ In young air" (*Selected*, 9). Another poem from *Some Trees*, "And You Know," shows Ashbery's characteristic verbal maneuvers evolving out of a prior coterie language, the local slang and in-jokes associated with the Audenesque and with the public school: "we carry your lessons in our hearts (the lessons and our hearts are the same) / Out of the humid classroom, into the forever. Goodbye, Old Dog Tray" (*Selected*, 23).[18]

Ashbery's subsequent poems can also infuse half-serious symbols of youth and school with homoerotic implications, and with existential frustrations. "Our Youth" warns "You will never have that young boy"; "the problem has not been solved" (*Selected*, 37–38). (Auden's "This Lunar Beauty" conveyed the same warnings.) In "The Big Cloud," youth—just as in Auden—represents a promise always betrayed: "laughter danced in the dim fields beyond the schoolhouse: / It was existence again in all its tautness, / Playing its adolescent joke. . . . But life was never the same again. Something faltered, / Something went away" (*April*, 58–59). It would be wrong to expect, throughout Ashbery's work, the kind of sustained attention to the social particularities of adolescence, to the cultural indicators of generational change, that I have noted in Williams and in the young Auden. Yet we have already seen a preoccupation with adolescence advance through "Soonest Mended," one of Ashbery's most famous poems. And the pathos and sense of loss that many critics consider Ashbery's primary subject acquires its distinctive relation to the slippery language that marks Ashbery's style in part through their common sources in the school codes, evasions, and deliberate "immaturity" that we recognize, in other contexts, as Audenesque.

❖ ❖ ❖ ❖ ❖

Philip Larkin declared that "deprivation was for me what daffodils were for Wordsworth" (*Further Requirements*, 47). One might add that he felt deprived of youth. Repudiating both childhood and maturity, Larkin's writings come close to identifying adolescence as the only desirable state. The desirable adolescence they imagine, however, is the adolescence of others, the youth he could not experience, being of the wrong temperament, gender, or generation. His poems thus imagine a double deprivation: the loss everyone will experience as he or she ages and the loss (or never-having-had) peculiar to Larkin or to those like him. Larkin's earliest work takes up—as does Auden's—young people imagined or observed in colleges and schools. His poetics of lost or occluded adolescence last (as Auden's did not) into the 1950s, when Britain developed a national youth culture; that culture gave Larkin (even when he denounced it) one more symbol of what he had missed, around which his late poems might crystallize. Adolescence in this sense may not create a basis for Larkin's style; instead, it becomes inseparable from his subjects.

Larkin's juvenilia replicate Auden's plots, depicting heroes in confined, school-like societies who "must escape, or perish saying no" (*CPL* 257, 243). "To read the *Journal of an Airman*," Larkin felt in 1939, "was like being allowed half an hour's phone conversation with God" (quoted in Motion, *A Writer's Life*, 44). Soon enough Larkin found styles unlike Auden's in which to describe regrets about missed youth: the very early "Ugly Sister" ends:

Since I was not bewitched in adolescence
And brought to love,
I will attend to the trees and their gracious silence,
To winds that move.
(*CPL* 292).

If Auden's school codes projected homosocial or homosexual cliques, the clarity and loneliness in Larkin's language suggest a young (heterosexual) man who has never had cherished codes to share, nor girls with whom to share them.

Larkin therefore made them up. During his last year at Oxford, Larkin wrote several hundred pages of fiction, poetry, and criticism in the persona of "Brunette Coleman." All are, or concern, British girls-school stories, of the kind popular since the late nineteenth century with audiences (mostly) of girls and young women; most of the Coleman material consists of two extended fictional works, *Trouble at Willow Gables* and the unfinished *Michaelmas Term at St. Brides*. Larkin showed this material to a few Oxford friends and preserved it throughout his life (*Trouble*, 205). Before its 2002 publication, *Trouble at Willow Gables* was heralded in the British press as Larkin's undergraduate lesbian fantasy; at least one reviewer savaged it as "pitiful pornography and feeble erotica" (Diski, "Damp-Lipped"). While surely designed to excite male readers with its scenes of spanking, tying-up, seduction, and repeatedly ripped trousers, *Trouble* and its unfinished sequel

reveal stranger aims than their reception suggests—aims that would inform Larkin's poems much later.

"Coleman" gave Larkin two things his own life had lacked: girls and the
public school. Larkin had lived with his parents while attending the single-
sex King Henry VIII School. "All the time I lived in Coventry I never
knew any girls," he recalled (*Further Requirements*, 9). John Kemp, in Larkin's novel *Jill*, believes public school life "was wild and extravagant . . .
compared with his own: it seemed to him that in their schooldays [his Oxford classmates] had won more than he would ever win during the whole
of his life" (57). Kemp makes up a sister, named Jill, who "writes" to him
from her boarding school, also named Willow Gables: "he liked to think of
her as preoccupied only with simple untroublesome things, like examina-
tions and friendships" (135–36).[19] Willow Gables in "Coleman" provided
Larkin—as Willow Gables in *Jill* provided John Kemp—with fantasies of
acceptance among safe erotic objects. The predatory sixth-former in *Trouble* expresses views that now might attract police: "Hilary thought, as so often before she had thought, that there was nothing so beautiful in the world
as a fourteen-year-old schoolgirl" (84) Her object of desire, Mary, "lived a
life so simple and rounded-off in its purity that it only remained for it to be
shattered" (84). Hilary decides not to shatter it after all, preferring to retain
her "vision of [Mary] embodying the purity of youth, dressed in white tennis things and haloed with a netball stand" (174).

So far, perhaps, so much undergraduate porn. Why, though, did "Coleman" also write essays and poems? In "Coleman's" adaptation of "Femmes
Damnées," Baudelaire's poem about a lesbian seduction, Larkin introduces
for the first time the contemporary, tawdry particulars that characterize his
later poems:

> The milk's been on the step,
> The "Guardian" in the letter-box, since dawn.
>
> Upstairs, the beds have not been touched, and thence
> Builders' estates, and the main road, are seen,
> With labourers, petrol-pumps, a Green Line 'bus,
> And plots of cabbages set in between.
> (*TROUBLE*, 246)

The Coleman materials provided not only an excuse for technical practice
(in verse and in prose) but a way to develop the outlook that would, later,

generate Larkin's best verse. "Coleman's" essay "What Are We Writing For?" consists of a serious and amply documented defense of the genre of girls-school fiction, which (she claims) has yet to produce its masterpiece. According to her "purist view-point," "a school story . . . is not a story about schoolgirls, but a story about a school with schoolgirls in it" (*Trouble*, 267). In writing school stories, "we are evoking that old, safe, happy beautiful world for our contemporaries, as well as creating a world of make-believe for our juniors, who are not yet old enough to savour the quintessence of their youth"; "we must construct a closed, single-sexed world" (268–69).

Larkin spent months, if not years, doing just that. Writing to Amis, Larkin belittled the Coleman works, including "WILLOWGABLISMUS" in a "list of sexual perversions" (*Selected Letters*, 103).[20] Letters to other correspondents, however, treat Coleman as a sort of Pessoan heteronym, a distinct person: writing *Jill* "is quite fun, because [John Kemp] writes a lot of imaginary stuff about her—diaries, letters, etc. Brunette Coleman, who wrote 'Trouble at Willow Gables,' is helping me. She also wrote a poem the other day called 'Bliss'" (*Selected Letters*, 63). If Larkin mocks Coleman, he also has Coleman mock him: the girls-school writer Nancy Breary, Coleman decides, "has moments of rapture," but "her writing suggests that by temperament she is a poet, for her characters are a little thin and her plots weak" (*Trouble*, 264). The naughty episodes also gave Larkin, so to speak, plausible deniability if Amis, or anyone else, should ask why he took such an interest in fictive girls. One answer might lie in the relative freedom Larkin imagined within their "closed single-sex world," so much like the boarding-school worlds in the early Auden. None of the people in the Coleman stories have visible parents, severe financial worries, dull jobs, or unsatisfied demands for heterosexual sex; these absences matter as much to the stories' wish-fulfillment aspects as does the presence of lesbian amours. Those absences are also what Larkin found in the (nonpornographic, "juvenile") school stories that "What Are We Writing For?" proves that he read in bulk.

The stories terminate, in fact, by emphasizing their status as closed and fictive worlds. Near the end of *Michaelmas Term*, the Oxford fresher Marie ventures into a bar to find a servant, Pat, who figured in *Trouble*:

"So it is you, Pat." Marie gulped. "I thought I . . . couldn't be mistaken. Why aren't you at Willow Gables, Pat? Have you left there?"

Pat's smile broadened, and her dimples became more pronounced.

"That story's over now, Miss Marie," she answered. "Willow Gables doesn't exist any more." . . .

"But if this is a story, Pat," persisted Marie, her caramel-coloured hair dipping in somebody-else's beer, "where's real life? If this is all untrue, where's reality?"

(*TROUBLE*, 228-29)

The manuscript terminates a few paragraphs later. Larkin's school-pastoral behaves here like the closed worlds we meet in dreams, whose fictive wish-fulfillments we recognize before we wake: it is an anxiously eroticized adolescence as pastoral, compelling because closed off from the adult world.

Larkin becomes a literary writer—first in his fiction, then in his poetry—when and as he recognized that sort of pastoral as historically contingent, and as always in some way insufficient. At the same time, he often fails to find consolation elsewhere. The protagonist in Larkin's last completed novel, *A Girl in Winter*, recalls the amorous disappointments of her sixteenth year, meditates on adulthood, and concludes that it holds no rewards: "in most lives there had to come a break, when the past dropped away and the maturity it had enclosed for so long stood painfully upright" (183). "Such a break," Larkin continues, "brings knowledge, but no additional strength":

In the past she thought she had found happiness through the interplay of herself and other people. The most important thing had been to please them, to love them, to learn them. . . . Now this brought happiness no longer. . . . And what had replaced it? Here she was at a loss. She was not sure if anything had replaced it.

She was not sure if anything had replaced it.

(183-84)

Here we have, starkly in prose, the situation behind so many of Larkin's poems: social life, life with others, brings rewards only in an inaccessible realm associated with the past, with other people's lives, and above all with youth. Maturity (however defined) removes those prizes and offers nothing in return. "The fault of the novels is they're about me," Larkin said (*Further Requirements*, 33).

Almost everything that happened to Larkin seemed to him to signal the end of youthful possibilities. In a sonnet of 1949, "interest passes / Always towards the young and more insistent" (*CPL* 22). The poems declare baldly, throughout Larkin's career, that maturity brings no satisfactions at all: "wanting . . . and finding out clash"; "Smiles are for youth" (*CPL* 146, 194). M.W. Rowe avers that after *Jill*, Larkin "no longer needed to be sustained or supported by fantasy" ("Unreal Girls," 92). Larkin's poems suggest otherwise. In "Breadfruit," "Boys dream of native girls who bring breadfruit, / Whatever they are," and grow up to marriage, mortgages, "nippers," and finally "absolute / Maturity . . . when old men sit and dream / Of naked native girls who bring breadfruit, / Whatever they are" (*CPL* 141). Since "Breadfruit" is its own plural, "they" can mean fruit or girls: old men know no more of voluptuous natives than they do of tropical fruit, and know no more than they knew as boys.

Andrew Swarbrick and others have shown how Larkin's poems set up oppositions (usually between happy, sociable other people and the unhappy or solitary poet) and then suggest that the opposites are really the same (or, at least, more similar than they appeared). "Reasons for Attendance" follows that pattern (as "Breadfruit" did) and depends (as "Breadfruit" did) on idealizations of youth. The poet approaches

>   the lighted glass
> To watch the dancers—all under twenty-five—
> Shifting intently, face to flushed face,
> Solemnly on the beat of happiness.
>
> Or so I fancy, sensing the smoke and sweat,
> The wonderful feel of girls. Why be out here?
> But then, why be in there? Sex, yes, but what
> Is sex?
>
> (*CPL* 80)

The poem reconsiders Larkin's choice of solitary "art" (a "lifted, rough-tongued bell") over the dance music's trumpet, and comes to find both choices dubious (*CPL* 80). Larkin in effect "rewrote" "Reasons for Attendance" several times, in the unfinished poem "The Dance" and again in "High Windows"; all these poems describe Larkin's exclusion from a space defined by distinctively youthful pastimes or tastes.

That exclusion produces the oppositions that the poems' endings lament (or, as Swarbrick argues, deconstruct). "Love Songs in Age" (1957) derives its pathos, and its verbal compression, partly from its compression of the life course: its old woman (based on Larkin's mother) rereads old sheet music and finds "the unfailing sense of being young / Spread out like a spring-woken tree" (*CPL* 113). "Lines on a Young Lady's Photograph Album" (1953) also casts youth as a "heaven" of last resort: the poet is

> left
> To mourn (without a chance of consequence)
> You, balanced on a bike against a fence;
> To wonder if you'd spot the theft
> Of this one of you bathing; to condense,
>
> In short, a past that no one now can share.
>
> (*CPL* 72)

The imaginary, the perfect, the beautiful, and the idea of youth here join hands to oppose the real, the adult, and "the future," which for this young woman (Winifred Arnott) would soon include marriage. "Maiden Name" (1955) rewrites "Lines," finding its impetus, and its version of "beauty," in "what we feel now about you then" (*CPL* 101).

To base one's poetry on an opposition between youth and age, vivid sociability and isolated decline, is to delete from the life course what social norms present as its fulfillment: responsible, "mature" adulthood, in which men and women settle down and establish careers or raise their families. Larkin wrote to Maeve Brennan in 1961, "At first one wants to get older in order to be grown up; then" (Larkin's own poem "On Being Twenty-Six" notwithstanding) "there's no difference between 25 and 26, it's just like wearing a different tie; but once past 35 it's impossible not to feel that each year is taking one further from what is desired . . . UNLESS . . . you have bound yourself thoroughly into life" (quoted in Motion, *A Writer's Life*, 315). "Looking back on my first 40 years," he told Brennan in 1962, "in a way I feel I am still waiting for life to start." Larkin added that this feeling "may be a sign of what the S[unday] Times calls 'second adolescence'" (*Selected Letters*, 344).

By that time the definition and experience of British adolescence had changed. "In the 1950s," writes Springhall, "the adolescent age group" acquired a "degree of self-awareness" that "marked a discontinuity from the previous history of their age group in Britain, if not in America" (*Coming of Age*, 190). *The Uses of Literacy* (1957), Richard Hoggart's influential book, complained of the "juke-box boys," who "spend the evening listening [to pop music] in harshly-lighted milk bars," "boys aged between fifteen and twenty, with drape-suits, picture ties and an American slouch" (189). Colin

MacInnes in 1958 called such boys parts of "an international movement": "a teenager . . . is a new kind of person" whose "songs, and even styles of clothing, are carried across Europe . . . by a sort of international adolescent *maquis*" (*England*, 47, 55, 57). "Never before," MacInnes concluded, "has the young generation been so *different* from its elders" (59; emphasis his).

Some poets noticed that difference almost immediately: "Meditation in a Coffee Bar" (1961), by the Cambridge don Graham Hough, compares the girl on whom the poet spies, with her "heart-breaking narcissistic gaze," to "Yeats's great rough beast that was to be / The god of a new age" (*Legends*, 36). Far from the academy, the "Liverpool Poets" (Adrian Henri, Roger McGough, Adrian Mitchell, and Brian Patten) began a series of local performances at coffee bars and "mixed media events" as early as 1961 and 1962, though their best-known documents (the Penguin Modern Poets "Mersey Sound" anthology, and Edward Lucie-Smith's *Liverpool Scene*) date to 1967 (Hewison, *Too Much*, 68). Poetry in general, and the Liverpool Poets in particular, became—along with the Beatles, the Rolling Stones, and the Kinks; the paintings and collages of Richard Hamilton; and the "Swinging London" fashion of Mary Quant—part of the decade's discussion of a revived, postimperial British pride built on youth and youth culture.

By 1970 George Melly could write that "pop," by which he meant a style in all the arts, might "present . . . an exact image of our rapidly changing society, particular in relation to its youth." "Its viewpoint is largely confined within an age limit extending (currently) from fourteen to the late twenties"; "pop is a young, almost adolescent culture" (*Revolt*, 5). A "pop" art in Melly's sense would combine elements of youth as pastoral—bright, new, immediate, innocent—with youth as rebellion, making something new in the world. Yet such an art had troubling limits: pop, Melly concludes, "is . . . tied only to the young, and therefore incapable of development beyond a certain point" (253). No one thought Larkin a "pop" poet or even a fashionable one: he appeared instead to match the sensibility of the immediate postwar generation, too young to feel heroic about the war, too old to experience 1960s youth. Yet Larkin's poems answer, even echo, "pop" ideas. Larkin had never envisioned maturity anyway (not, certainly, as something worth striving for); his dejected lyric outlook shared with pop its sense that adulthood had nothing to show.

No wonder, then that Larkin reacted to the new youth with strenuously mixed feelings.[21] Motion writes that Larkin "viewed the student revolution" of the late 1960s "with mingled fascination and contempt" (*A Writer's Life*, 376–77). In late 1969 Larkin read *The Beatles: The Authorised Biography* "with great interest & a good deal of fascinated repulsion. What a scene"

(*Selected Letters*, 423).[22] Compiled between 1966 and 1971, Larkin's *Oxford Book of Twentieth-Century English Verse* reflects not only his antimodernist preferences but also his attention to the new youth. Perhaps in response to commercial exigencies, Larkin included all four Liverpool Poets; Adrian Henri's "Mrs Albion You've Got a Lovely Daughter" apostrophized "*Beautiful boys with bright red guitars / in the spaces between the stars*" (607–8).

More important in thinking about Larkin's point of view, and more durable as verse, are several poems from his *Oxford Book* by poets who shared Larkin's tastes. Elizabeth Jennings's "Young Ones" (1967) is a direct antecedent for Larkin's "Sad Steps" and "High Windows," presenting the poet as an outsider both to the secret knowledge of the new youth and to the supposed consolation of age. Jennings's eponymous girls "slip on to the bus, hair piled up high, / New styles each month, it seems to me":

> They are fifteen or so. When I was thus
> I huddled in school coats, my satchel hung
> Lop-sided on my shoulder. Without fuss
> These enter adolescence; being young
>
> Seems good to them, a state we cannot reach,
> No talk of 'awkward ages' now. I see
> How childish gazes staring out of each
> Unfinished face prove me incredibly
>
> Old-fashioned.
>
> (LARKIN, OXFORD, 564)

The youth of the late 1960s seem to Jennings different in kind, more confident, and more unlike adults than the youth she experienced ten or twenty years before. "The Clothes Pit," by Douglas Dunn, sets the popular image of carefree mods against the material conditions of working-class Hull: Dunn's "young women . . . do not need to be seen / Carrying a copy of . . . *The Liverpool Poets*"; nevertheless, "The litter of pop rhetoric blows down Terry Street, / Bounces past their feet, into their lives" (Larkin, *Oxford*, 622).

For Larkin such "pop rhetoric" both amplified and debased the happiness he had earlier seen in adolescence, for others if never for him. Announcing "Sexual intercourse began / In nineteen sixty-three/ (Which was rather late for me)," "Annus Mirabilis" (1967) complains that the poet was born too soon for the sexual revolution (Larkin had "sexual intercourse," as Motion has proven, well before 1963). Originally entitled "History," the poem pursues not Larkin's biography but his attitude toward the youth that he felt he had missed (*Selected Letters*, 398). It is that youth from which Larkin articulates his exclusion: he belongs instead to the last generation defined by "the *Chatterley* ban," overturned in 1960.[23] Larkin's generation felt that male desire led "only" to

A sort of bargaining,
A wrangle for a ring,
A shame that started at sixteen
And spread to everything.

Then all at once the quarrel sank:
Everyone felt the same,
And every life became
A brilliant breaking of the bank,
A quite unlosable game.

So life was never better than
In nineteen sixty-three
(Though just too late for me)—
Between the end of the *Chatterley* ban
And the Beatles' first LP.

(*CPL* 146)

Larkin's tone and repetitions court sarcasm: has "every life" ever felt the same? How much do broad cultural narratives and signposts—Beatlemania and the *Chatterley* trial, the pill, the "sexual revolution"—really say about individual experience? Might they falsify as much as they show? Yet the young in this poem appear to seize, in fact, the pleasures Larkin ascribes to them in his fiction; in doing so they emphasize Larkin's difference from them.

Almost a year later, in April 1968, Larkin finished "Sad Steps"; the title comes from Sir Philip Sidney, whose sonnet asks whether lovers on the moon might feel as frustrated as those on Earth (part of Sidney's point is that we can never know). This poem, too, explores Larkin's distance from youth, identified this time not only with sex but with romance, and with a Romantic image: "the moon dashes through clouds," "High and preposterous and separate," becoming a "lozenge of love! Medallion of art!" (*CPL* 169) Sublime and inaccessible, though framed by everyday words and experiences ("curtains," "piss"), that moon for Larkin "Is a reminder of the strength and pain / Of being young; that it can't come again / But is for others undiminished somewhere" (*CPL* 169). The poem's equanimity seems more impressive if we recall that "the young" in Larkin's own life—"the young" he encountered five days a week in Hull—were several years past innocent Beatlemania; in late May 1968, student radicals would briefly take over the University of Hull.

Larkin's final engagement with ideas of youth came through diction. He told John Betjeman "that whenever he looked at" *High Windows*, "he found it was full of four letter words" (quoted in Motion, *A Writer's Life*, 444). If, as William Gass writes, "swearing consists of a series of cultural quotations" (*On Being Blue*, 49) most of Larkin's swear words quote youth: "they fuck you up, your mum and dad" is only the best-known example (*CPL* 142). Alan Bennett wrote that the "real Larkin" of the poems was the "one who feels shut out when he sees fifteen-year-olds necking at bus stops" ("Instead of a Present," 70). One of the ways he reacts in the title poem is to move into, and then away from, their language. Janice Rossen is wrong to call Larkin's verb "fuck" (attested as early as 1502) "a recent invention of the younger generation" (*Larkin*, 129). But Rossen is right to say that the gap in diction between the beginning of "High Windows"—"This Be the Verse" or "Sad Steps"—and the ends of those poems amounts to a generation gap. "I think [my use of swear-words] can take different forms," Larkin wrote to John Sparrow: "It can be *meant* to be shocking (we live in an odd era, when shocking language can be used, yet still shocks—it won't last)" (quoted in Motion, *A Writer's Life*, 444). Larkin's language calls attention to the "odd era" in which he wrote his late poems, when "the strength and pain of being young" seemed so unlike the experience of youth in previous generations, even though their underlying emotions may have been the same.

"High Windows," in particular, asks whether "being young" means in the late 1960s what it meant for the Larkin of the early 1940s, the Larkin who wrote *Willow Gables*: the poem gets energy from its contradictory answers. A preserved draft makes clear Larkin's scrutiny of his own envy, and the genuineness of his hopes for the young:

> When I see a couple of kids
> And guess he's fucking her
> And she's taking pills or wearing a diaphragm
> I feel I am walking in paradise
> Where shame has dried up like dew
> And remember how all the writers
> Born eighty years ago said this is what we wanted

(QUOTED IN MOTION, *A WRITER'S LIFE*, 354)

Larkin began the poem in 1965, when one writer "born eighty years ago" was D.H. Lawrence (1885–1930). The "couple of kids," or coupling kids, in "High Windows" enact Lawrence's dream of sexual freedom: the pill and the diaphragm segregate youth from adulthood, kids from Larkin, one generation from another. The "wonderful world" that Lawrence and Larkin imagined "held no one like them and no one like me / And now it's here / And God has wiped away all the tears from their eyes" (quoted in Motion, *A Writer's Life*, 354). That last line is a Miltonic and biblical reference: the angels in "Lycidas" "wipe the tears forever from his eyes," and Isaiah promises that the Lord will "wipe away tears from all faces" at the End of Days (Isaiah 25:8). Lawrence and Larkin, in other words, look down on "kids" as if from Heaven. Yet if Larkin believes the countercultural, free-loving "kids" are in Paradise, the young men and women themselves think no such thing; they are, as Brunette Coleman put it, "not yet old enough to savor the quintessence of youth."

That contrast between their unselfconscious view of themselves and Larkin's melancholy enters the contrast in form between the start and the end of the poem. "High Windows" moves from a deliberately jerky, halting quatrain with one half-rhyme on "she's" and "paradise," through *xaxa* and *abab* rhymes, to strong internal rhyme on "birds"/"words," to a fluent pair of rhymes on a sibilant, so that the last stanza could almost be one rhyme four times. The rhyme, in turn, emphasizes the shift in tone, as (in Barbara Everett's words) the "violent flatness of its opening . . . modulates into the exaltation of the close" ("Larkin: After Symbolism," 239). "High Windows" ends in a look up to wordless, endless radiant nothingness: death becomes both the end of the long slide everyone takes through life and an ascent into a mysterious void. Yet the poem—like "This Be the Verse" and "Sad Steps" and "Reasons for Attendance"—considers the relation of one generation to the next.

To read Larkin as always vexed by the youth he missed and by the changing cultural meanings of adolescence is to see how he speaks not just to his own time but to ours. Mark Greif, in an essay called "Afternoon of the Sex Children," finds in twenty-first-century America, with our tween pop stars and our moral panics over child porn, the final results of a postwar cult of youth: "The lure of a permanent childhood in America," Greif writes, "partly comes from the overwhelming feeling that one hasn't yet achieved one's true youth, because true youth would be defined by freedom so total that no one can attain it" (172). Modern adults can therefore see and envy such freedom only in social milieux they cannot themselves enter, in the closed worlds of teens and schools: "envy of one's sexual successors is now a recurrent feature of our portion of modernity" (174). "High Windows," which Greif then quotes, makes exactly that point.

So, in retrospect, does *Willow Gables*. Edna Longley finds in Larkin's poems evidence of a "narcissistic personality" that avoids "coming to terms with the adult world" ("Larkin, Decadence," 38). Yet that avoidance, in the poems, becomes a source of artistic strength. (Does anyone truly "come to terms with the adult world"?) Larkin explained, in a preface to his jazz writings, why he had given up record reviewing: "In a humanist society, art . . . assumes great importance, and to lose touch with it is parallel to losing one's faith in a religious age. Or, in this particular case, since jazz is the music of the young, it was like losing one's potency" (*All What Jazz*, 22). Yet losing touch with youthful power and freedom, and with the imagined communities these things represent, had been a theme of Larkin's work all along, even as the location of adolescence moved—in Larkin's imagination and in British culture—from boarding schools to Swinging London's streets. In *High Windows*, with its four-letter words and its "kids," the poet asks for the last time whether adolescence itself has changed, and he concludes that the succession of generations matters less than the experience each one has—an experience that for Larkin himself led always to vacancy, disappointment, self-declared (even flaunted) isolation, and the making of those feelings into art.

❖ ❖ ❖ ❖ ❖

Auden gave up an early style founded on the language peculiar to youth; Larkin found a subject in his felt distance from it. A third English poet would ground his own aesthetic on what he shared with successive generations of the self-consciously, subculturally, proudly young. "Every time some black-jacketed young sod thunders past me on a ghastly 450cc m'bike I mutter 'Thom Gunn made you up, you sod, you noisy little bounder,'" Larkin told Robert Conquest in 1961 (quoted in Motion, *A Writer's Life*, 344). It would be equally apt to say that black-jacketed bikers made up Thom Gunn. Only a few years younger than Larkin, and part of the same mid-1950s Movement, Gunn attended even more often than Larkin to ideas about youth, subcultures, and the adult poet's relations to them.

That relationship, as it developed over forty years, proved almost exactly the opposite of Larkin's. Where Larkin insists that he lacks the virtues of youth, Gunn insists that he and his poems can share them: representatives of successive adolescent subcultures (rockers, hippies, gay male hustlers, skateboarders) provide constant analogues for Gunn's own aesthetic goals. Gunn has written that his life "insists on continuities, between England and America, between metre and free verse" (*Occasions*, 194). His work also insists on the continuity of subcultures, from 1950s bikers to 1990s skaters, gay club kids, and radical Berkeley students. Early critics focused on Gunn's "nameless bikers and national servicemen, greasers and Teds, presided over by . . . James Dean and Elvis Presley" (Woods, *Articulate Flesh*, 213–14). Later admirers praised his celebrations of gay men's communities, sexual pleasures, and solidarity. Critics have been slower to see the unity in his work, which depends on a succession of similarly configured, usually (not always) male heroes from a succession of youth subcultures with which Gunn's poems identify their goals and their forms.

Gunn wrote, in a poem called "The Life-Artist," "I elevate not what I / have . . . but what I wish to have, / and see myself in others" (*CPG* 162). He also saw himself in America. In San Antonio, where Gunn's partner Mike Kitay taught in 1955 and 1956, Gunn "heard Elvis Presley's songs first" and acquired "a motorcycle which I rode for about one month" (*Occasions*, 188). Gunn has explained that during the mid-1950s he "was much taken by the American myth of the motorcyclist, then in its infancy, of the wild man part free spirit and part hoodlum, but even that I started to anglicize; when I thought of doing a series of motorcyclist poems I had Marvell's mower poems in my mind as my model" (*Occasions*, 187). He also recalled that during those years, "I had an irrational terror that on some visit back to England I might fall fatally ill, get *stuck* there, and die"; he calls the fear "absurdly romantic," "as through I would by dying there get wedged forever inside a purgatory of dissatisfied adolescence" (*Shelf Life*, 175–76). America, for him, meant a powerful, physically capable youth and youth culture; England connoted bad, weak, or failed coming-of-age.

And yet Gunn's poems took part in—even anticipated—a specifically English way of thinking about youth, one predicted by Hoggart, articulated by MacInnes, and codified by Dick Hebdige, whose *Subculture: The Meaning of Style* (1979) explains: "The cultivation of a quiff, the acquisition of a scooter or a record or a certain type of suit" serve "the construction of a style" and create "a gesture of defiance or contempt" (2–3). Gunn's poetry (like Hebdige's theory) traces the continuity of such gestures through the mid-1950s, when they first became evident in Britain, through three generations of increasingly international subcultures, from Teds and motorcyclists to punks, skateboarders, and club kids. The "resistance through rituals" and visual style, the reliance on "pose" or "stance," which Hebdige attributes to modern youth subcultures is precisely the "pose of self-confidence" that Gregory Woods finds in Gunn's characters (*Articulate Flesh*, 214). In Gunn's much-anthologized "On the Move," "Boys . . . in gleaming jackets trophied with the dust" become both existential heroes, who "join . . . the movement in a valueless world, / Choosing it," and paradigms of successful adolescence in an Eriksonian sense, "self-defined, astride the created will" (*CPG* 40). Jeff Nuttall recalls that in Britain around 1957, Bill Haley concerts and Elvis Presley films became sites of vandalism and violence, "trial gestures of tribal significance" (*Bomb Culture*, 23). He calls Gunn's poems about bikers, with their "aggressive masculinity" and their "atmosphere of oil and petrol," the first adult art works to capture that tribal power (28).[24]

"Elvis Presley" (1957) is perhaps the first literary poem about a rock and roll artist, and surely the first by an English poet. The poem provided the title for Melly's *Revolt Into Style*; when Gunn won a major award in 2003, the *Guardian* called him a "hip 1950s poet who revered Elvis" (Ezard, "Poetic Justice").[25] Gunn's stanzaic lyric deserves to be read entire:

> Two minutes long it pitches through some bar:
> Unreeling from a corner box, the sigh
> Of this one, in his gangling finery
> And crawling sideburns, wielding a guitar.
>
> The limitations where he found success
> Are ground on which he, panting, stretches out
> In turn, promiscuously, by every note.
> Our idiosyncrasy and our likeness.
>
> We keep ourselves in touch with a mere dime.
> Distorting hackneyed words in hackneyed songs
> He turns revolt into a style, prolongs
> The impulse to a habit of the time.
>
> Whether he poses or is real, no cat
> Bothers to say: the pose held is a stance
> Which, generation of the very chance
> It wars on, may be posture for combat.
>
> (*CPG* 57)

Each stanza reevaluates, and elevates, the Elvis of the stanza before: each seems designed to answer high-culture objections. Yes, Elvis seems limited, but therein lies his strength. Yes, the words are hackneyed, but his delivery gives them style; yes, it's an act, but it's also genuine. When we have worked out all the stanzas' oppositions we have come from a reflexive rejection of Elvis all the way to seeing in him the icon of a new culture: self-consciously adolescent and proud of it. "Generation" means both "demographic cohort" (as in "Beat Generation") and "effect, product, result": Elvis sets his hip against contingency itself. Gunn begins by belittling one of Elvis's hits, and assumes that Elvis's appeal requires an explanation: the poem translates what it takes to be adolescent energy, in a newly characteristic form, into words that adults can understand.

No wonder, then, that the poem positions Gunn in between adolescence as pastoral (where the same old forms suit each generation) and adolescence as "revolt." Robert K. Martin writes that the Elvis of 1957 "is Gunn's self-defined man . . . who creates himself, through the medium of style" (*Homosexual Tradition*, 184). Gunn's poems are full of such self-defined men, their styles (as in Hebdige) inseparable from the codes of defiant youth. Giving a "youngster" a tattoo, "Blackie, the Electric Rembrandt" initiates that youngster into a similar style of outlaw self-definition: "on / his arm . . . gleam ten / stars. . . . Now he is starlike" (*CPG* 118). In "Black Jackets," a "red-haired boy" in "cycle boots and jacket" also demonstrates an attitude Gunn admires: "The present was the things he stayed among" (*CPG* 108–09). What the boy cannot do for himself—what few of Gunn's strong-willed heroes do for themselves, and what Gunn tries to do (discreetly) for them—is articulate that attitude; the poems explain about each subcultural hero what he cannot explain but seems to prove in the stance he takes. With its verbal control and commitment to precise prose meaning, the poem makes clear for the adult poet, and for his readers, what the "red-haired boy" and the tattoo artist know without wanting to say. Their hyper-masculine armor and their self-possession suggest both the energetic young men in the later poems and the closet from which Gunn's later poems emerge.

Besides adolescence as new power and adolescence as eternal pastoral, Gunn outlines a third model that he goes out of his way to reject: a sub-Keatsian Romanticism of self-expression, extreme emotions, and literalized confessions, which had become associated for Gunn with the pained, fragile, and closeted youth he seems himself to have experienced. "Autobiography," for example, remembers "how it felt / to sit on Parliament / Hill on a May evening / studying for exams," "skinny / seventeen" and "dissatisfied"; to this teenaged Gunn (as to the aging Larkin),

life seemed all
loss, and what was more

I'd lost whatever it was
before I'd even had it.

(*CPG* 285)

This is the feeling that Gunn's subcultural heroes conceal entirely or never had. The young people in Gunn become tough, combative, armored, and empowered by subculture in order to avoid becoming like the seventeen-year-old Gunn, the helplessly self-conscious, solitary victim of an adult world. Gunn's poem "Adolescence" presents this paradigm elegantly:

After the history has been made
and when Wallace's shaggy head

glares on London from a spike, when
the exiled general is again

gliding into Athens harbour
now as embittered foreigner,

when the lean creatures crawl out of
camps and in silence try to live;

I pass foundations of houses,
walking through the wet spring, my knees

drenched from high grass charged with water,
and am part, still, of the done war.

(*CPG* 125)

These octosyllabics ("history" and "general" are disyllabic, "Wallace's" tri-syllabic) link the poem to others in *My Sad Captains* (1961); the half-rhymes, and the abbreviated sonnet form, link it instead to Auden, whose poems of young men on journeys ("Adolescence," for example) stand behind Gunn's. Adolescence is itself a "foundation," because future experience builds on it; the exposed foundations are both the beginnings of civilizations and lives (since ontogeny recapitulates phylogeny) and the bombed-out houses of post-Blitz London. The poet as former soldier, overlooking rebuilt cities and ruins in their "new spring," finds himself still dominated by the conflict which now belongs to his own "history," the conflict which for Gunn offers terms in which to interpret the rest of the world.

Gunn's commitment to adolescence as a subject dates from his earliest poems; after Stonewall and gay liberation, it entered his prose. A 1979 essay

finds the gay poet Robert Duncan's work dominated by three "human figures," one of whom, "the searcher," "is above all the adolescent and young
man. He is seeking something out but its shape is still unclear to him" (*Occasions*, 128–29). "The adolescent," Gunn continues, "is the perfect embodiment of the searcher, but the theme of sexual restlessness never completely
leaves Duncan's poetry, as it never completely leaves the human being"
(129).[26] Gunn's move in the 1970s toward openness about gay identity and
gay sex required no stylistic shift, and not even much of a change in his
subjects, since Gunn had already been writing about attractive young men
and their subcultural signs for more than a decade. Instead of soldiers and
motorcyclists in cafes, or (as in "Street Song") hippies and teenaged drug
dealers, *The Passages of Joy* (1981) pursued "Romantics in leather bars" with
"bottles and badboy uniforms" (*CPG* 207, 339). Gunn identified the continuity among subcultures in his own prose, calling the gay activists and the
clubgoers of the 1970s "the direct heirs of the hippies, drug-visionaries also,"
with "a shared sense of adventure, thrilling, hilarious, *experimental*" (*Shelf
Life*, 215).

The continuity of subcultures in Gunn's poetry signals the continuities
in his attitudes and ideals, and the continuities between past and present,
England and America, bikers and hippies, even rock and disco, which
Gunn's style tries to demonstrate. "New York" tries to bring disco's two-
four beat into Gunn's nevertheless unmetered verse:

> On the catwalk
> above the turning wheels, high
> on risk
>   his luck
> and the resources of his body
> kept him going we were
> balancing
>   up there
>   all night
> grinning and panting
> hands black with machine oil
> grease monkeys of risk
> and those wheels were turning *fast*.
> (*CPG* 317; EMPHASIS GUNN'S)

Young men like the young Gunn of "Autobiography," should (the poems
argue) admire young men like that dancer, rather than wallowing (like the

"confessional" poets Gunn abhorred) in their own pain (*CPG* 231). Later poems about athletic youths make the same point: take the pinball wizard in "Bally Power Play," or the young "Tow Head" of the later poem "Skate-board," his body all performance, his clothes emblematic, "chain round his waist,/ Hair dyed to show it is dyed" (*CPG* 433).

The Man with Night Sweats (1992) returned Gunn to prominence largely by virtue of its sensitive reactions to the HIV crisis among gay men. Those reactions, controlled versions of decline, mourning, and death, gained strength through their contrast with the figures of youthful vitality that continued to populate other poems. "Nasturtium" erects one tensely ex-tended figure for them all, a "prodigal" daffodil "Born in a sour waste lot," now ready

> To come forth into sun
> As if without a past,
> Done with it, re-begun . . .
>
> Not rare but beautiful
> —Street-handsome—as you wind
> And leap, hold after hold,
> A golden runaway,
> Still running, strewing gold
> From side to side all day.
>
> (*CPG* 454)

Gunn's eight-line stanzas reflect the young flower's exertions and mo-tions: doubled consonants (haNDsome . . . wiND, STill STrewing, for TH . . . wiTHout) hold the nasturtium "up" as it sways from side to side, while rhymes and syntax drive it forward in its growth. Those accomplished moves reflect the flower's character: as the "street-handsome," lithe, and blithe nasturtium stands to other flora, so the street kids stand to softer peers. Bodily skill and "street-handsome" style together denominate the poet's ideal, and the form reflects them. With "Hotblood on Friday," with the cycle-gang kids in "Black Jackets," with the disco acrobat, the pinball champion, and the stunt-turning boy in "Skateboard," the poems coalesce into intellectual defenses of heroic adolescents, members of particular sub-cultures, whose embodied self-creations the poems emulate as they describe.

Gunn's final collection, *Boss Cupid* (2001) did the same. "A GI in 1943" records, apparently, Gunn's very first sighting of a talismanically strong young man whose unusual clothes reflect his membership in a tough group. This soldier shows "Boy flesh / in a man's tunic," "rough animal stubble" on a calm "farm boy's face" (*Boss*, 53). Gunn's skateboarders, "forward boys in backward caps," and so on, would reincarnate the GI's "smooth look / of power. Power / as beauty, beauty / power"; Gunn's "focusing eye," trained to find such young men, "has learned nothing / fresh in fifty-three years" (*Boss*, 53–54). The poet seeks in "beauty" not "truth" but "power," a rawness against which Gunn counterposes his own discreet, abstract diction, his own set of rules. And it is power connoted not only by the young man's physique but by a generational "uniform"—in the 1940s, infantry; in the 1990s, "backward caps."

Such heroes' attraction is, of course, sexual, but it is rarely *merely* sexual. Sometimes the sex is sublimated entirely. "Office Hours" (another poem from *Boss Cupid*) describes "big handsome / sweaty boys / with their goatees / and skateboards," "sharp chic / ironic girls / with brisk hairstyles / and subtle tattoos": they are his undergraduate students at Berkeley, and with them "sexuality / is grandly deflected" into discussions of literature (*Boss*, 77). These young men and women in Gunn's office, with their distinctive, symbolic clothes and hair, descend directly from the motorcyclists and leatherboys in Gunn's poems of the 1950s. They represent for him, as surely as his frequent reuse of Elizabethan stanza forms, a continuity of history and character from early modern times to the present. Gunn's identification with successive generations of youth subcultures provides the wild hopes against which Gunn's chaste diction and explicit, almost didactic style plays. We might even venture that Gunn has achieved a reconciliation denied both to the more pessimistic Larkin and to the more ambitious, skeptical Auden: in Gunn's work adolescence as pastoral—as a style and self-enclosure that can be repeated—both contains and explains adolescence as newness, as rebellion. Each generation of a modern subculture finds new ways of self-definition, ways which can be understood (and praised) in inherited forms.

The schools in Auden; the spaces of exclusion in Larkin; and the clubs, biker bars, and street festivals in Gunn are spaces for nonprocreative creation, for a way of life that does not (necessarily) contribute to a normative, heterosexual, instrumentalizing adult economy, which is to say a way of life that might find a place for such "useless" things as modern poems. It would be anachronistic and probably unhelpful to say that adolescence itself, for these poets, is "always" "queer" (or "queered"). We can, though, say that adolescence in all three Britons becomes a space for nonutilitarian, nonreproductive pleasure and for specialized verbal exchange, devoted to self-construction, meant to give pleasure, and defined (by others, from the outside) as immature. That is the space of adolescence in schools, where British ideas about it began, and of adolescence in subcultures, where those ideas ended up; it is also the space we give poetry itself—as all three poets, in their strongest poems, seemed to know.

Such knowledge also suffuses the strongest single poem postwar Britain produced: Basil Bunting's *Briggflatts*. Without the inherited idea of youth as pastoral, refuge, and source, the poem would make no sense; without the rise of youth subcultures, without their challenge to early-1960s British society, the poem could not have been written. In 1963 the seventeen-year-old poet Tom Pickard called on the sixty-three-year-old Bunting for advice. Allied during the 1930s with Pound, Bunting had apparently given up writing after his *Poems* (1950) found few readers. Pickard, however, wanted to read and learn; he soon brought Bunting into the group readings at Newcastle's Morden Tower that Pickard and his friends set up. Soon afterward, Bunting began *Briggflatts*, dedicated to Peggy Greenbank, with whom Bunting had an intense, and apparently consummated, romance in their teens. *Briggflatts* contrasts its young lovers with frustrated traveling conquerors (Eric Bloodaxe, Alexander the Great) and with emblems of patience, humility, and endurance (a mason, a worm); all are aspects of Bunting, who suffered for conscience and traveled through a world at war but fled in shame from his first love. "Stocking to stocking, jersey to jersey, / head to a hard arm," Bunting's young lovers "kiss under the rain, / bruised by their marble bed" (*CPB* 60). "Take no notice of tears," the poet instructs himself, "letter the stone to stand / over love laid aside" (*CPB* 62)

The five "movements" of *Briggflatts* present conflicting versions of adolescence. Is it the crucible of the later self or a purgatory through which all selves must pass? Is it, instead, a height from which all adult experience is a falling away? Bunting told Jonathan Williams, "My autobiography is *Briggflatts*—there's nothing else worth speaking of" (quoted in Caddel and Flowers, *Basil Bunting*, 7). To read the poem without attention to the years (1963 through 1965) and the milieu in which Bunting wrote it is to see a pathos-charged version of adolescence in general, and of Bunting's early years in particular. To attend as well to the time and place of writing is to see how the growing counterculture, as Bunting encountered it, made the poem possible.

Briggflatts begins not with children nor with teens but with a "sweet tenor bull" in "late spring" and a stonemason who "times his mallet / to a lark's twitter," engraving—as the poem reveals—a tomb. In this rocky world, young lovers must take whatever hard bed they find, even a grave-stone. Boy and girl form a minimal household unit, expressed in minimal language: "Wetter, warmed, they watch / the mason meditate / on name and date." The couple then return home:

> Her parents in bed
> the children dry their clothes.
> He has untied the tape
> of her striped flannel drawers
> before the range. Naked
> on the pricked rag mat
> his fingers comb
> thatch of his manhood's home . . .
>
> Rainwater from the butt
> she fetches and flannel
> to wash him inch by inch,
> kissing the pebbles.
> Shining slowworm part of the marvel.
> The mason stirs:
> Words!
> Pens are too light.
> Take a chisel to write.
>
> (CPB 45)

M.L. Rosenthal found in these slow, spondee-rich passages "an almost pornographic glow of erotic transport" ("Streams," 191). As we realize that girl and boy have parted, the earlier image (mason carving letters on tomb) comes to describe the latter (boy and girl), as if he had carved the grave of their love.

The rest of the poem measures the adult Bunting's distance from that youthful communion. Bunting decries "love murdered," "love laid aside"; "What can he, changed, tell / her, changed, perhaps dead?" (*CPB* 46) The answer to that question is this poem, which doubles as a confession: Bunting's whole life seems, to him, corrupted by his infidelity to Peggy, "Guilty of spring / and spring's ending" (*CPB* 46, 47). "The abandoning of the girl," Peter Makin writes, "becomes the pivot," and "supplies the sense of an evasion, in the poet, that has to be explained or atoned for" (*Bunting*, 134). All pleasures (but especially sexual ones) seem "stained" by that first betrayal, as marble is "stained" by long rains (*CPB* 49). Even poetry itself

> looks well on the page, but never
> well enough. Something is lost
> when wind, sun, sea upbraid
> justly an unconvinced deserter.
>
> (*CPB* 49)

Bunting "deserted" neither in the Great War (when he endured imprisonment as a C.O.) nor in the Second World War (when he served in the RAF and in Persia). Rather, he has deserted Peggy, Northumbria, and the "spring" of his own, younger, local self. The death of King Eric Bloodaxe, who "ended in bale on the fellside," represents a loss of Northumbrian self-rule akin to Bunting's "flight" south (*CPB* 51).

And yet, as the poem gradually lets us realize, almost all of us have betrayed or broken some promises made in youth; Bunting's break with Peggy works almost as a secular Original Sin, as a means by which we may recall chances we did not take, potential powers and companions we did not pursue. The slowworm (a recurring emblem) is not a worm but a snakelike European lizard (*Anguis fragilis fragilis*) known for its exceptionally long life and its ability to lose its tail in order to escape when threatened. Both a phallus and a suggestion of potency lost, the lizard stands either for cowardice or for survival, for crafty reinvention or for a dishonorable abandoning of the best parts of one's younger self.

How should the grown poet think about the passion he abandoned in his youth? The dominant note remains regret: "Stars disperse. We too, / further from neighbors, / now the year ages" (*CPB* 59). Keith Alldritt explains that "the abandoned love is now perceived in the present tense," as "what was past becomes actual" (*Poet as Spy*, 162). Bunting continues:

> Then is Now. The star you steer by is gone,
> its tremulous thread spun in the hurricane
> spider floss on my cheek; light from the zenith
> spun when the slowworm lay in her lap
> fifty years ago . . .
>
> Sirius glows in the wind. Sparks on ripples
> mark his line, lures for spent fish.

Fifty years a letter unanswered;
a visit postponed fifty years.

She has been with me fifty years.

Starlight quivers. I had day enough.
For love uninterrupted night.

(CPB 62)

Short, spondee-loaded sentences emphasize the weight of time passed; Sirius casts its lines of light for "spent" fish because the time light from Sirius takes to reach Earth far exceeds the lifespan of fish. Bunting in 1965 remembers the Bunting of 1918, the adolescent whose "day" has become his "night," and who once hoped (in the manner of the troubadours) that no dawn would disturb his love.

Recent interpreters emphasize *Briggflatts*'s sonata structure, examine its use of early British history, or scrutinize its Quaker symbols. The poem's first readers, though, focused on Basil and Peggy. Cyril Connolly described "all-pervading nostalgia" (*Evening*, 366). John Peck wrote accurately that "musical patterns . . . weave around [Bunting's] recollection of a 'love murdered' and 'laid aside' in adolescence"; this "tender and traduced eros" finds itself uneasily enmeshed in Bunting's "pattern of heroic lament" ("Bardic," 169, 171). For Makin, *Briggflatts* describes "an artistic maturity ruined by its own evasions," which "seems to be finding a justification in saying that . . . evasion . . . fits in with the fundamental nature of things" (*Bunting*, 138).

But what nature, and what things? Bunting's "evasion" and its historical parallels seem alternately cowardly or despicable, to be condemned (like desertion) and inevitable, to be accepted (as the slowworm accepts its lowly, long life). Not the innocence or naturalness of presexual childhood but rather the initiative and freedom from shame of a reimagined adolescence, represent or instantiate the paradise from which Bunting has departed. The poem thus seems to ask: Is maturity necessary? Can we, as adult readers, imagine its abolition, or its cancellation, so that the innocent energies of the poem's adolescents become (again) accessible to us? That question has two sources in Bunting's own life. The first is his love affair with Peggy Greenbank. The second is the idea of an international youth culture, with its own art forms and its own manners, independent of inherited cultural authority—an idea that, as we have already seen, blossomed in Britain in the early 1960s. Bunting could not depict the first until he had encountered the second.

Bunting met Greenbank in 1913, when he was twelve and Peggy was eight. Their attachment continued for five years. "When [Bunting] was about seventeen and Peggy thirteen," Alldritt (Bunting's biographer) concludes, "they crept into the old whitewashed meeting house" and there "went through a pretend Quaker marriage ceremony" (*Poet as Spy*, 12–13). Bunting got back in touch with Greenbank after "Briggflatts" appeared; in 1965 and 1966, and again a few years later, the poet and his first love carried on an affair (165–66). We may find his continuing interest in her—and, perhaps, in substitutes for her—disturbing. "All his life," admits Alldritt, Bunting "would be drawn to pubescent or just post-pubescent girls" (84). "The Well of Lycopolis" (1935) presents pubescent sexuality in dysphemistic terms: "Daphnis investigated / bubless Chloe / behind a boulder"; "Abject poetry, infamous love ... After hours, is it? or under age? / Hack off his pendants! / Can a moment of madness make up for / an age of consent?" (*CPB* 24–25). Erotic life here seems disgusting, but so do the laws that restrict it. Set in the Canary Islands, "The Orotava Road" (also 1935) finds the poet watching "Milkmaids, friendly girls between / fourteen and twenty / or younger," who

> say 'Adios!' shyly but look back
> more than once, knowing our thoughts
>   and sharing our
> desires and lack of faith in desire.
>
> (*CPB* 107)

These earlier poems look now like failed attempts to make a poem from the same "lack of faith in desire" that produced *Briggflatts*; could Bunting have fulfilled the promise of his early romance with Peggy? Could he (could anyone) have made good on the potential we see in youth?

We saw these questions answered ambivalently or pessimistically in Auden's early poetry, wistfully or grimly in Larkin's verse. The only recent critic to find anything like these ideas in *Briggflatts* is Christian Wiman, who dislikes the ideas and the poem. "You're not a man at sixteen, you're a gland," Wiman quips; "To locate your life's ideal in that instant is, finally, deeply sentimental, and there is a direct connection between that psychological occlusion or willed immaturity and the idolatry of form, or technique, or style" which Wiman finds in Bunting and in modernism generally, very much as John Crowe Ransom had ("Free of Our Humbug," 40). Wiman, like Ransom, finds modernist poetics inadequate because unstable, overemotional, immature.

Yet Wiman sees what Bunting is trying to do: *Briggflatts* seeks a style as sensitive to the promise and ambition of adolescence as Wordsworth's *Prelude* (which Bunting acknowledged as an influence) is to the promise of childhood. Bunting also ends up less confident than Wordsworth about the recompense adulthood might bring. Youthful memories, as Randall Jarrell once wrote, "are deeply humiliating in two ways; they remind the adult that he once was more ignorant and gullible and emotional than he is; and they remind him that he once *was*, potentially, far more than he is" (*Third Book*, 19). That potential has no mention in Bunting's earlier poems. Its realization into Bunting's poetry depends on a concept of relatively autonomous adolescence, of teenage independence from adult institutions, which arrived in English culture long after Bunting's own youth.

Bunting became able to write *Briggflatts*—to make his poem of eternal disappointment—exactly when he discovered British youth culture, or when it discovered him. "Tom Pickard tapped an audience I didn't know existed," Bunting told Jonathan Williams (quoted in Alldritt, *Poet as Spy*, 150). Bunting remained close to Pickard and to his circle for several years, reading parts of *Briggflatts* to Pickard while it was still being written. In the preface to his 1968 *Collected Poems*, Bunting acknowledged a debt not just Pickard's circle but to youth counterculture generally. "I have set down words as a musician pricks his score," Bunting wrote, "not to be read in silence, but to trace in the air a pattern of sound that may sometimes, I hope, be pleasing. Unabashed boys and girls may enjoy them. This book is theirs" (*CPB* 3). Alldritt writes that "photographs of [Bunting] after he had become a part of the youthful set at the Morden Tower show how he had let his hair grow long" and adopted "the sort of clothes worn by the young men of Tom Pickard's generation: duffle coat, scarf and sweater"; "very visibly, and also clearly very happily, he aligned himself with the young" (*Poet as Spy*, 168).

Bunting also furnished a preface to Pickard's first book, *High on the Walls* (1966). Pickard, Bunting wrote, offered "few poems, but new and lasting, their maker very young. Tradition and fashion have no power over a man who has escaped education, with fresh eyes, a fresh voice, and skill to keep the line compact and musical." The same qualities which gave Pickard his appeal—his extreme youth, his status as an outsider—not coincidentally debarred him from institutional (perhaps from "adult") support: "He has to endure," Bunting continued, "the hatred of art which persists in the north of England, the insolence of officials, and of those who pirate the money subscribed 'for the arts'" (iii). One of Bunting's best-known short poems,

"What the Chairman Told Tom," recasts the reactions Pickard got when he sought local arts subsidies:

> Poetry? It's a hobby.
> I run model trains. . . .

> I want to wash when I meet a poet.

> They're Reds, addicts,
> delinquents.
> What you write is rot.

> Mr Hines says so, and he's a schoolteacher,
> he ought to know.
> Go and find work.
>
> (*CPB* 123)

Bunting's affiliations could scarcely be clearer: on one side, Bunting, Pickard, and their allies at Morden Tower; on the other, "the chairman," "an accountant," and "a schoolteacher," who consider all poets "delinquents." Bunting's appeal to "unabashed girls and boys" thus looks like his last, most satisfactory answer to the "problem of patronage" that Richard Price has seen throughout Bunting's work and which "What The Chairman Told Tom" brings up ("Basil Bunting," 99). At seventeen (the age when Bunting abandoned Peggy), Pickard had established a common-law marriage with his first love, started a family, and begun to create what Bunting had never quite had: a literary community that owed nothing to London, nothing to adult authorities, and nothing to the canons of respectability that would have condemned Basil's liason with Peggy.

No wonder, then, that *Briggflatts* as autobiography presents itself as a record of potential and of failure; no wonder it juxtaposed its sweet (and sexual) memories of Bunting's own adolescence with violently mixed feelings about adulthood. In asking why and how he failed his first love, in drawing on youth counterculture while doing so, the poem also places at its heart the contradiction between adolescence as perpetual pastoral, the same sort of thing in each generation, and adolescence as something new. Conscious of ancient history, dependent on 1960s youth, nostalgic for an erotic life conceived as at once transhistorically archaic and indissolubly personal, *Briggflatts* draws on the history of adolescence in Britain in order to ask whether and how we must grow up.

3

Soldiers, Babysitters, Delinquents, and Mutants

ADOLESCENCE IN MIDCENTURY AMERICAN POETRY

A LL HISTORIANS NOTE the importance of youth—of bobbysoxers, teenagers, rock and roll fans, juvenile delinquents, Beatniks, hippies, black revolutionaries, and white student radicals—in the United States after World War II. Few critics now see how that youth drove American poems. At one extreme, Karl Shapiro—Pulitzer Prize–winning poet of World War II and a former editor of *Poetry* magazine—asked with horror in 1970: "Is the Beatleization of American poetry becoming a reality?" (*The Poetry Wreck*, 361) At the other, Muriel Rukeyser in the late-1960s poem "For Kay Boyle" paid homage to another, older modernist by declaring their common cause with "the young bearded rebels and students tearing it all away" (*Collected Poems*, 545).

This chapter will see what aesthetic inventions took place before and between those two extremes. Shapiro, Randall Jarrell, and others responded in verse to the seeming contradiction between pastoral youth and endangered, violent soldiers during the war. Applying a polished 1950s formalism to domestic subjects, Phyllis McGinley became the first American poet to write seriously about teenage girls. Toward the end of the decade, Allen Ginsberg and others drew on new subcultural vocabularies to fashion a poetry received (if not intended) as part of a moral panic about juvenile delinquency.

Of the many poets who altered their practice drastically during the 1960s—switching from meter to free verse, adopting new influences, or resuming interrupted careers—most did not attribute their changes to the new cultural power of youth. A few of the most accomplished, though, did just that. The civil-rights marchers, draft protesters, and hippies in George Oppen's poems of the 1960s and early 1970s inaugurate new collective ways of being, and Oppen explores his ambivalence about whether they can succeed. For Gwendolyn Brooks, 1960s youth meant not a return to poetry but a change in poetic goals: changes in black America—and changes in the street life of black Chicago—convinced her to emulate, in the cadences of her own poems, the wildness of a rising generation. A more complicated response to youth movements and to the idea of adolescence came in the late-1960s poetry of Robert Lowell, whose sonnets emulate in their own piled-on, grinding lines the frustrations and losses that drastically misplaced youthful hopes might create.

❖ ❖ ❖ ❖ ❖

The word "teenager" appeared first in print in 1941, in *Popular Science Monthly*; later that year *Life* magazine mused that "teenagers . . . live in a jolly world of gangs, games, movies and music," "speak a curious lingo," and "drive like bats out of hell" (quoted in Mintz, *Huck's Raft*, 252). *Seventeen* published its first issue in 1944, by which time, as Grace Palladino concludes, teenagers "had a brand-new identity as an important social group"; "even the word was now popular" (*Teenagers*, 93). The word, and the idea, turned up in popular poetry. Phyllis McGinley achieved renown as an author of light verse for the *New Yorker* in the 1930s and 1940s, later attracting praise from Auden. McGinley's "Landscape Without Figures" described prewar Westchester County, New York, in terms of its teens, and wartime Westchester in terms of their disappearance:

> Where are they?—the boys, not children and not men,
>   In polo shirts or jeans or autographed blazers,
> With voices suddenly deep, and proud on each chin
>   The mark of new razors.

(*TIMES THREE*, 108)

Clearly a war poem, "Landscape" never mentions the war. Instead, McGinley invites her readers to ask what these "workers or players" have become, while she tells us what they used to be:

> They were lifeguards, self-conscious, with little whistles.
>   They owned the tennis courts and the Saturday dances.
> They were barbarous dark with sun. They were vain of their muscles
>   And the girls' glances.

They boasted, and swam, and lounged at the drugstore's portal.
    They sailed their boats and carried new records down.
They never took thought but that they were immortal,
    And neither did the town.

(*TIMES THREE*, 108).

Such pursuits as tennis and boating seemed frivolous (hence appropriate for teens); they have become appropriate topics for this somber, if unde-manding lyric only because their devotees have joined the military. The pe-riod before the war, or before Pearl Harbor, is like the summer before high school graduates enter college, but the war itself is shockingly unlike higher education. McGinley's vanished youth are formerly pastoral, formerly resi-dents of a protected space very much like any classical Green World, or like the youths from the "town" on Keats' urn. Yet all their pursuits—from re-cord collecting to suntans—seem distinctively modern, as does their never-named enterprise overseas.

No wartime poet paid more attention to youth culture than Karl Shapiro, whose "Drug Store" (1942) described a place designed for adolescents to gather; their "attractive symbols," "less serious than the living-room or bar," "[w]atch over puberty and leer" (*Poems* 11). Appalled by his own fascination, Shapiro attacked the drugstore as a place where "Youth comes to jingle nick-els and crack wise"; reading "magazines / Devoted to lust, the jazz, the Coca-Cola, / The lending-library of love's latest," young patrons "slump in booths like rags, not even drunk" (*Collected Poems*, 11). Teen culture here means con-sumption; each boy "becomes the customer; he is heroized," without even the politically attractive working-class solidarity or the achieved, supposedly adult masculinity represented by bars and pubs. Shapiro's "Hollywood" reached for sunnier descriptions of the emerging youth culture:

    Is adolescence just as vile
As this its architecture and its talk?

Or are they parvenus, like boys and girls?
Or ours and happy, cleverest of all?
Yes. Yes. Though glamorous to the ignorant
This is the simplest city, a new school.
What is more nearly ours? If soul can mean
    The civilization of the brain,
This is a soul, a possibly proud Florence.

(*COLLECTED POEMS*, 31-32)

Shapiro's awkward conclusion suggests that the movies *could* become a reason for American pride as their "school" improves.

Paul Fussell has written that "a notable feature of the Second World War is the youth of most who fought it." During the war, he notes, the draft age fell from twenty-one to eighteen; "soldiers played not just at being killers but at being grown-ups" (*The Great War*, 51). Shapiro's war poems, which earned him a Pulitzer Prize, portrayed his comrades as playful too, "the good-bad boys of circumstances and chance" (*Collected Poems*, 57). Randall Jarrell's more thoughtful poems about soldiers and airmen also focused on their youth. In "Second Air Force," a mother who visits an air base "thinks heavily: My son is grown," though neither her son nor his colleagues nor even their Flying Fortress bombers seem fully grown: "their Fortresses, all tail, / Stand wrong and flimsy on their skinny legs, / And the crews climb toward them clumsily as bears" (*Complete Poems*, 177). In one of Jarrell's best-known war poems, "Losses," the flyers "died like aunts or pets or foreigners. / (When we left high school nothing else had died / For us to figure we had died like)" (*Complete Poems*, 145).[1] Other war poets also depicted soldiers as adolescents, "not children and not men": John Frederick Nims's "Shot Down at Night" (1944) elegizes an airman who "Found in a foreign sky extravagant death" and therefore missed "the baseball-sounding spring, / The summer roadster," "the dance at Hallowe'en, / The skater's kiss" (*Five Young American Poets*, 69).

What separates poems like Nims's and Jarrell's from previous elegies on the American war dead is not their lament for a life cut off too soon but the specifics of what that life has lost: the trappings of a distinct, peer-dominated phase with its own pastimes, rituals, and tastes—roadsters, baseball, dances, popular song. Susan Schweik finds in verse from the Second World War "a sense of an often uncrossable gap between the male soldier who was understood to have experienced too much and the woman left behind who was understood to have experienced nothing at all" (*Gulf So Deeply Cut*, 6). Poems about soldiers that focused on their prewar lives— that is, on their lives as students and teens—gave civilian poets, especially women, a way to write about a war whose most prominent features they had not seen.[2] In their poems about uniformed adolescents, male and female poets, soldiers, sailors, and civilian writers may strike the same note, finding the same pathos in the same collision of new youth culture with old facts of war. Consider McGinley's "Valedictorian," subtitled "high school, 1943': her "young man with the pink and earnest face" anticipates, not the rewards of his high class rank, but "the rifle resting its equal weight / On every shoulder" (*Times Three*, 110–11). A soldier's corpse in Gwendolyn

Brooks's 1945 sequence "Gay Chaps at the Bar" seems, much like Nims's doomed airman, to retain its status as an American teen: "even in death a body . . . Shows the old personal art, the look. Shows what / It showed at baseball. What it showed in school" (*Blacks*, 65).

Postwar cultural critics, as Leerom Medovoi notes, could "adopt . . . youth as a national signifier"; the "striking celebrations" of *The Catcher in the Rye* (1951), by J.D. Salinger, "place youthful rebellion at the very core of Americanness" ("Democracy," 257, 261). At the same time, many adults "suspected" that a new peer culture of movies, comic books, and rock music would prevent the rising generation from ever becoming adults (271). This contradiction suffuses some postwar poems. As early as 1949, Jarrell's "Girl in a Library" made fun of young people's new "strange speech / In which each sound sets out to seek each other . . . And ends as one grand transcendental vowel" (*Complete Poems*, 15). The girl in the library represents everything troublesome (for Jarrell) about modern adolescence, whose peer group is both a debased pastoral and an enemy of the individual, inner life. Jarrrell's brighter conclusion makes her a worthy representative of premodern pastoral, a kind of person who is not so new after all: "I have seen, / Firm, fixed forever in your closing eyes, / The Corn King beckoning to his Spring Queen" (*Complete Poems*, 16). Jarrell's notes for *A Sad Heart at the Supermarket* (a book of cultural criticism published in 1962, but begun perhaps a decade earlier) include this revealing passage: "Norm now is / younger, more adolescent / to become grown-up faster, the quasi-grown-up category of teenagers is created, that can be reached fast—but grown-ups become more like teenagers, less adult" (quoted in Burt, *Randall Jarrell and His Age*, 162). Jarrell offered a counterproposal, a truly individual adolescent with a developed inner life, in his longest poem, "The Night Before the Night Before Christmas," the interior monologue of a fourteen-year-old girl.

Other poets reacted more wryly, or more optimistically, to the same new "quasi-grown-up category." Published in *Poetry* in 1950 (when Shapiro was the magazine's editor), William Stafford's "Juke Joint" also asked whether and how new teens replicated old pastoral:

When the chromium buds of America bloom
and they turn the springtime on,
smooth-cast youth fill the juke box room
and hunt the phonograph faun.

Stafford's youth are either the reincarnation or the empty parody of classical shepherds and nymphs. McGinley in 1946 celebrated "adolescent Sitters,"

"Those thrifty juveniles who keep . . . A watch upon our infants' sleep / For fifty cents an hour" (*Stones*, 150). Babysitters (McGinley's tight comic rhymes specify) wear braces, read comic books, enjoy Benny Goodman, eat candy, are "hep to jive and jitters" and "wear down the telephone" (150–51).

McGinley wrote accurately in 1965, "If I have done anything original, it is in my portrayals of childhood and adolescence" (quoted in Wagner, *McGinley*, 80). She rose above light entertainment when she saw herself and her readers as worried, ambivalent mothers of teenaged daughters. Her 1960 collection *Times Three* won that year's Pulitzer Prize; an entire section consisted of poems about teenagers. Some of those poems try to make elegant lyrics out of the necessarily restricted (and, the poems aver, too easily dismissed) emotional lives of suburban girls. "A Certain Age" takes on the conformist teen of the 1950s, about whom McGinley (like Jarrell) has complaints:

> This side of childhood lies a narrow land,
> Its laws unwritten, altering out of hand,
> But, more than Sparta's, savagely severe.
> Common or gentry,
> The same taboos prevail. One learns, by ear,
> The customs of the country
> Or pays her forfeit here.
>
> No bicycles. No outcast dungarees
> Over this season's round and scarless knees,
> No soft departures from the veering norm.
> But the same bangle,
> Marked with a nickname, now from every arm
> Identically must dangle,
> The speech be uniform—
>
> Uniform as the baubles round the throat,
> The ill-made wish, the stiffened petticoat,
> And beauty, blurred but burning in the face.
>
> (*TIMES THREE*, 45)

The conflict essential to youth does not (as in Housman) set fleeting beauty or glory against time; rather, it sets the conformity of a peer culture against the individuality which this girl yearns to express. The same girl, or one very like her, stars in McGinley's mock-chivalric "Launcelot with Bicycle," where she plays a sort of cul-de-sac Lady of Shalott, contemplating a boy on a paper route, "Wheeling heroic by"; "A wisful and a lily maid / In moccasins and jeans," the girl finds herself leaning on a "casement," "Despairing from the seventh grade / To match his lordly teens" (*Times Three*, 49).

"Portrait of Girl with Comic Book" focuses on the same transitional moment in a girl's life, with considerably more gravity: remembering "Gooseberry Fool," we might ask whether Amy Clampitt (a later *New Yorker* poet, and one just a generation younger than McGinley) had read it. McGinley begins:

> Thirteen's no age at all. Thirteen is nothing.
> It is not wit, or powder on the face,
> Or Wednesday matinees, or misses' clothing,
> Or intellect, or grace.
> Twelve has its tribal customs. But thirteen
> Is neither boys in battered cars nor dolls,
> Not *Sara Crewe*, or movie magazine,
> Or pennants on the walls.
>
> (*TIMES THREE*, 48)

"Thirteen" (the poem continues) represents a kind of zero point, a node between the habits and expectations of childhood, and those which mark, or imitate, the habits of adults. As such, "thirteen's anomalous—not that, not this," "the one age [which] defeats the metaphor." It comes with stereotypes, agreed-upon markers, but it bears—indeed, signifies—individuality too: in fact, it is the emblem of uniqueness itself, since nothing else can stand for it.

Wallace Fowlie wrote in *Poetry* in 1949, "Rimbaud is the poet of adolescence who is all beings at once, who desperately refuses to choose himself and thereby limit himself." Hence, Fowlie adds, "today every kind of reader recognizes himself in Rimbaud" ("Rimbaud in 1949," 168–69). McGinley recognizes this aspect of nothing-and-everything in her thirteen-year-old, who therefore deserves, and gets, the extremes and paradoxes that other poets reserve for metaphysics or for adults. "Thirteen," McGinley continues,

> Could not, would fortune grant it, name its wish;
> Wants nothing, everything;
> Has secrets from itself, friends it despises;
> Admits none to the terrors that it feels;
> Owns half a hundred masks but no disguises;
> And walks upon its heels.
>
> (*TIMES THREE*, 48)

The punning last line (meaning pride and unsteadiness and new shoes) lightens the generalities above it but does not invite us to dismiss them; it asks us, instead, to frame them, to take a generous but removed perspective. The poem, in other words, presents itself not only as wit but as wisdom; it takes the attitude mothers of thirteen-year-old girls ought to, need to take, an attitude of sympathetic and patient remove. These sudden transitions happen to all girls these days; mothers should take heart: this too will pass.

McGinley was not the only postwar poet to recommend such remove. Edward Brunner describes Richard Wilbur's odd status as both a popular poet of the 1950s and a paragon of learned technique: Wilbur "anticipates the charge that his poetry—or . . . the kind of experience in which his poetry specializes—might be inconsequential by displaying" the use his poems might have for their readers (*Cold War Poetry*, 33–34). McGinley's "Thirteen" works in that way as well, except that the "kind of experience" is not only the experience of reading the world aesthetically, of learning disinterestedness, but also the experience of raising a girl. McGinley describes what this young woman thinks and feels, but her calm stance and confidently balanced sentences suggest the point of view of a mother: in this poem and in a handful of others, she became the first twentieth-century American to write serious verse about young people from a mother's perspective, taking both mothers' and daughters' lives as seriously as other 1950s poets took baroque fountains, Old Master paintings, or the U.S. Navy. The poem's reception, in one way, mirrors its subjects: this poem that asks adults, in adult terms, to take girls seriously was not, itself, taken seriously enough—neither it nor anything else of McGinley's appears in most current anthologies (the Library of America's two-volume *American Poetry* being the happy exception).

We might recognize in these poems not just a neglected accomplishment but also a precedent (if not a foil) for later poems written—and later styles constructed—from daughters' points of view, poems that also take on what social researchers now call the transition to adult femininity. "Our images of the adolescent," Barbara Hudson writes, "are *masculine* images"; "the restless, searching youth; the Hamlet figure; the sower of wild oats; the tester of growing powers." Girls who want to be accepted as appropriately "feminine," Hudson continues, "are constantly open to subversion by judgments of their behavior as adolescent," that is, as flighty, willful, or wild, "whilst at the same time if they are too demonstrably acquiring a mature femininity they are told to have more fun, to be the zany, thoughtless, selfish person we see as the 'typical teenager'" ("Femininity," 51). Girls may therefore feel "that whatever they do, it is always wrong" (53). The results are a model of adolescence with a fixed (and heteronormative) endpoint and a set of double binds on the way there, on which McGinley's gentle ironies draw. Female poets of the 1970s and later—as we will see in chapter 4— would react to these double binds in fiercer, less reassuring poems.

❖ ❖ ❖ ❖ ❖

By the end of the 1950s, the assimilation of modern poetry into American universities, where adults taught late adolescents to read and write it, meant that stylistic innovation in postwar America would present itself as both a generational and an antischolastic revolt. Kenneth Koch's "Fresh Air" complained about "young poets in America . . . trembling in universities"; Koch imagined a "Strangler dressed in a cowboy suit / Leaping from his horse to annihilate the students of myth!" (Allen, *New American Poetry*, 231–32).[3] Poets and literary historians tend to describe this period by finding some sharp break—at Robert Lowell's *Life Studies* (1959), for example, or at Donald Allen's *New American Poetry* (1960), which included both Koch's "Fresh Air" and Frank O'Hara's 1955 elegy for James Dean. James Longenbach argues against such "'breakthrough' narratives," and their "association of personal or social liberation with formal transgression" (*Modern Poetry*, 8). Yet such associations may follow whenever poets and readers see their art as having come under too much (or the wrong sort of) institutional control. Applied to persons rather than to works of art, those associations—in which people discover who they really are by experimenting outlandishly, rejecting mentors, and setting out to break rules—are also, not coincidentally, one way in which we have defined adolescence.

Thinkers of the 1950s, in particular, defined it that way. Erik Erikson in *Childhood and Society* (1950), Edgar Z. Friedenberg in *The Vanishing Adolescent* (1959), and Paul Goodman in *Growing Up Absurd* (1960) all argued that postwar conformism had stifled the independence and the risk-taking that the teen years should include. "The American adolescent," Erikson wrote, "is . . . too immediately occupied with being efficient and being decent" to "know where he is not free" (*Childhood*, 321). W.D. Snodgrass versified such complaints in "The Campus on the Hill," collected in his first volume, *Heart's Needle* (1959). "My little ones lean not toward revolt," Snodgrass sighed, "with such passivity / As would make Quakers swear," the comfortable students at his private college "look out from their hill and say / To themselves, 'We have nowhere to go but down; / The great destination is to stay'" (*Not for Specialists*, 27). These students have made the pastoral ideal of youth into a parody of itself, a sub-Keatsian form of (un-masculine) inaction.[4] An America (or a literary culture or a university) that made adolescence impossible, that substituted a conformist peer culture for a true youth of chance and choice, was a republic (or a literary culture or a university) in decline.

And yet, Erikson also observed, even if young Americans were turning away from "real" opportunities for self-creation, symbols of teen peer culture, being symbols of independence, were becoming more prominent—coming, indeed, to represent America: "The adolescent . . . has, in fact, become the cultural arbiter" (*Childhood*, 340–41). Had teens and their new tastes eradicated the true adolescence on which real individuality and real art would depend? Or could the new teen subcultures furnish counterexamples for a conformist era? Steven Mintz writes that in the 1950s "the adolescent became the archetypal figure for the moral and sexual confusions of the age," citing *The Catcher in the Rye* along with the films *Blackboard Jungle* and *Rebel Without a Cause* (*Huck's Raft*, 297).

He might have added the Beats. Published in *Gasoline* (1958), Gregory Corso's "I Am 25" announced "the needy-yap of my youth: / I HATE OLD POETMEN!" (*Mindfield*, 35) Yet Corso's poem is an outlier; though they emphasized their distaste for staid, respectable adults, Beat *poets* did not usually describe their lives and writings as adolescent, transitional, or unusually immature. Critics, reviewers, and journalists, however, did. "The Beats were," Michael Davidson writes, "demonized as perpetual adolescents" (*Guys Like Us*, 55); debates about Beats became debates about youth, about whether (as *Newsweek* asserted in 1956) "Our Teenagers Are Out of Control" (quoted in Mintz, *Huck's Raft*, 291). Richard Eberhart in 1956 told the readers of the *New York Times Book Review* that San Francisco offered "a radical group movement of young poets" with "a young will to kick down the doors of older consciousness" ("West Coast," 70–71). "The youngest generation is in a state of revolt so absolute that its elders cannot even recognize it," explained a sympathetic Kenneth Rexroth in 1957; "the heroes of this generation," models for its poems, were "two great dead juvenile delinquents"—Charlie Parker and Dylan Thomas (*World Outside*, 42). Norman Podhoretz's famous 1958 attack compared Beat writers to "the young savages in leather jackets who have been running amuck in the last few years"; "fighting . . . what the Beat Generation stands for," Podhoretz concluded, "has to do with fighting the poisonous glorification of the adolescent in American popular culture" ("Know-Nothing Bohemians," 81).

Charles Bernstein has singled out Allen Ginsberg as "a poet of adolescent identification" largely on the strength of *Howl* (1956), in which "the best minds of my generation" met their destinies in a vocabulary deliberately alien to the "adult," academic poems Ginsberg no longer wanted to write (*My Way*, 270). It would be wrong to see in Ginsberg's jeremiad the kind of focus on youth as a phase of life or on adolescence as a model for style or as a principal subject, which we have seen (so far) in poems by Williams, Loy, Moore, Auden, Larkin, Gunn, Bunting, Jarrell, and McGinley. And yet parts of *Howl* do depict and celebrate the adolescent "moratorium," the period of self-conscious, risky freedom, which midcentury thinkers such as Erikson insisted that all young men (if not women) deserved, and which social critics such as Goodman would, a few years after *Howl*, insist that American teens were not getting. This is the freedom that Carl Solomon, "who threw potato salad at CCNY lecturers" and "drove crosscountry seventytwo hours to find out if I had a vision or you had a vision," exemplified, in Ginsberg's view, and for which an unjust America locked him up (*Howl*, 5). The country that diagnosed Solomon as insane is the country whose institutions make tame adults out of wild young men, a country where only juvenile delinquents feel free.[5]

Parts of *Howl* also flaunt linguistic registers new to American poetry, though not to American speech: registers associated with a (supposedly) new criminal class, with drug use, and with a gay male underground. (Midcentury psychiatric discourse, one of the explicit targets for *Howl*, considered homosexuality a form of immaturity.) Phrases like "angelheaded hipsters," "busted in their pubic beards," or "madman bum and angel beat in time" joined frank sexual words like "balled" and "snatched" in Ginsberg's effort "to recreate the syntax and measure of poor human prose," an effort that meant not the creation of new language from nothing but the appreciative quotation of young rebels' nonstandard speech (*Howl*, 3–6).

Other poets constructed gentler stanzas from the same youth argot. Robert Creeley hijacked Bohemian slang for comic and tender effects in "A Wicker Basket" (1956–58); the woman in that poem

> opens the door of her cadillac
> I step in back
> and we're gone.
> She turns me on. . . .
>
> And while certainly
> they are laughing at me, and all around me is racket
> of these cats not making it, I make it
> in my wicker basket.

(COLLECTED POEMS, 161)

Not only the cadences but the choice of phrase in almost every line reflect the nonstandard English associated with 1950s Bohemian youth—contemptible to some, and to others sublime.

Certain American poets in the 1960s would make adolescent preoccupations, language, and tastes into foundations for new styles; these in turn reflected changes in adolescence itself. Noting both the career of John F. Kennedy and the heroism of civil rights workers, the cultural historian Peter Braunstein finds in mid-1960s mass media "a new valuation of young people as valorous, crusading, and brimming with moral vitality" ("Forever Young," 248).[6] By 1966, "a teenage boy from Buffalo" could tell *Newsweek* that "adults live without a personal identity" (Palladino, *Teenagers*, 232). *Time* in January 1967 declared "the Man of the Year" to be "the Young Generation," "the man—and woman—of 25 and under": "The young have already staked out their own minisociety, a congruent culture that has both alarmed their elders and, stylistically at least, left an irresistible impression" ("Man of the Year," 18–19). During 1967, prevalent ideas of youth became less optimistic, more focused on confrontation and violence. Not coincidentally, that year saw many young activists shift their focus from gaining civil rights for African Americans to ending U.S. involvement in Vietnam.

Marshall Berman calls "arguments about what 'the kids' were up to, where they were leading our country and our culture," "the real sound of the '60s" ("Sympathy," 24). Published in the *Partisan Review* in 1965, Leslie Fiedler's essay "The New Mutants" became a frequent touchstone (Marvel Comics would later reuse Fiedler's title for a series about superpowered teens). The essay diagnosed in the rising generation's "beatniks or hipsters, layabouts and dropouts" "a growing sense of the irrelevance of the past and even of the present" (509, 507). These "new irrationalists" saw "the obsolescence of everything our society understands by maturity"; in consequence, they "are prepared to advocate prolonging adolescence to the grave" (511). The New Mutants (apparently all white men) "feel . . . they must not only become more Black than White but more female than male" (516). Fiedler warmed to youth movements later, but his label stuck: Frank Kermode, who taught at Wesleyan University during the student strike of 1970, described his "mixed feelings" about "the Rock generation, Mr. Fiedler's mutants," "the long-haired pot-smoking past-hating young" ("The Young," 191). (Richard Wilbur addressed an eloquent poem to the same Wesleyan strikers.)

The seriousness with which adults took youth culture and the prominence of youth in political news entered the poetry of the period, especially (but not only) after Robert Bly and others organized public events in which poets stood alongside student radicals to denounce the Vietnam War.[7] John Ciardi's exasperated poem "And You?" makes fun of such events; at his imaginary demonstration, "A manifesto named Bly will recite itself throughout," and "Victrolas from City Lights will improvise / the lucidity of 20,000 Berkeley undergraduates / in a march toward radiance and sugar for all" (*The Little*, 74). Other poets took the same phenomena far more seriously. Muriel Rukeyser saw in youth countercultures hopes for not just political but metaphysical change—her "young . . . resist a system of wars and rewards":

> Bringing their life   these young
> bringing their life   rise from their wakings
> bringing their life   come to a place
> where they make their gifts
> The grapes of life of death   of transformation
> round they hang at hand   desires   like peace
> or seed of revolutions that make all things new.
>
> (499)

Youth as innovative rebellion and youth as trans- or antihistorical pastoral, adolescence as individual (like lyric) and adolescence as collective (a youth movement) are for Rukeyser no longer at odds; rather, youth in revolt will restore Eden, the original "pastoral," making a Green World for us all. "These young," in Rukeyser's incantatory phrase, recall the ring of "savages" who worship the sun, "not as a god but as a god might be," in Stevens's "Sunday Morning" (*Collected Poetry*, 53). They recall, too, the Neolithic art in which Rukeyser's earlier poems (such as "Ajanta") took an interest, and they are vulnerable to the critiques set down by Stevens and Williams, who attacked other modernists' failure to distinguish between youth as social fact and youth as metaphor.

At the same pole of response, we can find Denise Levertov, whose poetry lauded antiwar activists, making a point of their newness, their innocence, their distance from compromised adult language and life. She wrote of one activist, "de Courcy Squire, war resister, / began her fast in jail. She is 18" (*To Stay Alive*, 22). Another activist "travels the country [as] a harbinger. / (He's 20. His golden beard was pulled and clipped / by a Wyoming sheriff, but no doubt has grown again" (*To Stay Alive*, 41). In Levertov's poems of radical sincerity, the stylistic marks of "open field" writing become signals of political commitment: declaratory short lines show the openness to experience that she identified with the young. Levertov even found hopes for radical change (which she identified with generational change) after the bloody debacle of the Chicago Democratic Convention in 1968: "*Which side are you on?* / Revolution, of course. Death is Mayor Daley. / This revolution has no blueprints and . . . is the first that laughter and pleasure aren't shot down in" (*To Stay Alive*, 29). Levertov, who taught in Berkeley during the People's Park siege of 1969, wrote that the violence had given her "not only the knowledge that there is no such thing as a generation gap when people are engaged in a common task," "but also the conviction that a meaningful education in the future" would take the form of a commune whose members "cook together . . . and grow vegetables and flowers together, and mend each other's clothes" (*Poet*, 196). In a commencement address at Bennington College in 1969, the poet "suggest[ed] that Bennington turn itself into just such a commune" (*Poet*, 198).

Poets unsympathetic to radical youth also conceived their 1960s poems and projects as responses to youth's demands. Shapiro paid tribute to the "juvenile delinquent" stereotype—even, perhaps, admired it—in his collection of prose poems, *The Bourgeois Poet* (1964):

> Waiting in front of the columnar high school (the old ones look like banks, or rather insurance companies) I glance over the top of my book. The bells go off like slow burglar alarms; innumerable sixteeners saunter out. . . . Here comes a surly defiance. As in a ritual, each lights a cigaret just at the boundary where the tabu ends. Each chews. The ones in cars rev up their motors and have bad complexions like gangsters. The sixteeners are all playing gangster.
>
> (11)

Waiting to pick his daughter up at school, Shapiro decides that the teen "sea of subjectivity" has "captured the telephone centers, the microphones, the magazine syndicates (they've left the movies to us)"; the high school strikes him as "enemy territory" (*Bourgeois*, 12). Poets younger than Shapiro are physical threats: "The term *generation* is a deadly weapon. When a poet says 'my generation,' move off a few feet. He probably has a switch-blade knife up his sleeve, and it's for 'my' generation" (*Bourgeois*, 100). By the time he finished his essay "The Poetry Wreck" (1970), Shapiro had turned entirely against all youth subcultures present and future. "The poetry of semi-literates and rock singers," he complained, "is equated with Shakespeare and Homer." "The poetry of adolescents, amateurs and psychotics seems equal to the poetry of masters," and "the kitsch-camp-op-pop-absurdist-revolutionary sweepings and swill with which [students] fill their wordless minds are what they bring to class" (*Wreck*, xvi–xvii, 357).

Shapiro and Levertov, as of 1970, disagreed on almost everything. Yet both believed that a new generation gap, and a new kind of American adolescent, inside and outside of colleges and universities, had worked substantial and likely permanent changes in the style and substance of contemporary verse. From the same premise, George Oppen, Gwendolyn Brooks, and Robert Lowell would create some of the decade's most powerful poems.

❖ ❖ ❖ ❖ ❖

Why did George Oppen return to the United States, and to the writing of verse, in 1958? Scholars cite the end of McCarthyite persecution, which had kept the committed communist Oppen, along with his wife and daughter, in Mexico. Oppen's own letters from those years suggest an additional reason: American youth seemed to Oppen to promise a renewal both of genuine art and of political hope. As Beats gave way to hippies, as the civil rights movement gave way to the New Left, Oppen's poetry began to emphasize his distance from the rising generation: his later poems could not wholly appreciate—though they still sought hope within—the new world of the young.

George and Mary Oppen moved back to New York City in 1958, after their daughter Linda matriculated at Sarah Lawrence College. Oppen wrote to Louis Zukofsky in 1958 that "the 'young generation' seems to me neither beat nor quiet. . . . They seem to me simply the healthiest in U.S. history" (*Selected Letters*, 8). "Surely these young people," Oppen wrote in 1962, "make art a part of their lives in a sense we never did" (*Selected Letters*, 66). Oppen tried to bring these lives into his poems. In the late 1950s, he completed (but did not publish) "The New People":

Crowding everywhere
Angrily perhaps
The world of stoops,
The new young people

With their new styles, the narrow trousers
Of the young men and the girls' bee hive
Hair-do's this year they seem a horde

Who have invaded.
And they are, they are!
And each is someone: the tragic

Flaw. That they are not the real,
The virgin
Forest, wilderness,

The mineral,
From which they come.
(*ONCP* 318)

The Oppen who, in Norman Finkelstein's words, "concentrates . . . upon the single crucial relationship of the self to community" asks whether the rising generation is different enough from its predecessors to save the community they purportedly share ("The Dialectic," 360). The "new young people / with their new styles" seemed to Oppen to have attained a more collective, and a less mediated, way of being (and of making art) than Oppen's generation could have imagined. Adolescent characters in novels, Julia Kristeva has written, become "metaphors of that which is not yet formed" (*New Maladies*, 151). Oppen plays on such metaphors but differentiates the new teens' temporary blankness from the absolute, and potentially permanent, "virgin" or "mineral" blankness of an uncarved rock, a wilderness, or a blank page.

Youth culture made its first appearance in Oppen's published poetry with "Pedestrian" (probably 1960 or 1961):

What generations could have dreamed
This grandchild of the shopping streets, her eyes

In the buyer's light, the store lights
Brighter than the lighthouses, brighter than moonrise

From the salt harbor so rich
So bright her city

In a soil of pavement, a mesh of wires where she walks
In the new winter among enormous buildings.
(*ONCP* 8

Brighter than the lights among which she moves, this young woman strides confidently through the networks and grids of New York while remaining apart from them: capitalism and car culture have perhaps governed her parents' generation, giving her the money that makes her a "buyer." She herself, however, sees a city not just "rich" but "bright."

Oppen told Diane Meyer in late 1964 that while *This In Which* had not been "a decisive expression of a period," he expected "to try in the next" book for just such a work (*Selected Letters*, 108). To Oppen as to so many others, the spirit of the age meant "the new, the 'new generation'" (*Selected Letters*, 109). In "A Language of New York" (the sequence that later evolved into "Of Being Numerous"), Oppen not only praises the young Bohemians, Fiedler's "new mutants," but tries to describe their subculture and purposes. He sees this endeavor as a response to his own times, but also as a response to William Carlos Williams's "To Elsie," with its signature line "The pure products of America / go crazy" (*CPW* 218). Oppen begins:

> Strange that the youngest people I know
> Like Mary-Anne live in the most ancient buildings
>
> Scattered about the city
> In the dark rooms
> Of the past—and the immigrants,
>
> The black
> Rectangular buildings
> Of the immigrants.
>
> They are the children of the middle class.
>
> 'The pure products of America—'
> (*ONCP* 118)

Charles Reznikoff (whom Oppen admired unreservedly) had traced his own poetic goals to Jewish immigrant culture; Oppen names the Bohemian youth of Manhattan and Brooklyn as immigrants' delayed heirs, returning to an authenticity that their middle-class parents appeared to lack.

Oppen considered his 1967 move from New York back to San Francisco "a homecoming to my adolescence" (*Selected Letters*, 394, 399). The city itself appeared "very familiar (our adolescence)—and ineffably distant"; the foggy port of Oppen's youth had become the center for the Summer of Love (*Selected Letters*, 170). In that city, he transformed "A Language of New York" into "Of Being Numerous" (1968). That longer sequence considers not only young people retaking old buildings but also their art forms— live events, "happenings," readings, partly improvised psychedelic rock—

which, as Oppen saw them, aspired to take up Whitman's project of representing American multitudes. The "bright light of shipwreck," the burning failures of bourgeois liberalism, might—in the searching gaze of the young—yet inspire:

> New arts! Dithyrambic, audience-as-artists!
> But I will listen to a man, I will listen to a man, and when I speak I will
>   speak, tho he will fail and I will fail. But I will listen to him speak. The
>   shuffling of a crowd is nothing—well, nothing but the many that we
>   are, but nothing.
>
> (ONCP 167-68)

This "new art" of multitudes is both a collective art, and an "art of the young":

> Urban art, art of the cities, art of the young in the cities—
> The isolated man is dead, his world around him exhausted
> And he fails! He fails, that meditative man! And indeed they cannot
>   'bear' it.
>
> (168)

"That meditative man" is W.B. Yeats's epithet for John Synge, who "dying chose the living world for text," making his plays from the folklife of the Aran Islands (Yeats, *Poems*, 243, 133). Oppen seems here to identify himself with Synge and with the modernist generation that (as we have seen) explored "the young" for inspiration and material, almost as Synge explored the Aran Islands. "The young," not "isolated" but collective, might now also represent themselves.

The lines quoted above formed segment 7 in "A Language of New York." They became segment 25 in "Of Being Numerous." Section 26 continues the investigation:

> How shall one know a generation, a new generation?
> Not by the dew on them! Where the earth is most torn
> And the wounds untended and the voices confused
> There is the head of the moving column
>
> Who if they cannot find
> Their generation
> Wither in the infirmaries

And the supply depots, supplying
Irrelevant objects.

(*ONCP* 178)

Oppen—who served in the infantry during the Second World War—here likens the young to an army, effective only en masse and only when identifiable as a group. This "column" also suggests the large-scale marches and demonstrations undertaken to oppose the war in Vietnam. Would this "column" overcome its confusion? Or would the succession of generations end?

"Of Being Numerous" achieved a hesitant style well adapted to these fears, which Oppen also cast as doubts about the young. "Route" complains that the virtues Oppen sees in youth may not last:

I have seen too many young people become adults, young friends be
    come old people, all that is not ours,
The sources
And the crude bone

        —we say

Took place

Like the mass of the hills.

(*ONCP* 194)

On the one hand, the young (the opposite of "adults") are the only source of social and even artistic hope. On the other, "the young" are (perhaps alarmingly) inchoate and unindividualized, like a geological "mass." "Route" compares historical change, and change in the human life course, to geological processes—slow, cumulative, unavoidable. At the same time, it appears to suggest that a "sane man" and a next generation, an accurate art and the social body it reflects, can come into being only if young people *stop* becoming adults, if they retain the qualities—idealism? openness to experience? distance from the cash nexus?—that for Oppen (as for Goodman, Friedenberg, and other observers) characterize adolescence, or ought to characterize it. Oppen strives to embody just those qualities in his open, idealistic, "unfinished" verse, which seems to have left open space for the nonadult, antihistorical, collective future it cannot directly describe.

The events of late 1967 and 1968—the March on the Pentagon, the disturbances on many campuses, the assassination of Martin Luther King Jr.

and the riots that followed—led Oppen to ask if that future had arrived. A 1967 letter asks if "social existence," "adequate status," might be "obtainable also by attaching oneself to a public event: as, the Beats, the Hippies, or even being young, which is rather public these days" (*Selected Letters*, 161). Oppen may have witnessed violence at Berkeley or at San Francisco State, where students occupied buildings in December 1967. Letters of 1968 show particular attention to the student occupations at Columbia and in Paris; Oppen wrote to William Bronk in May:

> The kids, the rioting kids! Amazing! . . . They want to do something else. Something that has not already been done. I don't mean they have found it, nor begun to. But this strange, world-wide 'rising'—revolt, despair, demand—! The life of the mind: what is left for them is the life of the mind. But for how many IS that a possible way of life? . . . surely I don't know. And what else is left for them?
>
> (*SELECTED LETTERS*, 175-76)

Another May 1968 letter tells Bronk, "I am elated by the rioting students, the rioting world . . . Strangely, they are zealots of catastrophe. Resembling, in this way, the poets" (*ONCP* 397). "The Students Gather" (1968) finds words for that elation:

> The puddles
> Shine with the sky's light
>
> A Public Demonstration
>
> Students gather in the square
> Between two skies
>
> Someone must speak
> I too agree
>
> We are able to live
> Only because some things have been said
>
> Not repeated
>
> Said
>
> (*ONCP* 296-97)

Oppen appears to claim that "we are able to live" (or to live with ourselves) only because student demonstrators articulate the moral demands around which "we" adults might then reorganize our lives: "we" (adults?) are to the demonstrators as the puddle is to the light of the sky.

Yet Oppen cannot quite join the hopeful collective that his poems from these years envision. "Of what I have witnessed and felt // The young do not yet possess so much time / It is not certain of any young man that he will" (*ONCP* 331–32). Oppen's grave tone and his aposiopeses—open spaces left for experience he has not had, will not have—rebuke other grown-up poets' naive beliefs that their inherited art and their students' tastes might merge in a seamless, revolutionary whole. One such poet, Kay Boyle, concluded a 1969 tribute to student radicals at San Francisco State by imagining canonical poets "there beside you on / The campus grass, Shakespeare, Rilke, Brontë . . . Their young arms cradling your bones" (Charters, *Portable Sixties Reader*, 228). Rather than embracing Boyle's vision of continuity between old poets and new students, Oppen suggests that 1960s art and culture—unlike all previous Western art and youth—reflect a sense that history might end. The 1962 Port Huron Statement (the founding manifesto of Students for a Democratic Society) declared flatly, "We may be the last generation" (quoted in Carroll, *It Seemed Like Nothing Happened*, 14). "An antigestalt became prevalent among young people" in the mid-1960s, Jeff Nuttall recalled, "an instinct to leave nothing complete," "to half-close doors, to half-finish letters . . . for an act completed is an identity established," and an identity established meant a commitment that might not last (*Bomb Culture*, 118). Nuttall's description of a new outlook that favored the unfinished, the incomplete—and which found in those preferences signals of youth—fits the style Oppen found. Consider the last segment in "Of Being Numerous," a prose quotation cut off, mid-sentence, by an ellipsis: . . . Few poems have seemed more "half-finished."

Nuttall did not wholly trust the style he described; its "weakness," he wrote, "is a kind of fatigue of communication and constructive action . . . as if the praxes of art were involved, to their detriment, in the processes of social dissolution" (*Bomb Culture*, 226). Donald Davie advanced the same objection to the poetry of Oppen and to much else in the arts after 1966, suggesting instead that "poetry should be responsible for giving to Californian youth that ballast which we may feel that it so perilously lacks" (*Two Ways*, 139). Davie added "Oppen does not agree"; for Oppen, youth "are to be, have to be, *trusted*, with whatever misgivings. The past will not help them, and perhaps we only thought that it helped us" (*Two Ways*, 139). Yet Oppen sometimes emphasized his misgivings and allowed his verse to incorporate them. A 1969 letter to Harvey Shapiro considers "A young man in imminent danger of being sent to Vietnam," who "does not, I suppose, consider it absolutely necessary that universities" (or any other institutions) "should function" at all (*Selected Letters*, 191). There follows a poem entitle "A Modern Incident," on the new American youth:

> The culture
> Of the draft-pool, an exotic poetry
> Between speech and action
>
> Between action and theatre
> A pop culture
> Of an elite
> Engaged in revolt
>
> Between act and environment,
> Hedonist, a property of the young,
> A popular song, a clean
> Sweep
>
> (*LETTERS* 191; *ONCP* 297-98)

Without a "Shadow" of original sin (as in T. S. Eliot's "Between the essence / And the descent / Falls the Shadow" [Eliot, *Poems*, 92]) "the young" advance a "Hedonist" "pop culture." Their "exotic poetry / Between speech and action" includes all the real-time interventions of art into ordinary life—from street theater to "be-ins"—that had come to characterize the era, and about which Michael Fried, for example, complained, writing in 1967 that "the survival . . . of the arts has come . . . to depend on their ability to defeat theater" (*Art and Objecthood*, 163). Oppen's antitheatrical terseness and his incomplete grammar allow his poem to resolve neither in confidence nor in fear. That irresolution enters the line break on "clean": the young promise a "clean" new art, but perhaps deliver only a "clean / Sweep," a negation of the old.

As the 1960s rolled on, Oppen's doubts accumulated, filling the open spaces in his lines. George and Mary attended the infamous rock festival at Altamont in 1969, in which a young man was killed while the Rolling Stones played. Altamont became the first subject in "Some San Francisco Poems," the sequence which anchored *Seascape: Needle's Eye* (1972). Crowds arrive at the festival, "moving over the hills":

> > in the multiple world of the fly's
> multiple eye the songs they go to hear on
> this occasion are no one's own

Needle's eyeneedle's eyebut in the ravine
again and again the massive spike the song
clangs

as the tremendous volume of the music takes
over obscured by their long hair they seem
to be mourning

(ONCP 221)

The "songs are no one's own" because they belong to the communal art of 1960s youth, the art that "Of Being Numerous" and "Route" compare, warily but favorably, to Oppen's own late modernist practice. "It is easier for a camel to go through the eye of a needle than for a rich man to enter the kingdom of God" (Mark 10:25): the repeated phrase "needle's eye" suggests that adult, middle-class America has become that rich man. Yet "needle's eye" may also mean that the "streams of women and men" with "their long hair" are trying to do the impossible: their failure (to enter Heaven; to construct, from their new arts, a countercultural utopia) explains their "mourning." Oppen likely had in mind, too, Yeats's "A Needle's Eye," which depicts history as an unresting "stream": "Things unborn, things that are gone / From needle's eye still goad it on" (*Poems*, 288).[8]

In January 1971 Elizabeth Hardwick reviewed *Gimme Shelter*, "a brilliant documentary film" about Altamont (*Bartleby*, 30). Hardwick saw "death everywhere," "in the dead, drugged eyes and in the jostling, nervous kicks and shoves"; she concluded that "something pitiless and pathological has seeped into youth's love of itself" (*Bartleby*, 38, 40). Oppen's poem makes no such grand claims; he said later, "we didn't know anything about the murder then" (Power, "Interview," 202). Nevertheless, "we knew something was wrong" (quoted in Mottram, "Political Responsibilities," 157). "Some San Francisco Poems" records (as Oppen seems to have seen it) the failure of New Left politics and of the new, collectivist art—especially, perhaps, rock and roll—to deliver the new beginnings they promised. San Francisco became failure's symbol:

Provincial city
Not alien enough

To naked eyes

This city died young

You too will be shown this

You will see the young couples

Leaving again in rags

(*ONCP* 223)

To end a poem this way is to equate the fans leaving Altamont and the im-poverished or disappointed hippies in post-1967 San Francisco with Adam and Eve leaving Eden. Youth movements' failure represents ("again") a sec-ond Fall. Adolescence as revolution, as force for permanent change, has al-ready proven false, though youth as pastoral, as eternal *hope* for future change, might (like the myth of Eden) endure.

These otherwise various "San Francisco Poems" are thus held together in part by Oppen's fear that the experiment of the American 1960s, the new youth and their new, collective outlook (which would replace the old liberal individualism), had already failed. "Something is wrong with the antiques, a black fluid / Has covered them," but something is wrong with the new constructions too (*ONCP* 231). Though symbols of youth remain, "green leaves / Of young plants," "we" can only "relinquish"

Sanity to redeem
Fragments and fragmentary
Histories in the towns and the temperate streets
Too shallow still to drown in or to mourn
The courageous and precarious children.

(*ONCP* 232-33)

"Some San Francisco Poems" explores what James Longenbach calls "Oppen's willingness not only to interrogate his own convictions but to suffer their collapse as well"; Oppen, Longenbach writes, "wants to bear failure, bear it willingly, openly" (*Resistance to Poetry*, 82). The fragmentation and the silences that mark the later Oppen—fragmentations different, in their refusal of grammar, in their frequent avoidance of visual data, from the terse unities of *Discrete Series* (1934)—look, we might say, like genera-tion gaps, like the spaces that separate Oppen's modernist consciousness from the necessarily incomplete new projects of the collective young. Yet Oppen will not allow *Seascape: Needle's Eye* to end in resignation. Instead, the volume concludes with "Exodus," whose crowds are not Adam and Eve leaving Eden but Israelites leaving Egypt:

When I was a child I read Exodus
To my daughter   'The children of Israel . . .'

Pillar of fire
Pillar of cloud

We stared at the end
Into each other's eyes   Where
She said hushed

Were the adults   We dreamed to each other
Miracle of the children
The brilliant children   Miracle

Of their brilliance   Miracle
of

(ONCP 234)

Oppen described these lines as "a sort of reference to Adam and Eve, to innocence" (Power, "Interview," 203). "Exodus" becomes a prayer or plea that
the "brilliant children" of the counterculture might accomplish their goals
and renew their innocence, whether or not "adults" witness or understand.

❖ ❖ ❖ ❖ ❖

For Gwendolyn Brooks, the changing models of adolescence in the 1960s—
along with changing models of urban community, black art, and black identity—prompted not a return to poetry but changes in how, what, and for
whom she wrote. The Brooks of *A Street in Bronzeville* (1945) and *Annie Allen*
(1949) found an attractive solution to one dilemma that vexed earlier African
American poets: whether to write of black experience in a "white," Anglo-
American idiom of pentameters and polysyllables, or to write of the same
experience in "black" folk diction and forms. Brooks simply did both, often
within the same poem. Consider "The Sundays of Satin-Legs Smith":

He wakes, unwinds, elaborately: a cat
Tawny, reluctant, royal. He is fat
And fine this morning. Definite. Reimbursed.
. . . .
At Joe's Eats
You get your fish or chicken on meat platters.
With coleslaw, macaroni, candied sweets,
Coffee and apple pie. You go out full.
(The end is—isn't it?—all that really matters.)

(BLACKS, 42, 47)

On the one hand, regular pentameters and end rhymes; on the other, syncopation, with words and phrases ("you get your," "cat") alien to standard written English. These effects of mixed diction, and the equally effective device of mixing blues quatrains with Anglo-American "high" forms, established (what Brooks's early poems had argued explicitly in any case) that the black Americans of Chicago's South Side deserved at least much dignity, attention, and beauty as anybody else. Yet Brooks's showy early style had a cost; it cast the poet herself (the speaker in these poems) as authoritative and nearly impersonal, as someone who stood slightly apart from the community of which she wrote. Brooks later remembered "1941 through 1949" as a "party era," when "we merry Bronzevillians could find each other and earnestly philosophize"; her poetry, though, presented her as a quiet journalist, chronicling the hardships and pleasures of a community which she simply observed (*Report from Part One*, 68).

To solve this emotional problem of felt remoteness, Brooks would turn first to children and then to adolescents. "A Song in the Front Yard" (also from *A Street in Bronzeville*) descends from "The Ruined Maid," by Thomas Hardy, and from Sterling Brown's "Chillun Got Shoes," poems in which innocent girls envy well-dressed prostitutes. Brooks's "Song," however, adopts a yearning first-person mode:

> I've stayed in the front yard all my life.
> I want a peek at the back
> Where it's rough and untended and hungry weed grows.
> A girl gets sick of a rose.
> (*BLACKS*, 28)

If "A Song in the Front Yard" belongs with Brooks's other investigations of childhood, it also belongs with her *Annie Allen* and with "Sadie and Maud," which followed the front-yard–back-yard, good-girl–bad-girl contrast through a life:[9]

> Maud went to college.
> Sadie stayed home.
> Sadie scraped life
> With a fine-tooth comb.
> (*BLACKS*, 32)

Maud, however, ends up "all alone," "a thin brown mouse," and a possible fate for her author (*Blacks*, 32). "When I was a teen," Brooks said in 1967, "my teen friends wondered, as they partied and danced, why I was happy to stay in my tiny room and write" (*Report from Part One*, 134). "I felt inferior," she added in a later interview, "because I was not one of the girls who danced" (172).

By contrast with these too-safe girls and teens, Brooks's early poems about showy young men and risky girls convey at once disapproval and excitement. Her most famous poem, "We Real Cool," has become a schoolroom chestnut partly by virtue of its contradictory "messages," since it warns young readers against emulating its speakers even as it shows their "cool." The pool players, "seven at the golden shovel," project (and the lines' syncopation famously reflects) a swagger which the poem tries to acknowledge, even as it says that they will "die soon" (*Blacks*, 331). The pool players, Brooks said later, "are supposedly dropouts," "probably young enough [for high school] or at least those I saw were when I looked in a poolroom" (*Report from Part One*, 155). (Chicago gangs did gather in pool rooms [Dawley, *Nation of Lords*, 115].) Poems from before 1963 celebrate—always with guilt or ambivalence—similar swagger in such characters as DeWitt Williams (who frequented "the Dance Halls, / Warwick and Savoy"), and "Cousin Vit," whose sexy vitality defies even death (*Blacks*, 39, 125). The divisions between respectable and "street," mature (or patient and studious) and immature (or wild) throughout Brooks's early poems reflects her city. St. Clair Drake and Horace Cayton in *Black Metropolis* (1945) described a "clear line between the 'shady' and the 'respectable'" among the adults and teens of the Southside (382).[10]

Young risk takers, "shady" types, in Brooks's early poems earn guilty admiration compared with her implicitly timid or prematurely wise, "respectable" poetic voice. When in the mid-1960s a discourse became available that gave adolescent wildness, rebellion, or "shady" behavior ethical value, Brooks embraced it, giving the new street youth not warnings but odes. Authentic, proud blackness, for Brooks, became in the late 1960s inseparable from encounters with the young: Brooks's daughter Nora remembers her mother exclaiming in 1968, when Brooks herself was fifty-one, "You middle-aged people make me so mad!" (Kent, *A Life*, 222). "Just now there's such a gush of raw vigor," Brooks commented in that year, "something very special happening in poetry today and I see it happening chiefly among the young blacks" (quoted in Kent, *A Life*, 227–28). Other black poets and critics—among them Brooks's friend (and later publisher) Don L. Lee (Haki R. Madhubuti)—saw something special too, something they tried to describe, encourage, and codify as the Black Arts Movement. "The black revolt is as palpable in letters as it is on the streets," wrote Hoyt Fuller ("Towards a Black Aesthetic," 199). Calls for writers to enact "revolt" resonated so strongly with Brooks—and led so consistently to poems idealizing the young—because she was already interested in how the young saw themselves, and in how she might stand in relation to them.

Completed in 1968, Brooks's second long poem, *In the Mecca*, started out as a novel for teenaged readers; the first of two surviving chapters begins with the protagonist on her way to her graduation, "tense, and wondering, and hot-hearted and oh-so-sixteen-going-on-seventeen" (quoted in Kent, *A Life*, 125). The finished poem, as Cheryl Clarke has put it, reflects "an artistic crisis in [Brooks's] writing life as she struggled to consider the issues of audience" in a bleak, dense exploration of black-on-black violence, pride, and social abandonment within the apartment complex from which the poem takes its name (*"After Mecca,"* 27). One of its strongest segments is an ode to girl gangs:

> A tough girl gets it. A rough
> Ruthie or Sue. It is unembarrassable,
> and will seem likely. It is very bad,
> but in its badness it is nearly grand,
> and is a crown that tops bald innocence
> and gentle fright.
> (*BLACKS*, 411)

The pronoun "it" has no obvious referent: Brooks has imported into poetry (perhaps for the first time) the idiom "gets it" (as in "he just doesn't get it"), and she uses it to describe the attitude—"bad" but "grand," immature and dangerous yet somehow admirable—that Ruthie and Sue espouse.

Ruthie and Sue, in other words, are Sadies—but more aggressive Sadies, in whose aggression Brooks finds a political meaning:

> Gang
> is health and mange.
> Gang
> is a bunch of ones and a singlicity.
> (*BLACKS*, 413)

The passage shows not just a new disposition toward aggressive teens (whom Brooks no longer sounds ashamed to admire) but new rhythms to match. Such broken-up lines try not just to praise and to justify but to re-

flect these teens' caustic, confrontational, and (for Brooks) politically meaningful style. The teen gangs in Brooks seem (to Brooks) to solve the one-
many problem that vexed Oppen's poems about young activists; the
collective being of these young people represents something new (hence
"single," individual) in the history of the language.

Brooks was not the only observer who looked at Chicago's street gangs
and saw hope. Starting in 1965, several gangs on the Southside and West
Side reorganized themselves as neighborhood-based social service organi-
zations. The activist David Dawley became in 1967 the only white member
of one such gang, the Conservative Vice Lords; "moving the Vice Lords
from gang to community organization," Dawley recalled, meant "less crime,
fewer homicides . . . and storefront programs that served the community"
(*Nation of Lords*, xii, xvi). One Vice Lord remembered that in 1967 "most
people still considered us a gang, but we were trying to get over to them
that we were . . . no longer out for killing and jive. . . . The militants came in
and say why be a gangbanger and kill each other when you can kill the
honky, and we began to see that the enemy was not black" (105, 107).

The same years saw lost credibility for the adult, official leaders of black
Chicago. For much of the 1960s the Chicago Coalition of Community Or-
ganizations, or CCCO—the subject of a voluminous study by Alan Anderson and George Pickering—tried to end de facto residential segregation,
help "children virtually imprisoned in public housing," and solve the in-
equalities of its school system (*Confronting the Color Line*, 145). The organization's efforts included repeated visits from Martin Luther King Jr.; Anderson and Pickering call this "Chicago campaign . . . the second major
failure of King's career" (3). 1966 and 1967 saw a rise in local violence, as
Southside and West Side teens clashed with police.

From those clashes, young spokespeople—some of them "gang leaders"—emerged (Anderson and Pickering, *Confronting the Color Line*, 210–
11). Reformed and politically minded but still ready for a fight, the gangs
struck some Chicagoans as attractive alternatives to a nonviolent movement that had not achieved many of its goals; "the civil rights organiza-
tions that came to Chicago" with King, Dawley explains, "were not working with the hard-core people anyway" (*Nation of Lords*, 108). Across the
nation, Black Power seemed an affair of youth, even of teens; William L.
Van Deburg notes that "top-ranking" Black Panthers in 1968 "ranged in
age from 26 to 34 while second-level leaders were between 21 and 26. 16
to 21-year-olds predominated among the rank and file" (*New Day in Babylon*, 156).

Brooks would respond to Black Power in Chicago with laudatory poems which emphasized its status as a youth movement, as something quintessentially unfixed and anti-adult. The ceremony to dedicate the Southside Wall of Respect, at which Brooks read "The Wall" and young black poets read their work, allowed Brooks to share that energy in public, paying homage to "Black / boy-men on roofs" (*Blacks*, 444). But "The Wall" was just the start of Brooks's attempt to shape a style for these "boy-men." The Blackstone Rangers on the Southside, like the Vice Lords on the West Side, had tried to become a social-service organization without abandoning their swagger and their insignia. In 1968 and 1969, Brooks recalled, she had "been hearing about the Blackstone Rangers for a couple of years, and I'd had this yearning—it sounds funny, I know—to 'do something for them'" (*Report from Part One*, 168). "Something" became the writing class Brooks, with Walter Bradford, taught for gang members and their friends.[11] That class inspired "The Blackstone Rangers," a kind of palinode to "We Real Cool." Brooks introduces the Rangers "As Seen by Disciplines" (not disciples, but disciplines, such as sociology): "Black, raw, ready. / Sores in the city / that do not want to heal" (*Black,* 446). As they see one another, however, the Rangers are not sores, but symbols of confidence:

> Jeff. Gene. Geronimo. And Bop.
> They cancel, cure and curry.
> Hardly the dupes of the downtown thing
> the cold bourbon,
> the rhinestone thing. And hardly
> in a hurry . . .
>
> Their country is a nation on no map.
>
> (BLACKS, 447)

Brooks's changing views about street gangs and her work with them led her to change her style in order to make it adequate for their praise; she even claimed that the Rangers began to respond to her only once she stopped "imposing . . . iambic pentameter" (quoted in Clarke, *"After Mecca,"* 43). Irregular alliterations and repetitions, along with sporadic full rhymes, give Brooks the forward momentum she had earlier used for poems about high livers, profligate rebels, and pleasure lovers (such as "The Rites for Cousin Vit"). Here, however, the profligate rebels are "The Leaders" (Brooks's subtitle); they conjure up a nation. "Gang Girls are sweet exotics"; the gang girl "Mary is / a rose in a whiskey glass" (*Blacks*, 449). Brooks encourages Mary to act like a Sadie, not like a Maud, and to accept the sexual advances her Ranger boyfriend is likely to make: "swallow, straight, the spirals of his flask / and assist him at your zipper; pet his lips / and help him clutch you" (*Blacks*, 450). Such advice in Brooks's earlier work must have sounded disapproving and ironic. Here, however, the bad girls are the best girls and deserve straightforward if shocking praise, since their expressive choices seem to empower the new nation of the militant young. Acknowledging Mary's need for "non-loneliness," the poem also comes close to the glorification of adolescent sexuality, of sexual and national energy in youth, which we have already seen, if not in Oppen, certainly in Williams and in Gunn.

When Brooks's late-1960s heroes are not adolescents, she sometimes treats them as if they were. Brooks's paean to Lee (another part of *In the Mecca*) finds parallels among political power, new kinds of loud music, and the "physical" prowess that Brooks's spondee-heavy, irregular lines emulate. Lee

> stands out in the auspices of fire
> and rock and jungle-flail;
> wants
> new art and anthem; will
> want a new music screaming in the sun.
>
> (*BLACKS*, 423-24)

Brooks sought for her own work the virtues she saw in Lee's, virtues identified explicitly with defiant youth; no wonder Lee singled out "The Blackstone Rangers" for praise (*Report from Part One*, 23).

Nor was Lee the only hero whom she treated in this way. Assassinated in July 1963 at the age of thirty-eight, after a very visible career in Mississippi's NAACP, the civil rights martyr Medgar Evers seems an appropriate subject for a laudatory memorial, but not necessarily for a poem about youthful exuberance. Yet Evers, in Brooks's version, achieved his prominence (and his martyrdom) by gleefully and violently refusing adult rules, adult tempers, adult restraints:

> Old styles, old tempos, all the engagement of
> the day—the sedate, the regulated fray—
> the antique light, the Moral rose, old gusts,
> tight whistlings from the past, the mothballs
> in the Love at last our man forswore.

Medgar Evers annoyed confetti and assorted
brands of businessmen's eyes.

(BLACKS, 440)

Brooks's off-balance lines—as rhythmically unpredictable as she could
make them, rendered more so by irregular internal rhymes—emphasize not
(for example) steadiness of resolve but vigor and speed. This Evers seems to
have made his mark by attacking not only segregationist traditions but also
the integrationist caution (the slow, "old tempos") that Brooks attributes to
previous generations. Brooks said of Evers in 1969, "He just up and decided
he wasn't going to have anything else to do with the stale traditions of the
past" (*Report from Part One*, 164).

Such vigor also sounds in the jagged lines of "Boy Breaking Glass." The
poem begins in medias res:

Whose broken window is a cry of art
(success, that winks aware
as elegance, as a treasonable faith)
is raw: is sonic: is old-eyed premiere.
Our beautiful flaw and terrible ornament.
Our barbarous and metal little man.

"I shall create! If not a note, a hole.
If not an overture, a desecration."

(BLACKS, 438)

The poem argues that a boy breaking a window has accomplished a valid
(political) protest and in some sense "created" a work of art. His spontaneous attack on a window demonstrates that no more sophisticated means to
contest his condition lies within his grasp: "It was you," the boy cries, "who
threw away my name!" Glossing her poem without saying so, Brooks
averred in 1972 that "Today's young people . . . want to be free to make, to
create. If they are not allowed to create, they break. In a vacuum, breaking
seems to them a form of creation" (*Report from Part One*, 82).

Completed in 1968, "Boy Breaking Glass" may address Chicago's local
violence of 1966 and 1967, the "long hot summer" riots of 1967, or the riots
in Chicago (and in more than a hundred other American cities) after the
1968 assassination of Martin Luther King Jr. Dawley, an eyewitness, explained why many black Chicagoans did not mind the destruction at the
time: "Violence was directed against property, not people, and the only

danger was for whites. There's no joy but there's a good feeling because in this riot there's integrity. Black people are standing up to The Man" (*Nation of Lords*, 119). Brooks depicted such reactions again in her 1969 poem "Riot," in which civil disturbances become Romantic uprisings of youth against age, of Black Power against Law:

> These candles curse—
>
> The young men run.
> The children in ritual chatter
> scatter upon
> their Own and old geography.
>
> The Law comes sirening across the town.
>
> (*BLACKS*, 475)

In Brooks's quasi-Homeric catalog of rioters, Gangster Disciples "stir / and thousandfold confer / with ranging Rangermen; / mutual in their 'Yeah'" (*Blacks*, 477); former gang rivals present a united front (*Blacks*, 477).[12]

What makes Brooks's poetry of the late 1960s so fascinating in retrospect—and so important to my argument in this book—is not simply that she embraced Black Power nor that embracing Black Power, for her, meant embracing ideas about the power in youth. What matters is that she altered her style—and wrote her most original poetry—as a direct result of that embrace and that the poetics that resulted—the broken-up, unpredictable, semimetrical, aggressive, sometimes fragmentary poetics of "The Blackstone Rangers" and *In the Mecca* and "Riot" and "Boy Breaking Glass"— seems particularly designed to capture the virtues Brooks ascribed to youth, virtues (aggression, rebellion, sexualized vigor, fresh attempts at independence) that she had described, but could not view *as* virtues, in the more careful poems of her earlier career. Youth as eternal pastoral appears in her poetry only to be repudiated entire; youth as rebellion created and sustained by peer groups (such as street gangs) can impose new language and energize the world.

After 1969, Brooks began to simplify her poetry, narrowing her range of diction, smoothing out her syntax, and shifting her interests from adolescents back to children. Brooks's 1971 sequence "In Montgomery" records her trip through Alabama on behalf of *Ebony* magazine: she arrived in the state "expecting / the strong young," feeling "that all of Before was rehearsal, / that the true trends, the splendors, the splurges, / were to be lit by the young" (*In Montgomery*, 2). A disappointed Brooks observed less confidence among black youth than late-1960s Chicago had led her to expect. She watches, for example,

> A spear of a Black girl
> in a glass-green skirt, tight, tiny
> below her sleeveless white blouse.
> She is Real Cool, munches candy,
> flicks a comb
> through the short black wires of her hair.
>
> (*IN MONTGOMERY*, 24)

In Montgomery consciously reprises Brooks's earlier work. This girl is "Real Cool"; near her, Brooks sees "bean-eaters" (the title of Brooks's 1960 book). These bean-eaters, however, look younger than those of 1960: one of them wears "dark glasses," another "blue jeans," and yet another plans on "'goin' up nawth where the money is. Young/ Jerry Johnson's not sure" (*In Montgomery*, 24–25).

Nor is Brooks sure. Montgomery is, still, "not free"; Brooks has not found here the energies she embraced in the Blackstone Rangers, and the poem marks the end of this phase in her work (*In Montgomery*, 28). Almost the only particularized adolescent in Brooks's post-1972 work is the troubled collegian of "The Coora Flower," caught between distress in her unlivable home and "learning nothing necessary" at her white-seeming school (*In Montgomery*, 81). The glorification of bad-boy and gang-girl vigor in such poems as "The Blackstone Rangers" could not last. Yet the confluence of Brooks's earlier shyness with late-1960s celebrations of confrontational African American youth made that glorification possible and generated some of Brooks's strongest poems.

❖ ❖ ❖ ❖ ❖

Of all the responses to 1960s youth in literary poetry, the most ambivalent and the most original took place in the work of Robert Lowell. Almost every phase of Lowell's career involved some quality (not always the same quality) that we might call—or that his peers dubbed—adolescent. David Kalstone found the key to Lowell's oeuvre in several poems (some entitled "Rebellion") that told and retold the story of how, in 1936, the nineteen-year-old Robert struck his father and knocked him to the floor in a dispute over the young poet's love life (Kalstone, *Five Temperaments*, 45–49). "Of course it was melodramatic and adolescent," Lowell recalled, "but I was a very melodramatic adolescent indeed" (*Letters*, 485).

If an adolescent is a kind of person characterized by rebellion rather than obedience, by becoming rather than being, and by challenging and testing rather than trusting, knowing, or believing, it is no wonder that Lowell associated his own work with adolescence throughout his career. His earliest poems, in their borrowings from Milton and their aggression against parent figures, exemplified Oedipal rebellion; his "confessional" verse of the 1950s and early 1960s explored psychoanalytic models of identity, guilt, and change. Regarded early on as a poetic authority, Lowell then used his powers to attack himself: the best accounts of his career highlight his successive rejections and revolts.

In *Notebook*, this self-canceling, self-attacking tendency entangles itself indissolubly with Lowell's thinking about the stages of life, about his own age, and about young people, from his ten- and twelve-year-old daughter to the antiwar students with whom he made common cause. The sonnets' self-canceling lines and sentences are aesthetic equivalents for both adolescent energy and adult unease; the sonnets often reject the seeming promise of adolescence even as they deny the authority of experience and of adulthood. Adolescence as pastoral, in these sonnets, has already collapsed—the green world is already iced-over, invaded, decayed—but adolescence as rebellion is bound to fail. The adult poet thus remains also adolescent, nostalgically and endlessly rebelling against himself. This disillusioned dilemma made its way not only into the free verse of Lowell's last phase (which often contrasts youthful vigor with middle-aged exhaustion) but also into other poets' work in the 1970s and afterward, where adolescence as a basis for poetry means not hope nor energy nor change but simply the absence of adult authority, the sense that we are all immature on our own.

To think about late Lowell and adolescence is thus to give an account of Lowell's late styles. Take, for example, these lines from "Through the Night":

We are firemen smashing holes in our own house.
We will each breath, and make our peace with war,
yearning to swoop with the swallow's brute joy,
indestructible as mercy—the round green weed
slipping free from the disappointment of the flower.
(*N* 47)[13]

Like the doomed students in Auden's *Orators*, the "I" and "we" in such lines depend for their identities and energies on what they oppose—as weeds, flowerbeds, or firefighters, fires. Moreover "I," "we," are always incomplete, resembling the green weed, not the flower or fruit. The strain and un-progress we feel in the sonnets involves the fiftyish Lowell identifying himself as both a father figure and an agent of youth in revolt. In "Memorial Day," he overhears Harvard students shouting to one another from their dorms:

> Sometimes I sink a thousand centuries,
> bone tired or stone asleep, to sleep ten seconds—
> voices, their future voices, adolescents
> go crowding through the chilling open windows;
> fathomless profundities of inanimation.
> And we will be, then, and as they are here.
> But nothing will be put back right in time,
> done over, thought through straight again—not my father
> revitalizing in a single Rhineland spa,
> Mussolini's misguiding roosterstep
> in the war year, just before our War began. . . .
> Ah, ah, this house of twenty-foot apartments,
> all the windows yawning—the voices of its tutees,
> their fortissimo *Figaro*, sunk into dead brick.
>
> (*N* 195–96)

The "house of twenty-foot apartments" in this sonnet contains rooms for fathers and sons, for teachers and students ("tutees"); where, if anywhere, does Lowell belong?

Lowell's desire to challenge his own authority and his consequent projection of a self violently divided and incomplete became the basis for the style on which the sonnets depend. Here are some of its salient features:

> choppy, broken-up, semi-iambic speech rhythms
> emphasized words repeated, repetitions used as rhymes
> aposiopesis, ellipsis, self-interruptions
> insistence on parallels whose content the reader has to uncover—"what
>   do A B and C have in common?"; puzzles
> verbs in the habitual or simple present or past, or counterfactual, almost
>   never future or conditional

hammered contrasts between past scenes and present moments, disar-
ranged chronology

sudden changes of perspective or time-scale

oxymorons and negations—"fathomless," "inanimation"

double and triple adjectives and adjective clauses—"bone-tired or stone
asleep," "chilling open windows"

chains of noun clauses with no verb—the implicit copula, with no clear
tense or mood

repeated apposition and parataxis

extended quotation—a whole poem, half a poem, or the first or last
phrase, in quotation marks, spoken by somebody else

All these devices collaborate to give a sense of self-invention balked, a self
frustrated by and tied to a turbulent, multivocal history. In a Lowell sonnet
each line, like each generation, has to decide what to do with and how
much to resist the line just before; the only relation each line *cannot* have to
its predecessors is complete independence.

Now this is the situation adolescents commonly face with parents. Friedenberg (writing in 1959) called adolescence "the period during which a
young person learns who he is . . . and differentiates himself from his culture, though on the culture's terms" (*Vanishing Adolescent*, 29). The adolescent can be in a relation of rejection to father and mother, to society and
culture, but never in *no* relation, never simply *without*. And this is how
Lowell regards and addresses history—his own and that of the nation. If
part of the strength of the early Lowell was the force with which he attacked his sources, part of the later Lowell's originality (as Vereen Bell has
shown) lay in the ways he credited those sources, insisting that we cannot
make everything new. The most persistent symbols in *Notebook*—rivers
clogged with "slush-ice," and the deciduous foliage that Lowell calls (following Gerard Manley Hopkins) "leafmeal" and also "leaf-lace"—suggest
Lowell's endless work on his always-rough drafts, his "carbon scarred with
ciphers," the self as never original and never finished (*N* 173).

No wonder, then, that the poems (to quote Bell's description of "Night
Sweat") "indicate an imperfect transition between childhood and maturity
and an arrested suspension between them" (*Lowell*, 73). In *Notebook* that
suspension becomes a principle of style. The sonnets' lines, each of which
might correct, improve, contradict, or simply rephrase the one before, become his symbols for generational succession and for the instability that
Bell describes. The Lowell of these poems has to keep moving, but to no

real destination—no future; his grammar maps his odd predicament with overlapping or ambiguous, bidirectional clauses: "The air is snow-touched, / fans our streaming backs, / blows in and in, a thousand snow-years back; / we were joined in love, a thousand snow-years back" (*N* 126). Boustrophedon (backward-then-forward, or right-to-left, then left-to-right—literally "ox-tread") becomes Lowell's figure for his relation to history and to the autobiography that leaves him neither certain nor mature. "I'm counterclockwise," he remarks elsewhere; "I come on walking off-stage backwards" (*Selected Poems*, 231, 237). Elsewhere, boustrophedon represents political change or its failure; college students graduate then "turn with the tread of an ox to serve the rich" (*N* 132).

Notebook dwells not just on youth and age but on ages and numbers, especially fifty and twenty. "Can I go on loving anyone at fifty?" (*N* 97)."It's as bad for me at fifty as nineteen— / the thirst for grownups, open cars and girls" (*CPRL* 610). "We're fifty / and free!" (*N* 22). The people in *Notebook* regularly tell us that they are, or are not, twenty: "You may have *joie de vivre*, but you're not twenty" (*N* 154); "I'm twenty, I've done badly, I'll do better" ("Saint-Just," *N* 169). Lowell's title "Gap" means both a military breach (an opportunity for an infantry charge) and a generation gap: "I wish to live my life back to twenty-one, / be ill-at-ease again as everyone," that sonnet muses, concluding instead, "My wooing at fifty would engulf the siren" (*N* 212). Rewritten for *History*, the poem became "Student" and declared "If I could stop growing, I would stop at twenty" (*CPRL* 549). These numbers triangulate the Lowell of 1967 and 1968 (age fifty), Lowell's own remembered teens and early twenties, and the lives of those who are twenty (give or take a few years) in the present time of the poems, which thus show him thinking both about which aspects of youth—and of poetic forms—remain constant over generations, and about which aspects had suddenly changed.

The years of Lowell's sonnets were also the first in which he took the mood stabilizer lithium carbonate. Frequently he connects his leveled-off disposition to health or to dejected maturity, the exhilaration of adolescence in political and cultural revolt to his own manic states. "Sound Mind, Sound Body" muses *Mens sana*? O at last; from twenty years / of the annual mania, thirty of adolescence" (*N* 216). Lowell's lithium carbonate regimen required self-administered blood tests: "High Blood" construes a blood test as a test for mania and for generational affiliation, since heartbeats and steady pulses suggest rock and roll: "the aorta and heartbeat of my life" are "acid rock turned high, teen-age record purring" (*N* 223). The psychiatrist Peter Blos in 1962 defined adolescence as an "individuation experience . . . which leads in its final step to a sense of identity" by way of "oppositional, rebellious and resistive strivings" (*On Adolescence*, 12). Such "strivings," with no "final step," are what *Notebook* depicts.

Those depictions, in turn, guide portrayals of public events. Between 1966 and 1969 the *New York Review of Books*, which Lowell and Elizabeth Hardwick had helped to found, became a conduit for communication between older literary figures and radical youth.[14] Leslie Fiedler's "On Being Busted at 50" appeared in the *New York Review of Books* in 1967; after Buffalo police (reacting to his stature as a campus leftist) invaded his house and planted drugs on his children and their friends, Fiedler discovered "an adult community more terrified . . . than I had then guessed of the gap between themselves and the young" ("Busted," 10). The same issue of the *New York Review* included Lowell's *Prometheus Bound*. This focus on radical youth and student movements among the adults with whom Lowell spent much of his time ought to be seen as central to *Notebook*, to both its sounds and its structure—correlated, albeit uneasily, with the year's most newsworthy scenes.

The first such scene is the October 1967 March on the Pentagon, which Lowell describes in both "The March 1" and "The March 2," and Norman Mailer in *The Armies of the Night*. Mailer alleged that Lowell happened on his plan for sonnets, or on his *Notebook* style, after the March on the Pentagon, even as a result of it; after the violence with which the march concluded, Lowell and Dwight Macdonald "left, unhurt, and eventually went home, Lowell to begin a long poem a few days later. (When next Mailer [who writes of himself in third person] saw [Lowell] a month later, 800 lines had already been written!)" (Mailer, *Armies*, 292).[15] The march gave the poet an experience of solidarity with the young ("lovely to lock arms, to march absurdly locked") against unjust, "marmoreal" authority (*N* 54). Yet it also showed his distance from them. Lowell's protesters "step off like green Union Army recruits / for the first Bull Run," the first land engagement of the Civil War—for the Union, a surprising and bloody setback; Melville wrote of that engagement, in lines the younger Lowell had used in another poem, "All wars are boyish and are fought by boys" (*N* 54; *CPRL* 20; Melville, *Battle-Pieces*, 43). Successive, conflicting lines of verse suggest the queues of protesters and guards; Lowell, with his wet glasses and shaky hand, feels out of place "march[ing] absurdly locked" with youth, even before confronting a young soldier, who in turn looks out of place defending the draft (*N* 54).

In this respect the march and "The March 1" stand for the whole of the book; over and over, *Notebook* depicts a failed or fraudulent spring or revolution, political and emotional promise wasted. "First Spring," for example, offers

> a smell, not taste, of life. For whom? For what?
> For the horses, six bets in ten misplaced,
> when another younger generation faces
> the firing squad and our blood is wiped from the pavement.
>
> (N 142)

Lowell's sonnet form looks and sounds new but proves incapable of narrative or argumentative progress; the sonnets repeat the same judgment on late-1960s youth. "Thanksgiving" and "Marching" liken hippies to seventeenth-century antinomians in New England: "They reel, arms locked, from luncheon into night: / bellbottom, barefoot, Christendom's wild hair; / words are what get in the way of what they say" (N 71). "Youth" compares the students of the late 1960s instead to Lowell's own cohort; he envies and identifies with the young but concludes that their hopes for "revolution" will not come true: "Many a youth will turn from student to tiger, / revolutionaries will sleep in the grave" (N 221). In "Harvard" what Geoffrey Hartman once called Lowell's "temporicide" (*Beyond Formalism*, 268), his habit of merging time-scales, lets him appear to sleep through thirty years; Lowell wakes as a teen, goes back to bed on a snowy morning, sleeps "through high-school, through college, through fall-term vacation," and wakes again in the 1960s (N 79).

In another sonnet, the middle-aged Lowell claims the same sexual and existential hungers as he had in the 1930s: "it's the same for me / at fifty as at thirteen, my childish thirst / to be the grown-up in his open car and girl" (N 44). "Thirteen" in *Notebook* became "Nineteen" in *History* (*CPRL* 610). The same sonnet ("Through the Night 1") pursues a three-way comparison among "the generations of leaves," the stages of a human life, and the endlessly revised but never-completed state of Lowell's own manuscripts:

> The pale green leaves cling white to the lit night;
> this has been written, and eaten out on carbons;
> incendiaries strike no spark from this moonlight;
> nothing less nutritive than the thirst at Harvard.
> Like the generation of leaves, the race of man;
> their long hair, beads, jeans, are early uniforms,
> rebellion that honors the liturgies.
>
> (N 44)

If the adolescent means for Lowell (as it did for Blos and for so many others) the unfinished, the energetic, the inconclusive, and that which threatens adults, then everything in the universe of *Notebook*—men, women, boys, girls, buildings, cities, trees—seems at times adolescent, even the night sky.

Among the recurring symbols in *Notebook*, none recurs so often as the color green—in leaves, in grass, in insects, in jealous people, in paint; almost always it signifies youth, spring, rebirth. Usually that rebirth is stalled, artificial, feigned, or *hors de combat*. At Eliot House, where Harvard students live, "cold makes the school's green copper cupola / greener over the defoliated playground" (*N* 79). The seals Lowell envies in "Seals" flee humanity and "head north—their haven / green ice in a greenland never grass" (*N* 250). "For Archie Smith: 1917–35" memorializes Lowell's classmate by comparing his early death to Dutch elm disease: "Our sick elms rise to breathe the peace of heaven, / at six the blighted leaves are green as mint" (*N* 220). By noon the leaves will appear less attractive, their shadows less clear; in a few years the tree will die. Green also marks standoffs, endless conflicts, and stalemates, as in the green opposing armies of "The March 2" (*N* 134). Another sonnet evokes "mercenary battles" whose "lines rushed, and Greek met Greek" in fights which at least came to (lethal) conclusions. By contrast, in contemporary "police-riots," "Our police hit more to terrorize than kill" (*N* 241).

"Police riot," for Lowell, would have had a particular meaning: it was the term by which official inquiries described the bloody confrontation between the New York City police and the students who occupied Columbia University buildings in April 1968. It seems impossible to overstate the attention that those events drew from literary writers; "non-Columbia people" (as the student newspaper, the Columbia *Spectator*, put it), among them "Dwight Macdonald, Conor Cruise O'Brien, Stephen Spender and Allen Ginsberg," "wandered about the campus inhaling revolution" (Avorn et al., *Up Against the Ivy Wall*, 148). In the *New York Review*, F.W. Dupee recalled the last night of the "uprising" as a kind of dissociative episode: "it was as if I were two different persons, one of them almost stifling in the blackout of his usual 'style,' character, profession, identity; the other vaguely exulting in the strange feeling of freedom" ("Uprising," 38). The uprising seemed to have split adult liberals into two people, one grimly respectable, one immature and energetic.

Lowell's split phrases reflect that uneasy division. "No destructive element emaciates / Columbia this Mayday afternoon," his "Pacification of Columbia" begins; the first line remembers Joseph Conrad's advice ("In the destructive element immerse"), which Stephen Spender used as the title of his once well known book about modernism (*N* 184). At the end of the sonnet, police officers'

> horses, higher artistic types than their grooms,
> forage Broadway's median trees, as if
> nature were liberated . . . the blue police
> lean on the burnished, nervous hides, show they,
> at least, have learned to meet and reason together.
>
> (*N* 184)

The officers' horses are like Swift's Houhynhyhms, more rational than any human being. They also suggest Isaiah 1:18–20:

> Come now, and let us reason together, saith the LORD: though your sins be as scarlet, they shall be as white as snow; though they be red like crimson, they shall be as wool. If ye be willing and obedient, ye shall eat the good of the land: But if ye refuse and rebel, ye shall be devoured with the sword: for the mouth of the LORD hath spoken it.
>
> (KING JAMES VERSION)

New Yorkers, Americans, Columbia students, police, have not learned to "meet and reason together," and so they have been, or will be, "devoured with the sword."

"Pacification" appeared on its own in the *New York Review*; in *Notebook*, it introduces the sequence "May." Lowell asks throughout that sequence whether youth movements and adolescent temperaments always seek violence and if political violence ever succeeds: "Guns / failed Che Guevara, Marie-Antoinette, / Leon Trotsky"; "arms given the people are always used against the people" (*N* 184–85). The third sonnet portrays a "Leader of the New Left," perhaps Columbia radical Mark Rudd, with "scars from the demonstrations / he bore like a Heidelberg student," as if the confrontation he helped to orchestrate had no more consequences (was as much a mere symptom of young men's hotheadedness) as Heidelberg's famous duels (*N* 185).

Alan Williamson finds in the Columbia sonnets "an almost mathematical pairing-off of attacks on Leftists with attacks on administrators" (*Pity the Monsters*, 174, 174–79). But the sonnets are also Lowell's attacks on himself. In a particularly well publicized episode, students took over the office of President Grayson Kirk and, in Dupee's summary, "smoked [Kirk's] cigars, drank his sherry, worked at his desk, lined up to use his bathroom, inspected the books on his shelves, slept wherever a surface offered, held interminable meetings, climbed in and out of the windows, and received guests" ("Uprising," 24). Reentering his office, Kirk exclaimed, "My God, how could human beings do a thing like this?" (Avorn et al., *Up Against the Ivy Wall*, 200). Much of the damage was later traced to the police.[16] In "The Restoration," Lowell sees and condemns himself both in the students and in President Kirk's ancién regime:

> The old king enters his study with the police;
> it's much like mine left in my hands a month:
> unopened letters, the thousand cigarettes . . .
>
> [Kirk] halts at woman-things that can't be his,
> he says, 'To think that human beings did this!'
> The sergeant picks up a defiled *White Goddess*, or is it
> *Secret Memoirs of the Courts of Europe*?
> "Would a human beings do this things to these book?"
>
> ([*SIC*]; N 85)

Lowell's psyche contains both the college president, the supposedly mature authority who owns the library, and the students who appropriated or defaced it.

Stephen Yenser notes the sonnets' "imagery of dust, draff, kitchen middens, and various wreckage"; Kirk's office makes just one example (*Circle*, 290). Helen Vendler, similarly, describes the sonnets' "nearly indigestible fragments of experience," "categories melted into one spew" (*Part of Nature*, 126; *The Given*, 22). These heaps and middens may owe some of their prominence to the trash, broken furniture, and waste piles so prominent in journalists' accounts of the Columbia takeover and its aftermath. In the "1930s" sequence from the 1976 *Selected Poems*, the same rubbish heaps suggest the wasted promise or husk of Lowell's own adolescence: "a boiled lobster / flung on the ash-heap of a soggy carton"; "old tins, dead vermin, ashes, eggshells, youth" (*CPRL* 505, 448). To think about politics in the 1960s means, for Lowell, both to think about his own youth and to think about garbage. With his green stalemates, trash piles, and failed revolutions, Lowell constructs a poetics of adolescence in which neither its pastoral nor its promised novelty succeeds: all that is left is the evidence, material and verbal, arranged into rubbish heaps or heaped into poems.[17]

One more public event in *Notebook* deserves note: the Chicago Democratic Convention of August 1968, in which Hubert Humphrey accepted the nomination amid horrific (and nationally televised) violence. Both Lowell and Hardwick attended; Hardwick's appalled coverage condemned both police and Yippies: "With this lawlessness of the law, misery fell from the sky" ("Chicago," 5). The carnage of the "children's crusade" confirmed, for Lowell, that people, events, and generations merely repeat themselves like tides, or like Lowell's own endlessly marching poetic lines (*N* 229). On the one hand, individuals do not improve (so that maturity is no better than youth); on the other, generations do not improve on their predecessors (so that youth movements will not make society good):

> the fall of the high tide waves is a straggling, joshing
> march of soldiers. . . . on the march for me. . . .
> How slender and graceful, the double line of trees,
> how slender, graceful, irregular and underweight,
> the young in black folk-fire circles below the trees—
> under their shadow, the green grass turns to hay.
>
> (*N* 230)

These public poems with their intractable parallels and endless standoffs show how the Lowell of *Notebook* found a form for his refusal either to endorse the student-radicals, or to condemn them. "Emotionally I am in sympathy with the 'Revolution,'" Lowell said to Williamson, but "intellectually I am doubtful that it would really make anything better" (quoted in Williamson, *Pity the Monsters*, 165). "The new blade is too sharp, the old poisons" (*N* 80). [18]

The ambivalence toward young activists; the seasonal symbols, in which spring leads to no renewal; the focus on the life course; the form, in which lines strain against one another, defying expectations of linear progress; and the attitude toward public, directly political events are of a piece. Yenser says that "Lowell's single most characteristic stance" is "a die-hard antimeliorism" (*Circle*, 312); Bell, that *Notebook* is "fundamentally antitelelogical" (*Lowell*, 142). That is, the volume denies that things, people, and society permanently, cumulatively, or naturally get better. One aspect of that denial is a dual suspicion, first of young people's beliefs that they can radically transform the world and second of adults' claims to know more than the young.[19] "We've so little faith that anyone / ever makes anything better," Lowell wrote in "For Eugene McCarthy," making McCarthy one of two exceptional politicians in *Notebook* whose failure proves a sad rule (*N* 204). "R.F.K." described the other: "I miss / you, you out of Plutarch, made by hand— / forever approaching our maturity" (*N* 197). Robert Kennedy "may have been our hero," Lowell wrote, defending his own phrase, but "he was never mature; nor would anyone who knew him well and loved him, have thought so" (*Letters*, 508). "We have struggled to where we are," Lowell's Prometheus says, "by living through a succession of tyrannies. Each ended . . . when a son cut down his father" (*Prometheus Bound*, 8). What if one has been the son and is now the father? One cannot remain adolescent or retain the hopes and energies of youth indefinitely, but for Lowell adulthood offers no stable place for critique and no attractive alternative, either in public life (where it represents an exhausted liberalism) or in the household (where it is ineffective fatherhood, failed sexual longing, muddling-through).

"Antimeliorism" describes Lowell's approach not just to history but also to biography: people grow up (from ten to thirteen, thirteen to twenty, twenty to fifty), but they do not improve. It also describes Lowell's technique: "I would have liked each line to be better than the last, and knew this was impossible," Lowell wrote of his *Notebook* style (*Letters*, 518). One of his most accomplished single poems, "New Year's Eve 1968," takes pains to describe that technique in its relation to the life course. In doing so he seems to compare himself by turns to John Donne, Grayson Kirk, Ulysses, and Prometheus: "These conquered kings pass angrily away," the poem begins, echoing Donne's "A Valediction Forbidding Mourning," in which "virtuous men passe mildly' away" (*N* 173; 87). But Lowell is neither virtuous nor mild, and no literary work can preserve virtue once it moves from potential to action: "each library is some injured tyrant's home." "This year" (that is, 1968) requires not virtue but "bad, straightforward, unscanning sentences— / mine were downtrodden, branded on backs of carbons"; "the typescript looked like a Rosetta Stone." Like the creator of the Rosetta Stone, Lowell leaves not a guide for the future but a way to translate the otherwise-inscrutable past. The future, meanwhile, like the sky at the New Year, looks as if someone had already written on it, looks, in fact, like Lowell's typescripts: "The slush-ice on the east water of the Hudson / is rose-heather this New Year sunset; the open channel, / bright sky, bright sky, carbon scarred with ciphers" (*N* 173). That ending is even more grim than it looks, since it echoes Lowell's *Prometheus Bound*: "Bright sky, bright sky, bright sky! . . . So helpless here, anything living can hurt me. Under this blank sky, nothing will open" (5).

Lowell's sonnets about his daughter Harriet, who turned thirteen in 1970, try to mediate less grimly between youth and middle age. *Notebook* opened with several such sonnets, and I conclude my discussion of it with two more. "These Winds" relies on an armature of repeated words and syl-

lables ("these," "winds," "upright," "all"), on abrupt, boustrophedon alterna-
tions between harshly enjambed lines and heavily end-stopped ones, and
on an unusual, complicating tenderness:

> I see these winds, these are the tops of trees,
> these are no heavier than green alder bushes;
> touched by a light wind, they begin to mingle
> and race for instability—too high placed
> to last a day in the brush, these are the winds . . .
> Downstairs, you correct notes at the upright piano,
> doubly upright this midday torn from the whole
> green cloth of summer; your room is dark as the cloakroom,
> the loose tap beats time, you hammer the formidable
> chords of The Nocturne, your second composition.
> Since you first began to bawl and crawl
> from sheltered lawn to this sheltered room, how often
> these winds have crossed the wind of inspiration—
> in these too, the unreliable touch of the all.
>
> (N 238)

Here the green of literary pastoral collides not with would-be revolutionary energy but with the gentler rhythms of Harriet's domestic space. Like
her father rewriting his poetry, Harriet does not compose or perform but
"corrects" her piano piece, going back to fix mistakes. The generations of
trees struggle unstably upward, as children learn to crawl, then walk. Lowell identifies, speaks for, both upstairs poet and downstairs child, as he does
for both trees and winds.

"The Hard Way," dedicated to Harriet, better typifies Lowell's difficulties; it begins with a warning and ends with yet another image of irresolv-
able conflict:

> Don't hate your parents, or your children will hire
> unknown men to bury you at your own expense.
> Child, forty years younger than mother or father,
> who will see the coruscations of your furrow,
> adolescence snap the feathered barb,
> your destiny written in our hands rewritten?
> Under the stars one sleeps, is freed from household,
> tufts of grass and dust and tufts of grass,
> night oriented to the star of youth—

heaven that held the gaze of Babylon—
by harshness, we won the stars. In backward Maine,
ice goes in season to the tropical,
then the mash freezes back to ice, and then
the ice is broken by another wave.

(*N* 215-16)

The poem offers all at once what so many of Lowell's sonnets offer separately or in pairs. Here are chiasmus (ice, melt, melt, ice), symmetry (tufts,
grass, dust, tufts, grass), and aposiopesis, rhetorical figures which avoid cumulative sequence. Here is the unknowable future, reason for qualified
hope in Lowell's daughter if nowhere else. Here is a way of seeing everything in nature as a symbol for generational conflict or generational succession; here are natural processes that do not progress but move ambivalently
"backward." Here is green grass as a failed symbol for flourishing youth.
Here is adolescence as violence (not guns but the feathered arrow). And
here is one more apologetic attempt to encapsulate changeable youth in
fixed poetry, asking—and doubting—whether adolescence can lead to anything better than itself.

By the time he wrote *The Dolphin* in 1971 and 1972, Lowell's interest in
adolescence focused more tightly on his biography and his mental illness.
"Fishnet" warns that this autobiographical poet will not find a clear plot for
his "illegible" life, then tries to generalize that plight: "Poets die adolescents, their beat embalms them, / the archetypal voices sing offkey" (*CPRL*
645). The sonnet "Ivana" addresses Lowell's "small-soul-pleasing" six-year-
old stepdaughter, who required plastic surgery after an accidental scalding;
almost catechistic in its stream of queries, the poem also sums up conclusions that *Notebook* had already drawn. No phase of life can know more
than another. Teenagers, youth, and adolescents have no special power, but
their angst is never outgrown:

Though burned, you are hopeful, accident cannot tell you
experience is what you do not want to experience.
Is the teenager the dominant of ache?
Or flirting seniles, their conversation three noises,
their life-expectancy shorter than the martyrs?
How all ages hate another age,

and lifelong wonder what was the perfect age!

(*CPRL* 694)

Lowell has rejected adolescence as enclosure, rejected adolescence as revolution, and rejected, too, the (Freudian) idea of adolescence as needed ordeal on the way to wise maturity. His style does almost nothing except to reject; if that is its limit, that is also its accomplishment.

In Lowell's last book, *Day by Day* (1977), the word *adolescence* represents not a set of energies and changes he seems unable to escape but one he *has* escaped. "Death of a Critic" portrays Lowell's exhaustion ("three parts iced-over," he calls himself, quoting Matthew Arnold) as an analogue, perhaps even a consequence, of students' failure to change the world. "The students whose enthusiasm / burned holes in the transitory / have graduated to not having been"; even revived, "they would have the fool's heartiness of ghosts . . . / without references or royalties, / out of work" (*CPRL* 757). Yet Lowell goes on comparing himself to the young:

> If I could go through it all again,
> the slender iron rungs of growing up,
> I would be as young as any,
> a child lost
> in unreality and loud music.
> (*CPRL* 776)

Literally the sentence means that if Lowell could grow up again, he would not grow up at all. These counterfactuals, these comparisons, establish how certain of his daily powerlessness the middle-aged Lowell now feels. In "This Golden Summer," to feel cut off from one's youth is to feel ready to die:

> We have plucked the illicit corn,
> seen the Scriptural
> fragility of flowers—
> where is our pastoral adolescence?
>
> I will leave earth
> with my shoes tied,
> as if the walk
> could cut bare feet.
> (*CPRL* 772)

Put this way, the carpe diem motif sounds not classical and eternal but scriptural and obsolete. Lowell moves from a rapid ten-syllable query into a series of weighty spondees; lines slow down as if to accept death. Perhaps the most affecting single poem in *Day by Day*, "St. Mark's, 1933," remembers Lowell's fifteenth year as an epitome of undignified, cruel revenge. "All term I had singled out classmates, / and made them listen to and remember / the imperfections of their friends," until, in retaliation, the classmates surrounded the young poet with scatological abuse: "I was fifteen; / they made me cry in public" (*CPRL* 801). How could such a state of mind, such a stage of life, prompt optimism, let alone revolution? Yet Lowell's *Notebook* testifies that it did.

The Lowell of "This Golden Summer" echoes (perhaps even remembers) Richard Poirier's essay "The War Against the Young" (1968), republished in *The Performing Self* (1972). "Every civilization has to invent a pastoral for itself," Poirier wrote, "and ours has been an idea of youth and of adolescence which has become socially and economically unprofitable, demographically unmanageable, and biologically comic. By a pastoral I mean any form of life which has, by common consent, been secured from the realities of time and history" (163). Poirier argued that the adolescent "pastoral" of the 1920s and 1950s had disappeared by the late 1960s, when young people sought not innocence but power. *The Performing Self* described Poirier's uncertainties as to what (if anything) could satisfy those demands. Lowell's disillusion thus both predicts and echoes the disillusion of the most cogent cultural critics of the 1970s, among them Poirier, Hardwick, and George W.S. Trow. For these critics, the student revolts and the new youth culture had diminished or abolished much of the cultural authority associated with maturity or adulthood, but nothing else had come to replace it. Adolescence, a time of rebellion and uncertainty, had become the default state, the right analogy, for American culture, as in Bourne's 1910s, but with a pessimistic bent. Teens, students, "youth" now turned to one another, to their peer culture, and adults acted like teens, not out of hope for a revolution but *faute de mieux*.

Some poets saw this turn as well. Stanley Kunitz would complain in the mid-1970s that "the generations live in separate camps, at odds with each other, with scarcely a language in common. The sons are in a hurry to reject the fathers" (*Kind of Order*, 140). Kunitz traced this supposed crisis to a new exaltation of youth: "One of the prevailing illusions is that youth itself is a kind of genius . . . instead of a biological condition" (304). Hardwick in 1977 suggested that adulthood itself had dissolved: "with parents authority seems to have become a burden. Part of it is the peculiar melding of parents and young adults in the way they look and dress, in their common reverence for sexual experience" (*Bartleby*, 95) We saw in the poetry of Oppen and Brooks the high points and then the partial recession of a hope that either youth itself or a particular generation of youth could use special powers to better the culture at large. We have seen in Lowell a style designed to record the collapse of similar hopes. Poets who formed their styles afterward could take an equal interest in adolescence—but for them it would mean not potency but nostalgia or uncertainty, not a confident vanguard but the absence of desirable adult roles, the perceived impossibility of supposedly more mature manners and forms.

4

Are You One of Those Girls?

W E H A V E N O W seen (in Williams and Lowell, among others) characterizations of adolescence in which its qualities—aggressive rebellion, for example, and attempted independence—seemed stereotypically though not exclusively male. We have seen the attractions Marianne Moore found in a women's college. We have seen Phyllis McGinley depict postwar teen culture from the point of view of a mother of daughters. And we have seen Gwendolyn Brooks (among others) celebrate the vigor she saw in youth of both sexes, to which she attributed revolutionary meanings. What we have not seen at any length are poems grounded in and modeled on young women and girls, in their changing bodies and their changing gendered roles, as other girls and women perceive and remember them.

Such poems are flourishing now. Simone de Beauvoir wrote that "adolescence is for a woman" an especially "difficult and decisive moment," in which "a conflict breaks out between her original claim to be subject, active, free, and, on the other hand, her erotic urges and the social pressures to accept herself as passive object" (*Second Sex*, 314). Gina Hausknecht has more recently described "a culture that, deeply ambivalent about teen female sexuality, both eroticizes and denies erotic agency to girls" ("Self-Possession," 23). That conflict informs the poetry about girls' experience, written from remembered or imagined girls' perspectives, that this chapter will describe. Though it might be extreme to say, with Ilana Nash, that "American culture has . . . collectively imagined the adolescent girl as a non-person," or that "teen girls are celebrated for their double emptiness" as a subaltern "foil for adult men," we can certainly say that teenage girls in the popular imagination have seemed aestheticized, inconsequential, given to specialized in-group speech—like poets or poems (*American Sweethearts*, 2–3, 22). At the same time, female adolescence has been, for many poets (and nonpoets) the locus of the traumatic experiences from which one postconfessional paradigm says that poems ought to be made. In many such poems, adolescence (defined, again, as the period after presexual dependent childhood and before the responsibilities and stable identities of an expected adulthood) means both power and danger. These poems incorporate and seek aesthetic equivalents for both glamour and hazard; they adopt dual, even conflicting aesthetic goals, on the one hand acknowledging the allure our culture can attribute to teenage girls (and that girls may attribute to themselves) and, on the other, attacking the roles such girls are enticed, convinced, or forced to play.

As early as 1963, Betty Friedan explored young women's "terror of growing up," describing "the terrifying blank which makes them unable to see themselves after twenty-one" (*Feminine Mystique*, 68, 64). Part of this terror might have looked familiar to Marianne Moore, who found in high schools and in colleges—but not afterward—encouragement to work and think independently.[1] The line of poems about girls' adolescence from recent decades emphasizes (by contrast with Moore's poems) not social roles alone but changing and socially visible bodies. Some of these poems take (as Williams and Auden had) adolescent potential as the ground and example for individuation, the moment from which lyric poetry ought to grow. Others, though, focus less on what girls discover as they enter adolescence than on what girls are instructed to leave behind.

This line of poems begins with Sylvia Plath—though not with the fully achieved Plath of *Ariel*. Plath's poetry of *The Colossus* and earlier sometimes demonstrates the discomfort with female embodiment, the queasy resistance to sexual maturity, that Beauvoir and others associate with adolescence (and which the mainstream Freudian thought of Plath's time would have considered problematic). In "Tale of a Tub," the poet's own body surprises and repels her: "two knees jut up / like icebergs, while minute brown hairs rise / on arms and legs in a fringe of kelp" (*Collected Poems*, 25). "Moonrise" associates summer, menarche, and death: "Grub-white mulberries redden among leaves. / I'll go out and sit in white like they do, / Doing nothing" (98). In "Two Sisters of Persephone" (a parallel in some ways to Brooks's "Sadie and Maud") one "barren" sister stays home and does math in the attic, while the other embraces an earthy fertility the poem only just manages to praise, comparing it to poppies' "red silk flare / Of petaled blood" (31–32).

Other figures in Plath try to put off adolescence indefinitely: the "particular girl" in "Spinster" "longed for winter" and rejected spring, making herself an impenetrable, unwakable Sleeping Beauty, with "such a barricade of barb and check . . . As no mere insurgent man could hope to break" (49–

50). In "Virgin in a Tree"—one of Plath's last and best poems on this topic—sexual maturity is frightening but refusing it is worse; the virgin Daphne figure, "ripe and unplucked," has

> Lain splayed too long in the tortuous boughs: overripe
> Now, dour-faced, her fingers
> Stiff as twigs, her body woodenly
> Askew.
>
> (67)

The language feels as insistently stuck, as contorted, as the girl, who remains virgin and more than half a tree. The rhyme scheme is "stuck" too; the first line of each stanza rhymes with the first line of all the others, and so on through nine stanzas of five lines each. Here female adolescence means resistance to adulthood and sexual maturity, a resistance Plath can neither celebrate (since, in her Freudian framework, it is an illness) nor quite give up.

And yet, even though she once worked for *Mademoiselle*, Plath never brings into her poetry the settings, vocabulary, or art forms associated, during her lifetime, with teen culture. "Above the Oxbow," her long locodescriptive poem about the Pioneer Valley in Massachusetts, calls it "this valley of discreet academies" but says nothing more about UMass or Amherst or Smith (87). Plath's mythic frameworks perhaps require that she leave the signifiers of 1950s teen and collegiate culture out of her poetry. She uses them, instead, in her novel, *The Bell Jar* (1963). The twenty-year-old narrator Esther Greenwood (whose first name suggests that she needs to attract men and whose last name suggests both inexperience and the Green World of *As You Like It*) encounters dancing, dating, a radio DJ, Hollywood film, "the most wonderful boy I'd ever seen," and "the Yale Junior Prom" (*The Bell Jar*, 43, 46).

Like Moore's classmates, like Friedan's terrified teens, the studious Greenwood has prepared herself to excel in a role specifically designated for adolescents (as a student, in schools) that will lead her to no clear place as an adult: "The one thing I was good at was winning scholarships and prizes, and that was coming to an end" (62). As with Larkin's Katharine, there is nothing Esther wants to be when she grows up: "I saw the years of my life spaced along a road in the form of telephone poles . . . and then the wires dangled into space, and try as I would I couldn't see a single space beyond the nineteenth" (101). Unlike Larkin's Katharine, however, Esther links her suicidal blankness to the restrictions and conventions of adult femininity in postwar America. Plath made that suicidal blankness into

poems. It is perhaps her wholly negative view of the social aspects of adolescence as much as her ambitions to classical permanence that prevented
her from building modern adolescence—its peer groups, tastes, subcultures,
and argot—into her poems as well.

Less original than Plath in other respects, Anne Sexton may have been
the first poet who used teen slang and teen culture to describe, from a girl's
perspective, the dilemmas of maturation and sexuality that feminist psychology would explore. The poems in Sexton's strongest book, *Transformations* (1971), which reworks fairy tales, focus on the trials of young women
entering (or refusing to enter) adult sexuality. Usually Sexton ruins the
happy endings; for her, heterosexual fulfillment is always a poor, guilty, and
tainted goal. The experience of physical maturation, new responsibility, or
heterosexual desire has no rewards that outweigh its costs; the poems often
permit both feminist interpretations (in which the young women fight
against or fall victim to patriarchal social structures) and Freudian ones (in
which they illustrate neuroses).

Sexton's prefatory poem tells all her readers that they are, in some sense,
like teens, lacking satisfactory answers to questions about how to represent
growing up:

> Attention,
> my dears,
> let me present to you this boy.
> He is sixteen and he wants some answers.
> He is each of us.
> I mean you.
> I mean me.
> (*TRANSFORMATIONS*, 2)

"He" gets not answers so much as examples and warnings. Snow White, a
"sleeping virgin" at thirteen, grows up to become as vain as her adversary,
the wicked queen, "rolling her china-blue doll eyes open and shut / and
sometimes referring to her mirror / as women do" (9). "Rapunzel" depicts
(but does it condemn?) lesbian sexuality as a way to avoid adulthood: "A
woman / who loves a woman / is forever young" (35). In "The Twelve Dancing Princesses," an intrepid soldier weds one of the princesses by invading
and destroying the dream life that their dormitory, and perhaps their vir-
ginity, allows them to share: "The princesses were torn from / their night
life like a baby from its pacifier"; "never / again would their hair be tangled
into diamonds, / never again their shoes worn down to a laugh" (92).

"The teen female body, even more than the mature female body," Ilana Nash writes, "is constructed as a public spectacle," organized around a "chrysalis moment" in which the girl becomes a visible (and sexually available) woman (*American Sweethearts*, 24). This moment of visibility is at once a moment of subjection (as Nash writes) and a moment of attempted self-definition (like a lyric poem); it therefore prompts contemporary poems about vulnerability, often hesitant or stuttering poems about the difficulty of being a woman and about the difficulty of self-knowledge, of being a coherent self.

According to the *Index of American Periodical Verse*, at least twenty-five poems entitled "Adolescence" or "Adolescent" have appeared in U.S. magazines since 1970. Many, perhaps most, are poems by women about girls and about the fear and risk that Nash (and Friedan) describe. In Mary Graham Lund's "Adolescence" (1974), for example, the teen years represent a fall into danger and meaning: "Our parents are shouting / warnings"; "It's important how we walk / and dance and dress." Alison Seevak in "Adolescence" (2001) (a poem tonally and thematically indebted to Sexton) imagines her thirteenth birthday as a secret and an omen; secretly trying on her mother's clothes, the poet "saw everything / coming towards me / that I did not want," from menstrual blood to "the small ways / we would disappoint one another."[2]

Typical among these poems in its ideas, but exceptional in its verbal elegance, is Nin Andrews's prose poem "Adolescence" (1997):

> The winter her body no longer fit, walking felt like swimming in blue jeans and a flannel shirt. Everything stuck to her skin: gum wrappers, Band-Aids, leaves. How she envied the other girls, especially the kind who turned into birds. They were the ones boys hand-tamed, training them to eat crumbs from their palms or sing on cue. What she would have done for a red crest and a sharp beak, for a little square of blue sky to enter her like wings. But it was her role to sink so the others could rise, hers to sleep so the others could dance. If only her legs weren't too sodden to lift, if only her buttons were unfastened by the water she kept swimming through, and she could extract from the shadow of her breasts a soul as soft as a silk brassiere, beautiful and useless, like a castle at the bottom of the sea.

Andrews's poem looks like a conscious rejoinder to an earlier, male conception of adolescence—and sexuality—as remembered power; the poet recalls, and her anxious, finally counterfactual clauses emphasize, a double deprivation. On the one hand, sexuality itself for young women constitutes a kind of fall: young women succeed when boys tame them or teach them to "sing on cue," when their bodies become permeable or "beautiful and useless," like the little mermaid in the fairy tale (not the Disney film) to which the poem refers. On the other hand, Andrews herself (compared to her peers) lacked even the compensatory rewards of sexuality, which turned other young women into lithe bird-girls but made her instead into a slow, un-mermaid-like fish.

Ruth Saxton argues that a "new emphasis on the psychology and development of the girl" emerged from the social sciences into American popular culture during the 1980s and 1990s. Saxton notes the controversial *In a Different Voice*, by Carol Gilligan; the journalist Mary Pipher's *Reviving Ophelia*; *The Body Project*, by the historian Joan Jacobs Brumberg; and the well-publicized writings of Naomi Wolf (Saxton, "Introduction," xxii–xxiii). She might have added, even more recently, Emily White's *Fast Girls: Teenage Tribes and the Myth of the Slut* or Rosalind Wiseman's *Queen Bees and Wannabes* (the acknowledged basis for the Hollywood movie *Mean Girls*). Gilligan posits a "relational crisis" that "occurs for women in adolescence," when "girls struggle against losing voice and against creating an inner division or split" (*In a Different Voice*, xxiii). Catherine Driscoll writes that in such models as Gilligan's, "girls provide a figure for a failure of development and thus a place to engage with the traps laid for the individual by the modern world" (*Girls*, 303).

Laura Kasischke has made that figure, that engagement, a basis for her poetic art, which depends more than any other poet's on the duality (glamour and hazard, protest and allure) our culture finds in teenage girls. Both the (sexualized) danger and the (sexualized) power that modern culture attributes to female adolescence find realization in her verse, where even the line breaks sometimes seem to enact the exhilarations and the disappointments of that unstable state. "Spring Break" (2005), part of the sequence "Impressions on Wax Tablets," begins:

> I'm sixteen in the Bahamas. A drunk girl
> on a balcony in a sundress
> with a pina colada.
> Burning, I'm about
>
> to slip out of my own memory altogether—
>
> still dancing, however, still
> talking nonsense to a stranger in a salmon-
> pink suit according to my friends.

(*GARDENING*, 15)

Kasischke did not know, then, that she was getting a sunburn. Nor did she know that she was entering the "burning world" of the Buddha's fire sermon, the world in which pain proves inseparable from desire. The in-between-ness of this moment—between the "naivete and luck" (her phrase) of childhood and the burden of maturity—prompts poetry both because it is a "chrysalis moment," and because it is a moment of risk: "Later, the football coach's son / will carry me to bed / and leave me there, untouched."

Kasischke's recent young-adult novel *Boy Heaven* (2006) includes the same incident—Bahamas, drunkenness, coach's son, sixteen-year-old girl unharmed (101–2). One difference between the prose narrative and the poetic version is that the poem manipulates verb tense and mood: part 1 of "Spring Break" uses only the present tense, part 2 the future ("will carry"), then the past perfect ("I had been wandering"), then a future tense along with verbs of state—"I'd // never be able to remember a thing, but my / friends would swear . . . I / lay laughing for a long time" (*Gardening*, 18–19). Her best poems examine the dislocations of self-conception, in time and space, that such strong identification with one's own former teenaged self can create. Here Kasischke's consciousness moves out in several directions from then returns to that one night, which she places (even though she can't remember it) at the core of her adult self; in the same way, the day of Persephone's kidnapping would define that mythical figure throughout her life as the queen of the underworld. The poet of "Spring Break" also likens her younger self to Persephone, "wandering in a staticky meadow / for a long time gathering / intangible flowers," making spring break, with its promise or threat of sexual initiation, into a middle-class American Hades (*Gardening*, 18).[3]

If the time described by a lyric poem is (by definition) a single moment, so that pivotal moments in a life become occasions for autobiographical lyric, each poem must fit its cadences to that moment's—or to that *type* of moment's—demands. In Kasischke such moments are pivot points for a specifically female adolescence defined by sexual peril, as in "Bike Ride with Older Boys":

The one I didn't go on.

I was thirteen,
and they were older.
I'd met them at the public pool. . . .

       I said
okay fine, I'd
meet them at the Stop-n-Go

at four o'clock.
And then I didn't show.

(*DANCE*, 47)

The ride could have become "the best / afternoon of my life," with "cute and older boys / pedaling beside me—respectful, awed . . . as I imagined it would be" (48). It might also have led to a rape: "bits of glass and gravel / ground into my knees," the violated girl never able to "love myself again" (48). Because neither outcome *did* happen, both *could have* happened; the poem takes place at the moment before the thirteen-year-old Kasischke's decision to skip the rendezvous made both impossible.

The poetry of female adolescence is often, for Kasischke, the poetry of risks not taken; the lyric moment becomes the moment before the "chrysalis moment," between innocence and experience, when the fate of the body and the place of the self within it is neither settled nor known. Kasischke's "Ravine" also records nostalgia for a girlhood defined by what had not (quite) yet happened, by the entry into heterosexuality for which the girls would consciously prepare; a onetime best friend

loved me enough to let me
go on and on as no one
ever has
about my body parts, my
optimistic theory
about development and growth
while we were in the bubbling
test-tube of it.

(*HOUSEKEEPING*, 80)

The girlhood friends find—and make a game from—a used condom, "dried-up and open-mouthed / as a baby bird": "We poked it up with a stick / and whipped it into the air," a game which "thrilled us as much / as sex ever would" (*Housekeeping*, 80). Their dismissal of inferior adult pleasure sounds as conclusive, though never as grotesque, as Louise Glück's famous "I hate sex" (*First Four Books*, 155).

And yet Kasischke's teens—unlike Glück's children and adults—remain invested in qualities we might call sexy. The moment of entry into sexuality—even when refused or postponed—becomes for Kasischke the moment where the poem locates the emergence of the self, not only for Kasischke in particular but for all women, all girls. Adolescence denotes both the quality of inwardness that makes it impossible to describe the embodied self completely and the eroticized demand that the self (through poetry, for example) become known. Set at a sleazy carnival, Kasischke's "Fatima" asks

> Am I wrong
> or has every teenage girl been
> at this same carnival in rain, in 19-
> 78, with four wild friends and a fifth of peach
> schnapps in her purse with its bit
> of rawhide fringe?
>
> (HOUSEKEEPING, 13)

This moment of risk and sexual excitement is for Kasischke the experience prior to language from which her poems draw analogies for almost everything else; they treat female adolescent embodiment as a kind of accessible universal, almost as a religious poet might treat a sense of God's presence in the world or as a Petrarchan lover might appeal to male desire. (Revenge on Petrarchan legacies that take the male for the universal thus becomes one of Kasischke's points.)

In Kasischke's early poetry, with its western Michigan, working-class Catholic background, teen sex takes the place of Catholic religiosity, even of Catholic miracles. The girls who drink at the fairgrounds in "Fatima" look to the older poet like the "peasant girls" who saw the Virgin in Portugal. The astonishing tale in "Local Legend" could have come from a 1980s teen exploitation film: "the last real miracle here was when / Catholic Central slaughtered Rockford" in football:

> They say
> two pom-pom girls in the Catholic cemetery
> took on the whole team
> themselves that night. There was
> the cold-sweat of marble
> in the air, stale
> green carnations, the earth-
> kiss of mulch in wild hair. I know
> I was there.
>
> (HOUSEKEEPING, 23-24)

The experience of initiation (like it or not) into patriarchy and the experience of sexual power are both truths to which the poem, with its flash of irregular internal rhymes, responds.

Kasischke's jagged enjambments, her wildly variable lines (which reject even the approximate regularities of most American free verse) suggest both the sometime urgency of her emotion, and the failure of sequence or measure in her life course. Seeking master narratives of that life course, she finds only the mystery of an inner life permanently associated with her own, and with other people's teens. In "Quiet" the visual memory of "a boy tapping his pencil on the table / all through Study Hall" (a boy whose attention she could not catch) feels to the poet

Like

drowning in a fountain—it was
my watery shroud of language and desire, and I

drank disastrously from it for the rest of my life.

(*GARDENING*, 34)

Here, perhaps, is Kasischke's ars poetica: the momentary glance exchanged in high school, the spark of a teen crush, encapsulates (as lyric, a genre of *multum in parvo*, also encapsulates) the thrill and "disaster" of having a female body and the "disaster" of having a body at all. That condition, or Kasischke's need to represent it, seems to her like both a thirst and a "fountain," a source that generates poems.

Other teens in Kasischke's poetry, the poet's alter egos and companions, stand for the traumas she, personally, escaped. The "sources of this life," "The Sorrows of Carrie M." implies, lie within adults' bonds to their own youth—in this case, in the poet's wish to stay in touch with her now-vanished friends, "Margaret of the scarves," "gentle-haired Clarisse . . . I email them, but I / don't think they'll email me" (*Gardening*, 39). The titular name suggests (though it may not denote) the protagonist of Stephen King's novel and film *Carrie*, whose telekinetic powers let her immolate everyone who shamed her in high school: "Carrie, tower / of fury and glory." The same poem evokes, with teasingly Freudian metaphors, "my teenage heart a little tear-drenched pillow // a pin-cushion without pins // a souvenir from a place/ I wished I'd never been" (*Gardening*, 37).

An earlier poem, "Candy, Stranger," portrays a lost sixteen-year-old girl (either a suicide or a murder victim) as a type of Christ. Amid "the birthday wind and the anorexic / star-song of suburban girls," this martyred girl becomes important because she has actually faced the sexualized danger that the other girls imagine; Kasischke speaks for the collective of girls her age, making their shared identity—shared dangers, shared desires—the dominant note of the reverent, halting poem (*Wild*, 22). After the murder (or suicide),

> The rest of us talk about it
> until we aren't teenagers anymore
> and the telephone lines stretch tight
> as female terror   where
>
> our voices shoot without our souls
> electric over the earth   across
> the dark time planet
> we don't understand   and through
> the red swirling dust of the one we do.
>
> (*WILD*, 22-23)

The mysteries of the human soul, here, are mysteries of female development: Why does it hurt? Why does it fascinate? Why does it create targets for male violence? Harder to solve these mysteries, Kasischke implies, than to find life on Mars.[4]

Traumas such as the fictional Carrie's, such as Fatima's, such as the kidnapped girl's in "Candy," help Kasischke contemplate her own passage into an adulthood less painful *than* her teen years but numb and uneventful by comparison *with* them:

> How awful
> resurrection
> for someone like me will be. The teenage
> girls are being dragged
> out of the earth by their hair.
>
> Tongues, testicles, plums and small hearts bloat
> sweetly in the trees. And then
>
> a silence like water
> poured into honey—
>
> the silence of middle age.
>
> (*GARDENING*, 20)

Does she mean that reliving her teen years will be "awful"? Or does she dread the "silence" of an afterlife, of failing to relive them? The teen Kasischke was lucky—the coach's son put her to bed, for example, without committing any depredations. And yet that luck allowed her nothing better than to become mature: "My love, all of it, a life of it, has been / too little" (20). Having evaded trauma, having settled uneasily into an adulthood (and into an uneasy poetic style, and into motherhood as well), Kasischke has become not sweet honey but bland water, not the flower but the wall: "through the years somehow I became / a high brick wall fully expecting / the little blue flowers to thrive in my shade" (*Gardening*, 23).

Three of Kasischke's six novels have teenage narrators, and all include traumatized teens. *The Life Before Her Eyes* (2002) imagines a Columbine-style high school shooting; *Boy Heaven*, aimed at teenage readers, takes its plot from a scary urban legend about cheerleaders at summer camp. In *White Bird in a Blizzard* (1999), Kat, the narrator, asks herself how

> the younger woman [her mother] was . . . became no more than a ghost. . . . Or she became *me*. Maybe I stepped into the skin my mother left behind, and became the girl my mother had been, the one she still wanted to be. Maybe I was wearing her youth now like . . . an accessory, all bright nerves and sticky pearls, and maybe that's why she spent so much time staring at me with that wistful look in her eyes.
>
> (14-15)

The same anxious envy animates "Spiritus," in which the poet remembers her own teen social circle: one girl's "beautiful / pale and drunken mother" always "wanted to dance with the girls / in beige stockings until morning, her / toe nails painted white" (*What It Wasn't*, 49). "That girl's mother wanted / to be us, and we dreaded / being ourselves, our mothers, our friends so much" that the girls in question drank themselves sick (50). The girls cannot stay as they are, but there is nothing they want to become: they would rather remain "drunk // and drowned" (51). If adolescent sexuality in Kasischke's poetry and fiction frightens adults who have finally outgrown it, adult orderliness can look—both to adults and to teens—like invisibility and vacancy, like a life no longer lived.

Thus far—despite her consistent interest in gender, despite her extremes of enjambment and her urgent tone—Kasischke may seem like Larkin or Auden, who also imagine growing up as loss. The dilemmas and double binds she depicts, however—in which a girl at best becomes a desirable teen, living under the threat of sexual violence and subordination after a "chrysalis moment," and then grows up to become undesirable, too old, unsexy, established, invisible—are not the dilemmas that male poets tell us they face.[5] Moreover, Kasischke in her poetry, if not in her prose, wants to envision a more complicated, more rewarding imaginative relation between adults and the teens whom they meet or whom they used to be.

Kasischke can do so (she is almost alone in doing so) by imagining herself convincingly as a grown-up mother and as a teenage daughter in the space of the same poem. "For / a long time I thought / I was the only one," a recent poem muses. "Then, I got old . . . I saw a girl today who was // the girl I was" (*Gardening*, 73). As early as "The Cyclone" (1992), Kasischke portrayed herself simultaneously as a girl yearning for erotic adventure—sixteen and "falling in love with a boy / who's learning to play the electric guitar"—and as "the mother of the boy who is learning / to play the electric guitar" (*Wild*, 17). The title poem in *Fire and Flower* (a book focused tightly on motherhood) begins by comparing the poet as she was—furtive and daring as Juliet—to the poet as she is, a giver of fertile shelter; once, a lover would "climb / the fire escape to me. The sky // was rocket fire. . . . Now // I sleep beside a child," "like a swan boat," "in our bed's unfolding flower" (3). In "Kiss," the memory of Kasischke's first kiss disturbs and saddens her precisely because (once recalled) it actually has the frightening sweetness attributed to first kisses in American popular culture. Kasischke's present-day children, who have never heard of her first boyfriend,

> are children.
> They know nothing
>
> but the trances of being children.
>
> When the light is dim
> I can see through them
> and on the other side, there's him.
> (*DANCE*, 39)

Remembered adolescence shines, at evening, through adult experience; the latter seems to the poet ("when the light is dim") merely a stage screen or scrim. Even though she has become a mother, and hence thinks she ought to focus on her children's future, teen experience for Kasischke here seems to be the foundation, the hidden meaning of the poet's adult life, more vivid and more important than whatever came next.

❖ ❖ ❖ ❖ ❖

Patterns that occur together in Kasischke—and from whose conjunction she gets her originality—turn up separately in other recent American poems. Rita Dove's two poems called "Adolescence" also portray erotically charged boundaries, thresholds that girls cross as they become women, as types for all knowledge, suggesting that experience will always disappoint. "Adolescence—I" presents a supposed revelation:

> Linda's face hung before us, pale as a pecan,
> And it grew wise as she said:
> "A boy's lips are soft,
> As soft as baby's skin."
>
> (SELECTED POEMS, 42)

The rest of this poem comprises only descriptions and similes; it displays the refusal to draw conclusions, the unsettling reliance only on directly available evidence, that characterizes much of Dove's early work.

That anxious unknowing dominates the more ambitious "Adolescence—II": "Although it is night, I sit in the bathroom, waiting," Dove begins (43). "Three seal men" out of a fairy tale arrive: "They bring the scent of licorice. One sits in the washbowl, // One on the bathtub edge; one leans against the door. / 'Can you feel it yet?' they whisper" (43). What is the young Dove, her "baby-breasts . . . alert," awaiting? Maturity? The end of childhood? Heterosexual desire? Evidence that she belongs in this world rather than in the consolingly imagined space of fairy tales and talking animals? Or evidence that she does not? The adult poet will not say, nor does she abandon the point of view ascribed to her younger self: "I clutch at the ragged holds / They [the seal-men] leave behind," the poem ends; "Night rests like a ball of fur on my tongue." Perfective present at the start of the poem, Dove's verbs by the end of the poem sound instead like recurring (imperfective) present, denoting actions that take place over and over, as if uncertainty and apprehension have rested on Dove's tongue from that night to this day.

Not so much the uncertainty as the necessarily temporary power in female adolescence offers the chief subject for Angela Sorby's *Distance Learning* (1998). If Phyllis McGinley's regular stanzas connoted reassurance, Sorby's rhymed forms often convey unease. In "Glossolalia" the fourteen-year-old Sorby's neighbor "is dying for me // to convert to Pentecostal / Christianity" (11). The neighbor, Rae Anne, who is probably Sorby's own age, fascinates Sorby for reasons the adult poet knows had little to do with religion:

> I'm fourteen and close
>
> enough to touch Rae Anne's
> braids, her bangs,

her birch white hair part.
How could I not feel

Christ's knuckles rap
hard on my heart?

(11)

Sorby here sets a pattern that her other poems about teens replicate: what looks like transcendence is actually adolescence; what looks like access to spiritual truths is in fact a power that comes from a phase of life and turns out to be temporary. Sorby's "Kate Fox" speaks for the girl once famous as a spirit medium in upstate New York:

When I was thirteen, I thought I would grow
pale as lace, forced to sew and sew
my brain into a filigree
of threads and holes. Then I learned

to crack my toe-bones until they echoed
like raps from beyond the grave.
Soon my body was a bag of tricks,
a telegraphic alphabet: croaks, moans, clicks.

(25)

For Sorby's Kate Fox, spirituality permitted an escape from the confining roles allotted to most nineteenth-century women and girls. That escape depended, though, on the "tricks" made possible by her growing "body," which produced no truth beyond itself, could not lead to any stable enlightenment or satisfying adult role: "I was the whole / heavenly host. I was as good as it gets" (25).

Whatever its pleasures, girls' and young women's experience in Sorby leads to no truth visible, no lessons usable in later life because it has no anchor and no source except the changing female body. "My *Distance Learning* poems," she writes, "suspect that no one ever really grows up, though lately I'm thinking that it's just some of us [who] can't/ won't despite mounting physical evidence to the contrary. My favorite poet in this vein is Laura Kasischke"; "it's funny," she adds, "that my poems are so *self-evidently* in sync" with hers (private communication). Both Sorby and Kasischke see adulthood as a perpetually unfinished project of managing loss, but their nostalgia also grounds a feminist argument: what our culture does to girls' bodies, what it asks girls to do, creates the risks that the girls in the poems at once anticipate and recall.

"The quality of embeddedness in social interaction and personal rela-
tionships that characterizes women's lives in contrast to men's," Gilligan
contends, "becomes not only a descriptive difference but also a develop-
mental liability" as teen social pressures and adult expectations encourage
girls to abandon their families and their childhood friends (*In a Different
Voice*, 9). Gilligan herself finds this conundrum, along with moving reactions to it, in poems about girls' transitions from childhood to adolescence
by Michelle Cliff and Sharon Olds ("Preface," 12–14). Such reactions have
become a staple for poets concerned (as Olds is not) with bringing into
contemporary poetry a specifically adolescent language, a *form* in some way
responsive to adolescent social being. A poet who believes, with Gilligan,
that girls "lose voice" as they become women—and who wishes to project
and defend that "voice" (however defined)—might think herself logically
obligated to find a voice or a style that does not sound "adult."

Thylias Moss has at times created such a style.[6] Moss's "When I Was
'Bout Ten We Didn't Play Baseball" merges the reflective adult poet with
the knowing girl she may have been, not only in its sentiments and identi-
fications but in its choice of nonstandard English:

> There's a wedding and I was not invited and that's
> cool; what I would want to know, how pretty is
> her dress, I can see from here. Not bad.
> I like how the bride's all covered going into
> the storefront church. She's made out like
> an overcast day.
>
> (SMALL, 45)

Though some phrases sound descriptively sophisticated, clearly "adult,"
others indicate the persona's youth even more clearly than they indicate
race. The poem assumes as much when it goes on to place its fidgety speaker
within her protective family: "The heat does hug. / It isn't shy and proper. My mother wouldn't want me / to play with it" (45). Moss's figures
of identification sound younger than Gunn's, younger than Brooks's,
younger than Kasischke's, and for good reason: to retain their independence they must remain not just pre-adult but immediately presexual, or at
least preheterosexual.

Such poems adapt from recent feminist theory two theses: first, that
movement into adolescence represents for many girls a loss of power, confidence, and independence (Gilligan's argument); second, that there are special properties in "girls' talk" (as the sociolinguist Jennifer Coates has argued), syntactic, lexical and even phonological features through which

"teenage girls negotiate their identity during adolescence as they move from girlhood to womanhood" (Coates, "Changing Femininities," 123). In her poems of the 1980s and 1990s, Moss's linguistic choices—her run-on sentences, apparent "chattiness" or digressiveness, and mix of colloquial with academic language—can align her with "girls' talk," suggesting ways in which she tries to remain outside both fixed adult and dangerous late-adolescent heterosexual gender roles. Her prose poem "An Anointing" promises to avoid those roles; its italics suggest a manifesto:

> *Me and Molly are in eighth grade for good. We like it there. We adore the view. We looked both ways and decided not to cross the street. Others who'd been to the other side didn't return. It was a trap.*
>
> *Me and Molly don't double date. We don't multiply anything. We don't know our multiplication tables from a coffee table. . . .*
>
> *Me and Molly, that's M and M, melt in your mouth.*
>
> *What are we doing in your mouth? Me and Molly bet you'll never guess. Not in a million years.*
>
> (SMALL, 142)

Elizabeth Grosz writes that "the female body has been constructed not only as a lack or absence but . . . as a leaking, uncontrollable, seeping liquid," "as formless flow," requiring patriarchal or phallogocentric control (*Volatile Bodies*, 203). Refusing any such control, Moss's girls punningly refuse to date, decline to "*multiply*," and defy adult taboos: "*Me and Molly have wiped each other's asses with ferns. Made emergency tampons of our fingers.*" Refusing to "*cross the street*" into a heterosexual adult space where men might impregnate them, the girls promise instead to give birth to one another, "*Molly down my canal binnacle first, her water breaking in me like an anointing*" (*Small*, 143). The "me and Molly" of "An Anointing," like the girl in "When I Was 'Bout Ten We Didn't Play Baseball" (who stayed away from a wedding) establish solidarity within a pre- or non-heterosexual world defined in part by its distance from adult speech. Moss's liminal—and dual rather than isolated and singular—girls replace patriarchy with menarche. By locating a claim about girls' power at the precise point in girls' lives when they, supposedly, enter heterosexual and patriarchal dominion, when their flow literally requires control (which the girls here provide for each other), Moss makes her fluid, fluent prose poem at once an unsettling, playful entertainment and a determined attack on the social constraints that girls face.

With characters specified by age or grade, Moss identifies girls' adolescence as a state of potential resistance to Gilligan's "loss of voice." Yet Moss has no use for the sense (so important to Kasischke) of female adolescence as attractive despite its risks, as a source of interiority and passion (so that adult women want to remember it) even if it can also be risky and horrifying (so that adult women are glad they never have to go through it again). The most ambitious single poems about female adolescence do encompass that duality; they belong not to Moss, nor to Kasischke, nor to Sexton, but to Jorie Graham. Graham's versions of lyric have always portrayed the self as a temporal process, as something one has to discover or become; in "The Geese" (from her first book, *Hybrids of Plants and of Ghosts*) "the real / is crossing you // your body an arrival / you know is false but can't outrun" (*Dream*, 12–13). Analogies between the self of lyric (as Graham conceives it) and the self of adolescence (as twentieth-century culture has defined it) enter Graham's work in her most autobiographical volume, *Region of Unlikeness* (1991). I conclude by describing some of that volume's best poems.

"Fission," the first in the book, takes place in a movie theater in Italy in November 1963, when Graham would have been thirteen. As the poem begins, the young poet watches the famous scene in Stanley Kubrick's *Lolita* in which both James Mason as Humbert Humbert and the viewers first encounter the title character (played by Sue Lyon); Lyon looks back at Humbert (and at us) through her iconic sunglasses. The young Graham then watches as "a man" announces that President Kennedy has been shot; the house lights come up and the theater's skylight opens. The poet's discovery that she has one body and no other, that her life story will be the story of that mortal body, is like the discovery that Kennedy has been shot; the poet's discovery of a new verbal form resembles the adolescent discovery that one's body has changed, is changing, and that the social form imposed on a girl's body will involve an imagined or real male gaze.[7]

Helen Vendler writes that "in the autobiographical poems of *Region of Unlikeness* . . . memory oscillates . . . between a past moment . . . and the same past moment revived as a present-tense moment" ("Indigo," 14). In "Fission," this double focus invites readers to compare the two people involved in the memory (Graham the adult poet and Graham at thirteen), asking to what extent those people differ. Yet the poem begins not with temporal but with spatial comparisons: "real electric light upon the full-sized / screen / on which the greater-than-life-size girl appears" (*R* 3). Sue Lyon's Lolita looks "greater-than-life-size," both physically larger (since she's on a movie screen) and more developed than a real "girl" at Lolita's age might be.[8] This Lolita not only accepts a spectator's gaze but looks back; to become the object of a sexualized gaze seems to Graham here the cost of becoming an agent of any kind—one is seen sexually or else "never . . . seen."

This stopped moment of interlocking gazes (Humbert's at Lolita, Lyon's at the audience and "the man," Graham's and ours at Lyon) creates a moment of initiation, of firstness, much like the moments Graham depicts in earlier poems—the moment, for example, in "San Sepolcro" "before / the birth of God" (*Dream*, 21). Here, however, it is also a "chrysalis moment," a girl's entry into sexuality, like the moment Kasischke postponed in "Bike Ride," the moment Moss's girls refuse. As in "San Sepolcro," Graham will depict our understanding of such an encounter as a journey away from it; we understand innocence or initiation only from a position of experience. But where "San Sepolcro" depicts the moment before a birth, "Fission" (like the film it describes) begins at the moment before a fall:

> as the houselights come on—midscene—
> not quite killing the picture which keeps flowing beneath,
> a man comes running down the aisle
> asking for our attention—
> Ladies and Gentlemen.
> I watch the houselights lap against the other light—the tunnel
> of image—making dots licking the white sheet awake—
> a man, a girl, her desperate mother—daisies growing in the corner—.
>
> (R 3)

Since *Lolita* is a film (and a book) devoted to moments of fall, of innocence lost, Graham can depict such a fall (or separation, "fission") at once in herself (as she stands in the theater), in the crowd (as they realize that Kennedy has been shot), and on screen (as Dolores approaches her encounter with Humbert). "Like the movie heroine," writes Laurence Goldstein, Graham's "spectator . . . is now abandoned to a fate rushing towards her with the single-mindedness of Humbert himself" (*The American Poet at the Movies*, 234). She looks back because she is ready to be looked at: "her sun-barred shoulders . . . accompany / her neck, her face, the / looking-up" (R 4).

As the film fades, "the theater's skylight is opened and noon slides in"; Lyon appears at once to grow up and to become less visible (to spectators generally as to Graham in particular). Her incipient story gives way to an absence of story; events pile up in apparent simultaneity:

> a grave of possible shapes called *likeness*—see it?—something
> scrawling up there that could be skin or daylight or even

the expressway now that he's gotten her to leave with him—
    (it happened rather fast) (do you recall)—

the man up front screaming the President's been shot, waving
    his hat, slamming one hand flat
over the open
    to somehow get
our attention,

in Dallas, behind him the scorcher—
    laying themselves across his face—
him like a beggar in front of us, holding his hat—
    I don't recall what I did,
I don't recall what the right thing to do would be,
    I wanted someone to love . . .

(R 6)

The Kennedy assassination wrecks not just the confidence of Americans but the progress of Kubrick's film, and by extension the progress of American girls (like Lyon onscreen, like Graham below it) through time on their way to becoming women, finding "someone to love."

Given her descriptions of the film up to this point, we might *expect* the young Graham to hope the story would resume, to rejoin in imagination the story about growing up that Lyon's character seemed about to tell. But such a story (as we know, as the adult Graham knows) has a tragic or at least a traumatic ending. That ending has informed, in different ways, the tonal and linguistic decisions in Kasischke, Sorby, and Moss, and it informs Graham here. The next line becomes a turning point—the first time Graham uses past tense to describe herself and one of only two places where a new sentence coincides with the start of a stanza. Graham seeks not a way to *resume* the story of becoming a woman but (as in Moss's "An Anointing") a way to avoid stories and womanhood entirely. Graham then projects that search onto the Dolores Haze of the film. Recalling "a way she lay down on that lawn / to begin with," Graham imagines that there must be "a way to not yet be wanted," "a way to lie there at twenty-four frames / per second—no faster" (R 6). Once admitted to the ongoing plot, there will be "no telling what we'll have to see next," "no telling what on earth we'll have to marry marry marry" (R 6). That last phrase echoes "The Applicant" by Sylvia Plath: "My boy, it's your last resort. / Will you marry it, marry it, marry it" (*Collected Poems*, 222). The apparent allusion to Plath (rare in Graham) reminds us to look for Plath's concerns; what would 1950s or early-

1960s femininity do to the young women who embraced it? What "plot," what "desire" would it make young women accept?

Now this way of thinking about time and narrative, looking and "being-seen"—an initial fascination with its allure followed by a discovery of its dangers and a wish to withdraw or postpone—describes (a) Graham's thirteen-year-old self as "Fission" depicts her; (b) the adult Graham of *Region* and of *The End of Beauty* and many of her mythological alter egos (Daphne, Penelope, Saint Teresa, Eurydice); and (c) girls or female adolescents generally, as depicted by every one of the cultural critics and psychological thinkers this chapter has quoted so far, beginning with Beauvoir:

> The young girl feels that her body is getting away from her, it is no longer the straightforward expression of her individuality; it becomes foreign to her and at the same time she becomes for others a thing: on the street men follow her with their eyes and comment on her anatomy. She would like to be invisible; it frightens her to become flesh and to show her flesh.
>
> (*SECOND SEX*, 288)

The "young girl" for Beauvoir wants "to be a child no longer, but she does not accept becoming an adult"; hence she occupies "a position of continual denial," since "she does not accept the destiny assigned to her by nature and by society; and yet she does not repudiate it completely." Instead, Beauvoir's typical girl "limits herself to a flight from reality or a symbolic struggle against it" (314). Such a symbolic struggle appears, in "Fission," twice: in Lyon's Dolores (as the young Graham viewed her) and in the young Graham as the older poet remembers her.

"Fission" thus derives power in part from the analogy between Graham's general resistance to teleology, narrative, closure, and Western history, on the one hand, and girls' resistance to womanhood, on the other. The poem suggests not only an analogy but a homology (a single source): What if the resistance to narrative time Graham so often depicts derives from a resistance to ways of "being-seen," to ways of becoming a woman? These suggestions make "Fission" not just one of Graham's most affecting poems but one of her most effectively feminist. Graham returns (as Gilligan asks women to return) to an immediately presexual (or preheterosexual) moment as a source of power, a chance to resist being told "what to want next."[9]

That return also looks like a withdrawal from the situations the film depicts—a withdrawal, in turn, for which Graham (once a film student herself) solicits useful analogues in film theory. Laura Mulvey famously discovered the Lacanian mirror phase in the condition of cinema viewing, where "the image recognized is conceived as the reflected body of the self, but its misrecognition as superior" ("larger-than-life-size," Graham says) "projects the body outside itself as an ideal ego" ("Visual Pleasure," 241). We might name Graham's next experience not fission but fusion: as "three lights" (skylight, house lights, movie-projector light) interrupt her reverie by "merging" across her person: "the image licked my small body from the front, the story playing // all over my face my / forwardness" (R 7). She now seems doomed to inhabit the plot of *Lolita*, moving ahead into history and womanhood, already caressed, obscenely, by filmic light. After this fusion, however, the lights come apart, illuminating Graham's body as something incomplete, "outside itself"; the lights are "there flaming,"

> mixing the split second into the long haul—
> flanking me—undressing something there where my
>   body is
> though not my body—
>   where they play on the field of my willingness,
>
> where they kiss and brood, filtering each other to no avail,
>   all over my solo
> appearance.
>
> (R 7)

Emily White compares girls' adolescence to "a psychological morning, disorienting in its brightness"; "the girl who develops [physically] ahead of time," White adds, "feels like she is being pulled forward, suddenly thrust into the harsh light of the world's gaze" (*Fast Girls*, 24, 51). Kristy, in Kasischke's *Boy Heaven*, realizes "that it was possible to *feel* boys' eyes on you" (57). Graham's lines evoke just such feelings and metaphors. Graham connects these concerns about female development over weeks, months, and years to her concerns about how we experience time in minutes, moments, and seconds; her lyric strategies for exploring, stretching out, and dissecting time can therefore come to represent her own (and other characters') resistance to the limiting, sexist "story" of feminine development. To reenter the social world—to spend "the dollar bill / in my hand"—would be to make a "choice," and "choice" is "the thing that wrecks the sensuous here the glorious here— / that wrecks the beauty" of lyric exemption from time.[10] Having contemplated and rejected "choice," Graham's poem mirrors many of her generation's stories of adolescence in refusing any kind of conclusive or satisfying end. It concludes instead on a dash, on a held breath: "Don't move, don't / wreck the shroud, don't move—" (8). The poem thus (like Moss's work) valorizes a refusal: Graham imagines withholding her consent from the story her culture wants her to tell about her body, her age, and her time.

Graham's drive against closure and teleology, against systems of all sorts, has precedents in her personal history. Graham attended the Sorbonne in 1968 (aged seventeen or eighteen) along with the protest leader Daniel Cohn-Bendit; she was arrested twice during the Paris upheaval and then "expelled for taking part in student protests" (Casper). Those protests and their associated ideas inform Graham's work. The sociologist Deena Weinstein writes that while "children are taught to have ideas of what they would like to 'be' when they grow up," "adolescents have the privilege and torment of raising the question of whether they want to be anything that society holds out for them" ("Rock," 10). Such questions—and the refusals that serve as their answers—pervaded both the protests of May 1968 and the poem from *Region* which recalls them, "The Hiding Place."

That poem resembles "Fission" in telling a story about a turning point in public history; in describing a crowded, dark place from which the young Graham emerges into shocking light; and in making that emergence stand for a transition in her life course. Once again, Graham identifies a valuable, even heroic resistance (to narrative and authority) with the stage she feels she has left behind. Where that stage had (in "Fission") a mute and phantasmatic representative (the "larger-than-life" Lyon/Lolita), here youth and resistance acquire "a certain leader":

> I found his face above an open streetfire.
> *No* he said, tell them *no concessions.*
> His voice above the fire as if there were no fire—
>
> language floating everywhere above the sleeping bodies;
>   and crates of fruit donated in secret;
> and torn sheets (for tear gas) tossed down from shuttered windows;
>   and bread; and blankets, stolen from the firehouse.
> (*R* 19)

That Whitmanesque leader (perhaps Cohn-Bendit, or a man whose name Graham never knew) represents and unifies the dispossessed Parisians of the poem, whom Graham also encountered in jail: "In the cell we were so crowded no one could sit or lean. / People peed on each other," and guards beat a "girl in her eighth month" of pregnancy (*R* 19). These scenes of heroism and horror (like the unrolling film at the start of "Fission") introduce the longer, more personal part of the poem, which takes place after Graham's release from jail: walking in Paris, she breathes "air thick with dwellings," and envisions

> The open squeezed for space until the hollows spill out,
> story upon story of them
> starting to light up as I walked out.
> How thick was the empty meant to be?
> What were we finding in the air?
>
> (R 20)

Newly released from jail, Graham feels she does not belong (in a repeated pun) to any of the "stories" around her—a foreigner and a defeated student rebel, she has neither a home nor a clear course of action, and in this she stands for all the defeated young radicals of 1968, not so much for their political programs (which she describes vaguely as "claims") but for their mood: "Was I meant to get up again? I was inside. The century clicked by." Public history has slipped back into its ordinary, adult-driven course: "They made agreements we all returned to work. / The government fell but then it was alright again." Graham ends not in that tone of flat dejection but on the exhilarating student leader, a hero of imagination resisting what Stevens named "the pressure of reality" (*Collected Poetry*, 656)—what Graham might call the pressure of history. At the end of the poem, we see, not the "helicopters" nor "the government" but

> The man above the fire, listening to my question,
>
> the red wool shirt he wore: where is it? who has it?
> He looked back straight into the century: no concessions.
> I took the message back.
> The look in his eyes—shoving out—into the open—
>   expressionless with thought:
>
> *no*—tell them *no*—
>
> (R 21)

"The Hiding Place," like "Fission," ends on an em-dash, avoiding (in print) the visible symbol of closure as it avoids (aloud) the tone of voice that might make closure seem apt.[11] The student, the girl, in these poems of adolescence wish "to postpone closure" in their own life courses just as the poems "postpone closure" in their grammatical elaborations (Gardner, *Regions of Unlikeness*, 219). Once again Graham celebrates a youthful figure who appears momentarily able to stop adults' public time, and once again the poem both valorizes that resistance and shows that it could not last.

Nor are "The Hiding Place" and "Fission" alone in that project; other poems in *Region* focus on other traumatic moments of adolescence—learning to wear makeup and discovering her father's affair ("Picnic"), a sexual encounter at age thirteen ("The Region of Unlikeness"). The resistance to time and teleology, the mobilization of long lines, enjambments, and grammar on behalf of such resistance, which characterized "Fission" and "The Hiding Place," also informs those other poems. In "The Region of Unlikeness," an early fall into sexual experience prompts self-consciousness about time, a source of solidarity with other women, and (conjecturally) a reason the adult Graham writes as she does:

> The window is open, it is raining, then it has just
> ceased. What is the purpose of poetry, friend?
> And you, are you one of those girls?
> (R 37)

What was prospective in "Fission" becomes retrospective in "Region," the sexual initiation having already happened; the poem's resistance to compulsory heterosexuality, to teleologies of womanhood, appears not as a wish to stop time before a fall, before a "chrysalis moment," but as an ambiguity between two ways to see the same girl afterward. Both versions rewrite the myth of Persephone, whose spatial path the young Graham's flight downstairs, into open sunlight, reverses. In one version of the rewritten myth, the girl's footsteps are "plantings," destined to root her in one place as woman and mother and wife. In the other version, she remains always in motion, undertaking an incomplete escape: she descends

> the
> wrought-iron banister—three floors of it—now the *clack*
> *clack* of her sandals on stone—
> each a new planting—different from all the others—
> each planted fast, there into that soil,
> and the thin strip of light from the heavy street-door,
> and the other light after her self has slipped through.
> (R 38)

The girl, Graham says, "is still running down the Santo Spirito, and I push her / to go faster, faster, little one," much as she encouraged her younger self in "Fission"; around her, the women of Rome sell produce, "calling the price out, handling / each fruit" (*R* 40).

James Longenbach has critiqued Graham's "dream of openness" in *Region* (what we might call her perpetual escape) as politically (or even ontologically) unrealistic; Longenbach suggests that Graham's more recent poetry views the avoidance of narrative closure more reasonably, as a mere postponement of "patterns and laws" (*Modern Poetry*, 170–71). We might say that Graham's poems of adolescence in *Region* make that concession already; the desires to stand outside history, to avoid shape and story, to avoid the passage of time itself, to avoid the development of the female body into the light of a harsh male gaze all appear in these poems as linked and finally unachievable wishes. Those wishes prove inseparable from what Gilligan calls "girls' resistance" ("Preface," xxiii), from what Kasischke and other younger poets have revealed as a partly feminist and hence ethically charged wish not to accept any inherited story about what a girl must become—a wish, in at least one sense, not to grow up.

Recent American women poets find tonal, linguistic, and conceptual fits for difficulties that girls face as they enter their teens. One such difficulty involves sexual risk, dangerous self-exposure; another involves the loss of homosocial girlhood bonds; and a third (which grows out of the first two) has to do with entry into fixed narrative, into a limiting "life story" as such. All three topics can both prompt and represent lyric poetry, understood as the opposite, or the opponent, of a heteronormative, instrumentalizing, confining adult world. Some poets embrace "girls' talk" as part of a resistance to adult demands. These poets, and others, organize poems around a duality by which teen girlhood means both inward discovery and unwilling self-subjection, and in which teen girlhood inspires both awe and fear. Consciously if not programmatically feminist, such poems—of which we have seen only some examples—represent late entries into the larger twentieth-century project of describing adolescence in poems, of finding verbal forms to fit that life stage.

5

An Excess of Dreamy Possibilities

B Y THE END of the 1960s, ideas of teenagers and of youth culture had spread through much of the industrialized world.[1] "Los *teenagers*," wrote the Spanish poet Jaime Gil de Biedma, in his essay on Barcelona nightlife, "viven su existencia entre el-los, puros, hermosos y un poco irreales [the 'teenagers' live among the other patrons, pure, beautiful, and a little unreal]" (*El Pie*, 206). Though European and Asian critics decry "teenagers' taste for US films, television and music," writes the anthropologist Charles Acland, new works "portraying global teens" are "celebrating this aspect of a new, transnational generation" ("Fresh Contacts," 44). This is a book about some poets writing in English, not about all poetry worldwide. It can, though, acknowledge the international spread of teen culture in two countries where it emerged rather late and where major poets have either pursued or angrily rejected comparisons between the kind of person that a teenager or an adolescent is and the kind of poetry those poets want to create. The countries are Ireland and Australia; the poets, Paul Muldoon, John Tranter, and Les Murray.

Partly in response to Seamus Heaney, partly in response to Northern Ireland's Troubles, and (perhaps most of all) out of his own temperament, Paul Muldoon makes both adolescence and uncertainty organizing principles for many of his poems, using each to represent the other, in a skeptical poetics resistant to both ideas of pastoral self-seclusion and hopes for social (even for emotional) change. In Australia, John Tranter emerged from the utopianism of 1960s youth revolt (and from the would-be poetic avant-garde with which, in Sydney, that revolt was associated); during the 1970s and afterward, Tranter incorporates emblems of teen culture into his skeptical, poststructuralist-inflected style, reviving adolescence as pastoral in order to replace failed hopes of adolescence as utopian revolution. In doing so, Tranter—almost alone among the contemporary poets in this book—looks steadily, directly, and self-consciously at the legacy of Rimbaud. Tranter's Australian archrival Les Murray stands alone in another way; he takes note of modern adolescence and its implications for modern writing in order to denounce everything it represents.

❖ ❖ ❖ ❖ ❖

Muldoon's poems regularly include phrases like these: "Mercy was thirteen, maybe fourteen" ("Boon"); "Internal exiles at thirteen or fourteen" ("The Geography Lesson"); "I was thirteen or fourteen" ("Making the Move"); "she was twenty / or twenty-one" ("Big Foot") (*PMP* 54, 76, 90, 112). The same mannerism appears in his prose; Muldoon writes that he "first read Donne . . . at the age of fifteen or sixteen" ("Getting Round," 108). The youngest age such phrases mention is "ten"; the oldest is "twenty-one." These paired ages (I have not listed them all) are only one of the many ways in which Muldoon's work has used his—and our—notions of adolescence. From the adventure tales and drug-lore of "Yarrow" to the schooltime pranks of "Twice," from the embarrassed chastity of "Cuba" to the lubriciousness of "De Secretis Mulierum," from recurring phrases to recurring characters (such as the schoolmate Will Hunter), many of Muldoon's poems include teenaged protagonists or feelings and situations we associate with adolescence.

Muldoon's poetry has long struck readers (both hostile and friendly) as somehow immature. Mark Ford described *Meeting the British* (admiringly) as "outlandish" and "emotionally discontinuous," comparing Muldoon's provocative personae to Heaney's "absolutely solid poetic personality" ("Out of the Blue," 20). For Calvin Bedient, Muldoon's "brilliant callowness" "fit[s] . . . Ortega y Gasset's characterization of [modernism] as masculine and youthful" ("The Crabbed Genius," 210–11).[2] Other critics have described Muldoon's "elusiveness," his "chimerical . . . first-person voice," and his attraction to the "contingent and provisional" (McDonald, *Mistaken Identities*, 149; Wilson, "Paul Muldoon," 349; Matthews, *Irish Poetry*, 186). Muldoon's versions of youth and young people explain and act out the elusive, provocative stances so often remarked in his work.

Muldoon's poems, with their slippery, shifting shapes, explore frustrated or confused identities, presenting people who do not yet know who they are or what to do. The poems imagine—with tenderness or brutality—teen romance and its failures, comparing it favorably to adults' doctrines and disciplines. Refusing both the stable, "mature" perspectives associated with adult authority and the childhood innocence other poets associate with lyric, Muldoon imagines failed, stalled, incomplete, or continually reen- acted comings of age. His interest in adolescence works in tandem with his tendency to entangle or even destroy the narrative lines of his long poems; the result is a world in which most sorts of intellectual and emotional clo- sure are simply not possible. Instead, Muldoon's poems tend to present people who cannot or will not complete their life stories by settling on one identity or growing up; at their happiest, these presentations celebrate the artifice displayed by his playful, defiant, or coy personae.

Muldoon has been viewed as notably, or exceptionally young from the time he began to publish—in part because he *was* young (twenty-one when his first book, *New Weather*, appeared), and in part because he was fre- quently (and still is) viewed as Heaney's younger counterpart or successor. "I was seventeen or eighteen," Muldoon told Michael Donaghy, when he first encountered Heaney (Donaghy, "A Conversation," 77). "Clonfeacle" (from *New Weather*) responds to the *dinnseanchas* genre (poems on Irish place names), which Heaney replicated in English, in the trimeter qua- trains Heaney used. "Walk[ing] along / The river where [Patrick] washed, / That translates stone to silt," Muldoon imagines that

The river would preach

As well as Patrick did.
A tongue of water passing
Between teeth of stones.
Making itself clear,
Living by what it says.
(*PMP* 12)

The point of the poem seems to be that Muldoon and his companion, "I" and "you," cannot or will not "translate" these natural certainties into any part of their own lives:

You turn towards me,
Coming round to my way

Of thinking, holding
Your tongue between your teeth.
I turn my back on the river

And Patrick, their sermons

Ending in air.

"I" and "you" are perhaps coming to some agreement about a date or a romance or the end of one (Tim Kendall suggests a first kiss [*Paul Muldoon*, 34]). The hesitation in the lines maps hesitations in the actors they chronicle, a hesitation that concludes in silence, in mid-stanza. This youthful uncertainty is where "I" and "you" and the poem's sound agree; all are set against the older certainties that Patrick and the river (and, perhaps, implicitly, Heaney) embody.

"Whatever the mottoes are," Muldoon has remarked, "when they become organized, codified, there's a very fine line between organized religion and organized crime" (Keller, "An Interview," 17). The uncertain young lovers of "The Kissing Seat" seem about to cross a related line: "The organized crime / Of the kissing seat, /How well it holds us," the poem begins. Its lovers seem of two minds about each other; both are looking

> Elsewhere.
> It's getting late now,
> You've only a linen shift
> Between you and harm.
>
> (*PMP* 27)

Muldoon seems to be quoting a girl's parents (as he would do explicitly in "Cuba"), placing their language into his own poem, without telling us how ironically we ought to read it, whether a kiss, or more than a kiss, would indeed be "harm."

Such hesitancies are not Muldoon's alone (Heaney signed his own earliest poems *Incertus*). Yet more than most young poets the Muldoon of the 1970s liked to present himself as young and uncertain, even in poems with few or no autobiographical elements. Muldoon's youthful personae can take their ambivalent perspectives—and offer the insights that come with them—precisely because they are distant from adult authority. "I was only the girl under the stairs," "The Big House" begins, "But I was the first to notice something was wrong" (*PMP* 43). It is because the guests and the mistress have paid her little attention that she can report on the Big House so well, and it is because she is the servant girl (up first in the morning) that she has seen the squire arrive, dead, on horseback. Nor is the serving-girl who speaks the poem the only young person whom we might identify with its author; one of the guests at the haunted estate is "a young man who wrote stories for children," though "The young man's stories were for grown-ups, really."

Another early poem, "February," likens its man or boy ("he") to a tree:

He heard that in Derryscollop there is a tree
For every day of the year,
And the extra tree is believed to grow
One year in every four.

He had never yet taken time to grieve
For this one without breasts
Or that one wearing her heart on her sleeve
Or another with her belly slashed.

He had never yet taken time to love
The blind pink fledgling fallen out of the nest
Of one sleeping with open mouth
And her head at a list.

What was he watching and waiting for,
Walking Scollop every day?
For one intending to leave at the end of the year,
Who would break the laws of time and stay.

(*PMP* 13)

The poem is the first of many in Muldoon's oeuvre to mingle remembered sex with imagined violence or to portray the former in terms of the latter, and it requires conjecture as well as decoding.[3] Yet the poem coheres only if we take its subject to be, first and last, youth: the poem imagines that stage of life as a condition of rural, or village, isolation, a condition at once magical, limiting, violent, and subject to "laws of time" that send the residents away (in Muldoon's own case, to university) despite their mixed feelings about it. The "fledgling," the girl or woman with her "belly slashed" (a wound or an appendectomy—or an abortion), the "one wearing her heart on her sleeve" and the "one without breasts" may share not only victimhood but youth. The Romantic figure the poem awaits can redeem them all, apparently, by "break[ing] the laws of time." "They" are, perhaps, the girls of a village, and the poem's final lines seem to reverse its implicit situation; it may be "he" who plans to leave but asks if he should stay.

From *New Weather* on, Muldoon has written poems that look back critically at his own failed romances—from divorces to difficult dates. The first such poem to achieve tonal control was "Elizabeth." In it, unexpected migrations of birds (arriving "inland, they belong to the sea") stand for the uncertainties of the young woman Muldoon names:

> You are inside yet, pacing the floor,
>
> Having been trapped in every way.
> You hold yourself as your own captive.
> My promised children are in your hands,
> Hostaged by you in your father's old house.
> I call you now for all the names of the day,
> Lizzie and Liz and plain Beth.
>
> (PMP 27)

These figures of self-enclosure and self-imprisonment are the "self-inwoven similes" Christopher Ricks identifies with Northern Irish poetry in general (*Force*, 51–55). Their use here, though, suggests not civil war (much less reconciliation) but a baffled or balked self-creation. Muldoon does not know what to call Elizabeth because Elizabeth does not know who she is, what name she prefers, or what she wants, and no one—not her father, not her lover—stands in any position to tell her. Without the ability to make such decisions (or to let them be made for her) she seems to be fading away: the birds "will stay long / Enough to underline how soon they will be gone, / As you seem thinner than you were before." That ending suggests both a figurative "shrinking" (from the imposing outdoor birds) and anorexia (which reappears in *Quoof*). Elizabeth's unsettled, in-between status is not a source of power (as it can be for Muldoon's male juveniles) but a debilitating condition.

An earlier, cruder romantic-erotic failure takes place in "How to Play Championship Tennis," whose lonely "third-form" narrator flees the groping advances of the ironically titled "school caretaker" (*PMP* 46). Heterosexual initiations guide still other poems from this period, among them the tender "Boon" (which features Mercy, along with Will Hunter) and "The Girls in the Poolroom," whose speaker delights in malapropism:

> The girls in the poolroom
> Were out on their own limbs.
> How could I help
> But make men of them?
>
> (PMP 53)

It is they, and in particular a confused girl called Emily, who "make a man" of him; the reversed language suggests that no one in the poem has got very far toward maturity.

A far stronger poem of sexual initiation, "Cuba," also sets the absurdities of adults' beliefs against teenagers' tentative search for something else. "My eldest sister" (named May) has been out all night, and returns home "in her white muslin evening dress" (*PMP* 78). First-time readers assume she has been out with a man, and perhaps that they have had sex. "My father," too, knows, or thinks he knows, that May has done something sinful, instructing her to "'make your peace with God.'" In the same way the father feels sure that President Kennedy will start a nuclear war over Cuba because he is "'nearly an Irishman,'" hence temperamental, "'not much better than ourselves'"; the young siblings can only listen in fear. May then proceeds to the confessional:

> I could hear May from beyond the curtain.
> "Bless me, Father, for I have sinned.
> I told a lie once, I was disobedient once.
> And, Father, a boy touched me once."
> "Tell me, child. Was this touch immodest?
> Did he touch your breast, for example?"
> "He brushed against me, Father. Very gently."
> (PMP 79)

It may be that May has simply lied to the priest. Most readers, however, are likely to imagine that she has told the truth; her night out in evening wear has led to nothing more indecent than that. Against her, the poem's grown men (and perhaps its readers) seem prurient in their assumptions, and this may be part of the point: May's body is none of the Father's business, and perhaps not much of her father's either. "The poem's fathers manipulate May," Kendall writes, "imposing their narrow prejudices upon her; 'Cuba' is a parable of innocence destroyed . . . by their sanctimonious codes" (*Paul Muldoon*, 76). Yet her innocence seems to have been preserved, almost against her wishes. What the poem has to set against its fathers is a youthful solidarity and curiosity; we identify with the more benign snooping represented by the poem's young narrator and with the innocent curiosity represented by his sister's night out.

Set in 1963 (rather than 1962) the sonnet "Profumo" works as a sequel to "Cuba." Its innocent teen romance involves Muldoon himself:

> My mother had slapped a month-long news embargo
> on his very name. The inhalation
> of my first, damp
> menthol fag behind the Junior Common Room.

The violet-scented Thirteenth Birthday Card
to which I would affix a stamp
with the Queen's head upside down, swalk,
and post to Frances Hagan.

The spontaneously-combustible *News of the World*
under my mother's cushion
as she shifted from ham to snobbish ham;
'Haven't I told you, time and time again,
that you and she are chalk
and cheese? Away and read Masefield's "Cargoes."

(*PMP* 155)

The "snobbish" mother works as a blocking agent, parallel to the father in "Cuba." As in that earlier poem, public affairs, mediated by distracted adults, interfere with the private world of the young people in the poem, a world with code words such as "swalk" (sealed with a loving kiss). The discreditable sexual secrets of the Profumo affair of 1963 emphasize the relative innocence of the young Muldoon's secretive actions, from cigarette to birthday card to the tabloid under the cushion. John Masefield's once-famous poem about nautical voyages, meanwhile, stands in mocking contrast to Muldoon's domestic troubles; "Cargoes" sets a "Quinquereme of Nineveh from distant Ophir" against the humdrum, practical freight of England (Masefield, *Poems*, 43–44).

Even more than "Cuba," this poem emphasizes the tentative, furtive attitudes of its youthful actors. After the abrupt first sentence, most of the poem consists of noun phrases, the verbs buried in dependent clauses. Those clauses, moreover, introduce actions recalled or contemplated rather than undertaken and completed. Muldoon has not yet stamped and sent the birthday card; "my mother," at the edge of her seat, has not uncovered the tabloid, perhaps never will. Muldoon's rhyme scheme, meanwhile, seems exceptionally tangled even for him: *abcd ecfg ebdgfa*, with no completed rhyme until line six. It could be overreading to connect the rhymes' hidden couplings to the couples the poem considers (Muldoon and Frances Hagan, John Profumo and Christine Keeler). One can, though, say that the rhyme scheme suggests connections that have to be kept from the wrong eyes.

Muldoon's poems of failed or comic romance belong to a larger pattern; his characters try to come of age and find they cannot. In "Making the Move" the powerlessness that the adult Muldoon feels as his first marriage breaks up and the compensatory fantasies of male heroism it prompts re-produce the comically simple fantasies and adventures of teenaged boys. Its couplets, with their deliberately obvious rhymes, mime the speaker's juve-nile failures; Muldoon remembers

> A primus stove, a sleeping-bag
> The bow I bought through a catalog
>
> When I was thirteen or fourteen
> That would bend, and break, for anyone,
>
> Its boyish length of maple
> Unseasoned and unsupple.
>
> Were I embarking on that wine-dark sea
> I would bring my bow along with me.
> (*PMP* 90-91)

Ulysses' bow "would bend for no one but himself"; he used it as he traveled circuitously back to his own "good wife." Muldoon's journey away from his marriage will instead return him to the juvenile state in which he identified with "bad Lord Byron" and hoped to emulate Ulysses.[4] Muldoon would later say he had been "taken by the idea of the 'self' bow, the bow 'made all of one piece', as opposed to 'backed' or composite. . . . The yew self bow is traditionally six feet long, man-tall" ("Getting Round," 119). From these sources Muldoon has derived not only a young man in a collapsing marriage but a man who returns ambiguously to his teenage preoccupa-tions as part of a continuing effort to make some sense of himself, a self who is not and will not soon be "all of one piece"—even if he has long been "man-tall."

"Making the Move" also names Raymond Chandler, whom Muldoon has characterized as "a pure stylist," "a man who pretended to be engaged in narratives but wasn't the least interested" (Donaghy, "A Conversation," 79–80). Muldoon's attraction to versions of adolescence, to baffled or failed or unfinished growing up, makes itself evident in his own narrative poems, not only in their incidents of adventure but in their frustrated and frustrat-ing plots. "The More a Man Has the More a Man Wants" ends in symp-tomatically, confrontationally anticlosural gestures—ellipses, an incomplete sentence, the final line "'Huh'" (*PMP* 147). Tales told within the poems be-come shaggy-dog stories; land and sea journeys, quests, and even paved roads come to sudden and baffling endings.

As "Incantata" (with its meditation on "the word 'might'") acknowledges, Muldoon has been drawn to verb forms that suggest uncertainty; Jane Stabler calls his verse "slyly interrogated by conditionals and subjunctives" (Stabler, "Alive," 55). Andrew Osborn has shown how Muldoon's skepticisms inform his intricate rhymes, which "spurn . . . all-or-nothing dichotomies in favor of greater or lesser probabilities" ("Skirmishes," 328). Muldoon's preference for young and aggressively uncertain characters— from his Irish schoolboys to a snappy girl in a Toronto disco—works in tandem with his abrupt or random endings, his odd tastes in verb moods, his elusive rhymes, and his stated attraction to indeterminacy; they let him depict sympathetic beginnings followed by vexing or indeterminate middles and relieve him of having to draw conclusions.

The adolescents in his 1990s poetry are less frequent and less tormented. Yet up to *The Annals of Chile* (1994) they do the same kinds of representative work. Expansive and hyperallusive where the earliest poems seem cannily restrained, the long poem "Yarrow" may seem (like Muldoon's other recent verse) the stylistic opposite of *New Weather*. Muldoon's uses of youth, however, suggest that the early and late poems share concerns. "Yarrow" juxtaposes punningly related incidents from Muldoon's own life with symbols and quotations from Plath, *King Lear*, and other sources, including boys' adventure stories; the assembled fragments serve, among other purposes, to mourn Muldoon's mother. Much of the putative autobiography takes place in "the winter of 1962–63," when Muldoon would have been aged eleven; much of the rest imagines his later romance with an almost comically self-destructive woman called S——, addicted to New York City, to heroin, and to self-dramatization (Redmond, "Interview," 4). Other parts of the poem revisit "Profumo"—"the mouth of Christine Keel- // er," "a photo of Mandy Rice-Davies," the profaned head of the Queen (*Annals*, 74, 110, 79). As in "Making the Move," Muldoon's failed romance prompts him to recall youthful adventures that reached no conclusion:

> It was thirty years till I reached back for the quiver
> in which I'd hidden the carbon-slip
> from Tohill's of the Moy: my hand found the hilt
>
> of the dirk I confiscated from Israel . . .
> I'd been diverted from my quest.
>
> (ANNALS, 137)

In the course of "Yarrow," the young Muldoon discovers adventure, heroic (impossible) versions of himself, sex (and the idea of the erotic), Latin (and the idea of translation), danger (and the thrill of the forbidden). He discovers, moreover, that for him these things are confusingly, but compellingly, related. These discoveries seem to lead directly into the glamorous, absurd affair with S——. And if they begin in Muldoon's 1963, they continue throughout his teens:

> That was the year I stumbled on Publius Ovidius Naso
> vying with Charlie Gunn in an elegiac distich:
> the year Eric and Jimi rode the packet
>
> on the Chisolm
> Trail and Mike Fink declaimed from his Advanced Reader
> the salascient passages from *Amores*.
>
> (*ANNALS*, 75)

Though the previous page refers to the extreme cold and the Profumo scandal of 1963, the "year" this page describes must have been later, since Jimi (Hendrix) released his first single ("Hey Joe") in December 1966. Almost all of "Yarrow" contains such mixed and plot-defeating signals. "The polylingual parodying of . . . noble heroic deeds . . . and of romance," concludes Steven Matthews, "continues Muldoon's attack on all idealisms," while its "demotic measures of time" repudiate any "fixed sense of history" (*Irish Poetry*, 205). "Yarrow" offers instead an antinarrative antihistory, starting from Muldoon's twelfth year, and festooned with red herrings, hyperactive allusions, and double entendres, in which Muldoon in effect fails to grow up.

From this angle "Yarrow" seems consistent with much of Muldoon's first two decades of work. Girls just old enough to walk out with boys; boys old enough to devour (or try to act out) adventure tales; and men and women in their late teens or twenties (often seeking sexual exploits or taking hallucinogens) are the usual, almost the only, centers of consciousness in *New Weather*, *Mules*, *Why Brownlee Left*, and even in *Quoof* (whose poems about Muldoon's father see him through the eyes of an admiring son). With the brief exception of "The Right Arm," Muldoon's corpus before *Hay* seems almost devoid of young children, since (among other reasons) he does not seem to believe in childhood innocence; his poems begin with the entry into experience, and with the uncertainties and missteps attendant upon it (*PMP* 107).[5]

The uncollected sonnet "Under Saturn" announces much more coarsely Muldoon's dissent from childhood innocence, painting its formative encounter—apparently a first kiss—as excitingly "dirty," always already sexual. The octave recalls "a child's vow / Sworn in all integrity . . . To a girl with hair in braids"; the sestet then recasts the memory in decidedly un-Yeatsian terms:

> I grasp the nitty-gritty
> Plait between her shoulder-blades.
>
> My mouth on her faintly urinous
> Mouth. Brisket-bone.
>
> And now, blah-blah, now
> At a snail's lick across a stone.
>
> (219)

Yeats's poem "Under Saturn" invoked "lost love, inseparable from my thought / Because I have no other youth" (*Poems*, 179). Muldoon's point seems to be that this is how formative experiences really feel: messy, vertiginous, smelly, exciting, wet—and, in retrospect, sometimes comic.

These poems' disbelief in childhood innocence matches their lack of trustworthy, or even sympathetic adults. In Muldoon's world to grow up is to know more facts, to have more experience, to see more of the conjunctions and resemblances that could link anyone to anything. It is not, however, to learn how the world makes any final, stable sense. To try to condense from the world a foundational truth (on which codes of conduct or institutions might rest) might be as irrational, as destructive, as trying to "squeeze" "a moral for our times" out of a frog (*PMP* 120). Almost the only figure in Muldoon's early poems who does grow up—whom we see in his youth and as an adult—is Joseph Mary Plunkett Ward, in "Anseo," whose adult role as a republican militarist ironically repeats his role as school rebel (*PMP* 83). And one of the admirable aspects of Muldoon's father, as the poems present him, seems to be his distance from authorities; he exerts himself to demonstrate farm skills or shares a decidedly noninstructive moment (watching "our favoured wrestler, the Mohawk Indian") rather than promulgating rules and judgments (*PMP* 111).

"What I resist very strenuously," Muldoon has declared, "is . . . any kind of *ism*, that insists on everything falling into place very neatly. . . . I'm antiprescriptive" (Keller, "An Interview," 18). Many readers link this "antiprescriptive" bent to his background and his generation. Muldoon arrived at Queen's University–Belfast in 1969; his frequently quoted, unpublished essay "Chez Moy" recalls those times.[6] "Unlike Heaney and slightly older writers," whose university days coincided with the Northern civil rights movement (Clair Wills argues), "Muldoon's adolescence was overshadowed by the beginning of the Troubles, perhaps fostering a feeling of political

impotence rather than ethical responsibility" (*Reading*, 21). His earliest poems on political violence share a terse, difficult attitude of *non serviam*: "We
answer to no grey South / Nor blue North," the U.S. Civil War soldiers in
"The Field Hospital" declare (*PMP* 33).

We might compare Muldoon's refusals and obliquities not only to those
of the committed, violent men and religious believers Muldoon can depict
(from Joseph Mary Plunkett Ward to Gallogly) but to the real young people
studied by social psychologists such as Ed Cairns, whose research suggests
that *children* in Northern Ireland after 1969 sensed *less* "complexity of moral
problems," became *more* ready to accept adults' rules and norms, than children in England or the United States (*Caught in Crossfire*, 76). Even more
than in another milieu, skepticism in this one might come to seem a form of
individuation; individual doubt becomes odder and more powerful as a component of character and poetry the more the people and works around it
seem committed to violent certainties. While Heaney wrote newspaper col-
umns and book reviews, Muldoon's only remotely "civic" publication from
the 1970s would be *The Scrake of Dawn*, a commissioned anthology of poems
by Northern Ireland's students aged eight through sixteen.

If there are logical stopping-points to Muldoon's representations of adolescence, they occur in short poems of the 1980s and 1990s that recall particular young people with admiration. One such poem, the sonnet "Twice,"
seems to remember deceased schoolmates, among them the prank-loving
"Lefty" Clery:

> It was so cold last night the water in the barrel grew a sod
> of water: I asked Taggart and McAnespie to come over
> and we sawed and sawed
> for half an hour until, using a crowbar as a lever
>
> in the way Archimedes always said
> would shift the balance, we were somehow able to manoeuvre
> out and, finally, stand on its side
> in the snow that fifteen- or eighteen-inch thick manhole cover;
>
> that 'manhole cover' was surely no more ice
> than are McAnespie and Taggart still of this earth;
> when I squinnied through I saw 'Lefty' Clery, 'An Ciotach,'
>
> grinning from both ends of the school photograph,
> having jooked behind the three-deep rest of us to meet the Kodak's
> leisurely pan; 'Two places at once, was it, or one place twice?'

(*PMP* 320)

"Fifteen- or eighteen inch[es] thick," the manhole cover has taken unto it-self the distinctively uncertain adjectival phrases that Muldoon's other po-ems attach to people. (That "lever" may be a riposte to Heaney, too.)[7] That symbolic photograph, like the fictive ice disc, turns individuals into illu-sions or doubles of themselves. The poem has done likewise with its key words. *Ciotach* is Irish for "lefthanded" or "lefty"; "sawed," "water," and "manhole cover" each appear twice close together, while the homophones *saw* ("cut"), *saw* ("viewed"), *said*, *sawed*, and *sod* trade places throughout.

It makes no sense to ask which of the two "Lefty" Clerys in the school picture is real—no more sense than to ask, faced with Muldoon's eye-rhymes, whether "sod," "sawed," "said," or "side" is the original word. The prank, played in a *school* photograph, mocks the official, school-standard view of the world. It allies Muldoon and his language with the unofficial ("subversive," even) gestures practiced by the schoolmates he remembers, sets his sense of himself apart from the stabilities of an adult world. More-over, it works to *commemorate* those schoolmates and their tricky sense of themselves; they may no longer be "of this earth," but Muldoon's poem, like their ghostly image, still is.

Muldoon's verbal strategy has struck other readers as a "postmodern dis-avowal of origins" (Batten, "He Could Barely Tell," 188). Poems like "Twice" indeed depict copies without originals, dual and multiple chains of shifting selves whose narratives fail to reach clear ends. Yet Muldoon's youthful personae, with their tenuous romances and school pranks, "attempt to take both roads" (as Kendall has put it) and try to conceal or joke about those attempts, not because they have no sense of self but because the selves they sense are dual, multiple, tricky (*Paul Muldoon*, 17). Readers who seek pur-chase on Muldoon's language from social and cultural theorists might turn instead to recent studies of youth and youth culture, which, the anthropol-ogist Vered Amit-Talai argues, encourage "an especially acute awareness of the contingent character of any cultural experience," "impart[ing] a con-stant edge of private scepticism to social action" ("The 'Multi' Cultural," 232, 228). The adolescence that in Brooks or Oppen promises to change society and in Lowell has already failed to do so succeeds in Muldoon at refusing to settle down.

"Muldoon's subject," McDonald observes, "has often been, not discon-nectedness (or "deconstruction") per se, but "the connectedness which the 'arbitrary' brings about" (*Mistaken Identities*, 160). This sort of connected-ness cannot lead the narrative poems to clear and firm conclusions, the lyric poems to ringing affirmations, or the characters in them to stable, ma-ture self-knowledge. What it can do is enable a verbal art that—in its early tenderness, in its frequent outrage, in its unpredictability—Muldoon has always associated with the unstable self of youth. It is such a self that "Lefty" Clery celebrates, or once did, and such a self that Muldoon runs aground or "los[es] with all hands," in "Yarrow" (*Annals*, 189).

Such a self, too, distinguishes Gypsy Rose Lee, perhaps the least remarked of the many personae in Muldoon's "7, Middagh Street"—and the only person in Muldoon's poems before *Hay* (1998) who can be called happy. In her section of "7, Middagh Street," the vaudevillian turned ecdysiast tells stories from her early career. At the same time, she explains how she discovered (to put it more flatfootedly than Muldoon does) that art is our nature, that to become oneself is to learn concealment and evasion, that to grow up successfully, in her line of work, is not to grow up at all. Muldoon has pieced her monologue together from anecdotes in Lee's memoir, some of them pages or years apart.[8] In his poem, she remembers a show with horses onstage:

> the first five rows
> were showered with horse-dung.
> I've rarely felt so close to nature
> as in Billy Minsky's Burlesque Theatre.
>
> This was Brooklyn, 1931. I was an under-age
> sixteen. Abbott and Costello
> were sent out front while the stage
> was hosed down.
> (PMP 181)

Impatient "customers" boo not only the comedians but the scenery, an imitation Garden of Eden, until Gypsy shows up:

> Gradually the clamor
> faded as I shed
> all but three of my green taffeta fig-leaves
> and stood naked as Eve.

Even "naked as Eve," the young stripper still wears three fig-leaves, reversing Yeats by "walking not quite naked"; it seems an appropriate compliment when Nudina the snake-dancer tells her "I loved the *act*" (emphasis added).

Most readers of "7, Middagh Street" find Muldoon's spokesman (rightly) in Louis MacNeice. We might also see his points of view in Gypsy Rose Lee, whose entertaining story is the story of how to become Muldoon's sort of artist. Existing between her own famous past and the present in which she speaks, Gypsy Rose Lee becomes at once the silliest and the happiest of Muldoon's expert representations of immaturity. Lee's act, even her costume, mocks received notions of innocence (Eden) as it stretches decorum (and local laws). As an adult, she enjoys retelling, and even interpreting her stories of underage exploits; she, too, has "grown accustomed" to "a life-size cut-out of" herself—another of Muldoon's flexible, doubled identities. At the same time, she holds on to the props of other acts and of her own youth: "I keep that papier-mâché cow's head packed," she quips, "just in case vaudeville does come back" (*PMP* 182).

❖ ❖ ❖ ❖ ❖

We have seen in Muldoon a new way to use adolescence, speaking from within it, denying that his own poems or attitudes can get beyond it, never ascribing to it any revolutionary power, and never even trying out an "adult" voice. The Australian poet John Tranter also pursues uncertainty and instability through forms and properties that suggest modern youth; Tranter also responds, as Muldoon does not, to the legacy of youthful, prophetic radicalism that runs from the New Left of 1968 all the way back to Arthur Rimbaud. The historian John Rickard writes that in Australia, "much of the cultural creativity of the late 1960s and early 1970s had [the] intoxication of [a] generational revolt" (*Australia*, 241).[9] Australian poets whose work began in those years, among them Michael Dransfield, Laurie Duggan, John Forbes, and John Tranter, became known as the Generation of '68. Duggan's comic poem "(Do) The Modernism" echoes the Who: older Australian versifiers, Duggan complains, "never busted a pentameter or stayed out late / till the g-g-g-generation of s-s-sixty eight" (quoted in Johnston, "Surviving").[10] As the coeditor of new magazines such as *Leatherjacket* and *Transit*, Tranter became a representative for the generation; his 1979 anthology, *The New Australian Poetry*, became its definitive document.

Tranter's early participation in supposedly revolutionary literary communities did not lead to a continued faith in radical improvement led by youth (either in literature or in society). Instead, as with late Lowell—and perhaps more decisively—versions of adolescence in Tranter's later poetry describe not a continued faith in youth so much as a disillusion with everything else. As early as *Red Movie* (1972), Tranter tried to represent simultaneously youth, instability, power, and velocity: "Cracking the speedo at a hundred plus, / adolescent, on a faster highway, I caught myself dreaming of you in the distant future" (*Trio*, 25). (An Australian "speedo" is a speedometer, not a bathing suit.) Australian critics regularly compare Tranter's poems, "built for speed, you might say," to fast cars (Dobrez, *Parnassus*, 154). Martin Duwell writes that Tranter "allow[ed] the fast life of youth, drugs, sex and cars into poetry" (quoted in Johnston, "Surviving"). Yet these speedy vehicles represent not confidence so much as instability. For Andrew Taylor, Tranter's poems "remain ungrounded in any 'truth,'" just as the automobiles and aircraft remain on the move ("Resisting").[11]

Tranter has described a "striking discontinuity between my generation and that immediately preceding it" in Australian letters, "between those born before the Second World War and those born after, say, 1940" who "had grown up with Dylan and the Beatles, with Kerouac and Zen, with Frank O'Hara and rock and roll" (Duwell, *Possible Contemporary*, 26, 27). Yet his poetry of endless and antiteleological motion and his use of adolescence to stand for it links Tranter not so much to rockers nor to Beats nor even very firmly to O'Hara but instead to Ashbery, late Lowell, and Muldoon. His poems' quickly changing tones and attitudes; their interest in forms of power that prove temporary; their tendency toward in-group speak, argot, and shorthand; and their deliberate failure to stick with one voice all fit the teenaged characters, whom Tranter (like Lowell) plays off against baffled, disillusioned elders, as if in unfinishable competition to become the (one) voice of the poem.

Tranter began the sonnet sequence *Crying in Early Infancy* in 1971 and completed it in 1977; since he did not arrange the sonnets in order of composition, they cannot reflect "development" in his thinking (Duwell, *Possible Contemporary*, 31). Their vividly unstable verbal registers convey a consistent pessimism about maturity and authority. One sonnet from *Crying*, entitled "(after American Graffitti)," imagines the taste of "marsh water . . . which illuminates our adolescence." In it, "hot machines [i.e. fast cars?] are broken and a promise / is a memory" (*Trio*, 59). Another sonnet, "The Student Prince," ends up as angry and direct as Tranter ever becomes; its burden is that neither educational institutions nor inherited concepts of *bildung* nor prior standards of aesthetic success retain any worth for him:

> I went to college like a privilege
> and learnt to wield a metaphor in each hand
> and got a kiss on the arse for being good.
> Who made a million? The Student Prince?

> Who made a profit from a lasting work of art?
> Who was improved by the perfect landscape?
>
> (*TRIO*, 78)

Over and over in Tranter growing up brings nothing new. The sonnet "Half Moon" implies that an adequate representation of so-called puppy love, of first crushes and crushing break-ups, would also be an adequate representation of adult emotion, since social adulthood adds nothing to experience but only subtracts from its range:

> You and the bubblegum
> shock me into an understanding, it's like
> breaking up permanently at fourteen and
> you're broken-hearted before you're middle-aged
> and yet you're lucky, if that response
> is really automatic. What's broken?
> Who's lost? Anything? At all?
>
> (*TRIO*, 82)

The voice here (if we can call it one voice) tries out an effect common in Tranter's later work; the speaker sounds disillusioned enough that we associate him with "middle age" and yet tells us that he feels as he did in his teens. Nothing in language, art, or experience seems to Tranter *more* trustworthy than what might have been said and done in the back of a car at age seventeen; the volatility of tone and the semantic uncertainty in Tranter's work create a space that the shifting attitudes and excitements of the very young seem to fill.

In that uncertainty they invoke Rimbaud. "The first, say, fifteen years of my writing," Tranter has said, were "undertaken in the shadow of Rimbaud," "the prototype of all modern poets" (Duwell, *Possible Contemporary*, 21). Rimbaud became for Tranter, as for some of the American modernists we saw in chapter 1, the ideal-typical adolescent, as well as the first modern poet. Published in several versions during the 1970s (I quote the latest, from 1979), Tranter's long associative poem "Rimbaud and the Modernist Heresy" replaces or misplaces Rimbaud amid 1950s teens, conflating international modernism with a cultural history of English-speaking youth:

> After the lost generation we find the single
> beatnik emerging, it's like Castaways in Space

with a drug supply at the corner store
and we're getting fresh on adrenalin milk-shakes
when the beatnik declines as a focus for the novel
and the word 'hippie' surfaces in the dictionary.

(*TRIO*, 98)

Tranter has said that "when [he] was very young," he believed—thanks to his reading of Rimbaud—"that the role of the poet was rather visionary and prophetic" and that poets could "see . . . patterns of meaning in the universe" (quoted in David Brooks, "Feral Symbolists," n.p.). After 1971 he ceased to believe in that role; "Rimbaud and the Modernist Heresy" began as a record of that disillusion, working out, as the Australian critic David Brooks put it, "the apparently duplicitous role Rimbaud has played in Tranter's own thinking and the damage his influence may have done to Tranter's generation" ("Feral Symbolists,").

Rimbaud is for Tranter the spirit of the Generation of '68, almost as the self-mythologizing heroin addict Michael Dransfield, another *poete maudit*, became for other Sydneyside '68ers a reincarnated Rimbaud, the doomed apostle of "Visionary Impressionism" who intended "living as a form of art" (Dobrez, *Parnassus*, 428–29). "*Arthur! We needed you in '68,*" Tranter exclaims near the end of "Modernist Heresy"; "*you / cannot accept this burden of pity*" (*Trio*, 105). "Arthur" never arrives and cannot save a generation if he does. Yet Tranter does not repudiate his early admiration for Rimbaud's poems. Tranter instead presents poetry in general, and Rimbaud's attractive example in particular, as a continuing, collaborative, almost furtive enterprise; the poem therefore describes "an adolescent growing up crooked; / in the universities, a small profit in a great / decline" (*Trio*, 99). Tranter's long poem pursues the questions many readers of Rimbaud have asked: Why did he give up poetry? If we no longer believe, as Tranter had ceased to believe, in a sacred or visionary mission for poetry, why should we read or write it? Is there value in secular, non- or anti-prophetic, representations of contemporary life? Must a poet raised on Rimbaud's untenable hopes, or on the related hopes of 1968, come up with new representations of crisis states, of fluid identity, that retain Rimbaud's investment in youth without writing (as Rimbaud did) metaphysical checks no experience can cash?

We might say that readers of Rimbaud after 1968, after the international failure of utopian youth movements in public life, must choose among versions of him; *either* he is a poet of adolescence, recording a biologically and culturally catalyzed transitional state heightened by drugs and literary technique, *or* he is a visionary poet, a seer whose discoveries transcend body, style, and place. It requires a lengthy counterintuitive essay, if not a book like Kristin Ross's, to show how Rimbaud might be both at once. Tranter, as his interviews make clear, embraced in his verse the paraphernalia of youth culture—the swimming pools, the slang, the speeding cars—exactly when, perhaps even because, he switched allegiance from the "visionary" to the "adolescent" Rimbaud.[12]

That switch produced Tranter's unusual diction. Tranter turns to his clashing array of tones and socioloects, and to teen lingo in particular, in order to avoid implying that any particular kind of language is the best, effective, sacred, or right one. In this he resembles but goes beyond Robert Lowell; what Lowell did with colliding lines and statements, Tranter does with jangling, "inappropriate," or "unserious" phrases and words. "I think you're stoned again / or is that true love?" Tranter asks in "Parallel Lines" (*Under*, 49). The lingo in "Boarding School" seems to him as least as good as any other way to express amours:

> Bright gods, trust me to play
> the game properly. Meeting you
> suddenly, I think you're tops;
> I'm absolutely riddled by lust,
>
> at least I think it's lust.
> (*UNDER*, 67)

"Radio Traffic 1: Lipstick" opens with a burst of almost campy slang, an invocation to the excessive and immature:

> Debbie is too much, Maureen divine, & Sue-Anne
> an excess of dreamy possibilities. What shall we
> do tonight? The High School game is washed out,
> but your new perm wasn't meant to be wasted, &
> a cracked flask of vodka spills a trickle on the
> back seat of Dad's Chev in a message—
> Wait for me after the Labomba, near the Gym!
> (*TRIO* 127)

Here the uncertainties and excitement of teen life are neither resolved nor replaced by anything weightier; the assumptions adults tend to make about teen argot—that it pertains to an in-group, that it changes constantly, that it may accomplish nothing of consequence—for Tranter simply describe language in general (*Trio*, 127).

The recent pantoum "Rimbaud in Sydney" suggests that the difference between the nineteenth-century French Rimbaud (a last flowering of Romanticism who battles and fails to defeat the world as it is) and the contemporary Australian Tranter (who battles with subways and swears in comic frustration) is the difference between a Romantic youthfulness and a contemporary, perhaps interminable adolescence. Tranter's poem begins:

> Romanticism has never been properly judged—
> it is a simple as a phrase of music.
> We grappled and triumphed over the subway map.
> What the fuck is going on around here?
>
> It is as simple as a phrase of music
> when you are seventeen. You aren't really serious:
> What the fuck is going on around here?
> I'm a fiery passionate woman—I'm not a raving loony.
>
> When you are seventeen you aren't really serious.
> Reality being too thorny for my great personality,
> I'm a fiery passionate woman.
>
> (*STUDIO*, 88)

Tranter is quoting not only Rimbaud's poem "Roman" ("On n'est pas sérieux, quand on a dix-sept ans") but Rimbaud's letters; in Wyatt Mason's translation, "Romanticism has never been fairly appraised; who would have? Critics!! The Romantics, who so clearly prove that the song is infrequently the work of a singer. . . . For I is someone else [Je est un autre]" (*Rimbaud Complete*, 366). Romanticism has never been properly judged (Tranter's juxtapositions imply) because there can be no place, no point of view, not even a proper diction from which to judge it; anything we can say will sound immature.[13]

Less concerned with the 1960s than Tranter's earlier writings, *Under Berlin* (1988) seems even more interested in the 1950s teen culture that spread so swiftly from America into Australia. "South Coast After Rain, 1960" invokes the year when Tranter himself turned seventeen; in one of its brief sketches,

> A car hurries along the road
> in the distance—you can just hear it—

a teenager driving his dad's new Holden
to meet the prettiest girl in town.

(*UNDER*, 10)

The teenager may be Tranter himself, and his experience then, the poem insists, is as serious as anything that happened later on:

Ah, the girl, how lovely she is:
at sixteen, how grown up.
He thinks of meeting her in twenty minutes,
    nothing else.

The radio glows in the dashboard,
the rock'n'roll sounds brand new.
Things will be like this
    forever.

(*UNDER*, 11)

A reader may add that adults know better—but Tranter asks whether we do; the boy and girl may "meet," "fight, separate, / grow old" (he elides marriage and childbirth), but the moment of their first encounter will matter more than all their subsequent lives: "Parked in the darkened driveway / they sink into a kiss. The radio / fills the car with emotion" (*Under*, 11).

Other parts of *Under Berlin* read like outright sequels to Tranter's earlier works. In "Debbie & Co." the chaotic self-display of the very young appears to be as good an example of human interaction as anything else. The poem takes place at a "Council" (public swimming) pool:

Half the school's there, screaming,
skylarking, and bombing the deep end.
Nicky picks up her Nikon
and takes it all in, the racket
and the glare. Debbie strikes a pose. . . .

            Under the democratic sun
her future drifts in and out of focus—
Tracey, Nicky, Chris, the whole arena
sinking into silence. Yet this is almost
Paradise, the Coke, the takeaway pizza,
a packet of Camels, Nicky's dark glassees

reflecting the way the light glitters on
anything wet.

(*UNDER*, 18)

We have observed similar scenes in Larkin: the young people in groups,
doing things only teens tend to do, reflect a kind of paradise. Yet this poem
(unlike "High Windows") contains no adult "I," no framing consciousness
of the poet's own, only Debbie and her friends. Noel Rowe writes that
"Debbie & Co." depicts "a world on the raw edge of adolescent ambiguity"
as "Debbie is momentarily aware of some trade-off between the past and
the future" (*Modern Australian Poets*, 40–41). This moment represents,
Rowe suggests, the "recognition of ambiguity" and the linguistic indeterminacy that Tranter highlights in his poetry generally: "the poem itself is
chemical gossip," a watery, splashy language that hopes to remain unfixed
(41).

"High School Confidential," another poem from *Under Berlin*, relates
only glancingly to the kitschy scare film about marijuana whose title it
shares but insistently to the legacy of teen culture (and of parodies, even
self-parodies, of teen culture) that the title suggests. Tranter depicts a mesh
of subcultures with their own proliferatingly associative talk—a realm like
poetry (or like Tranter's poetry) itself. The poem begins:

> Remember blotting paper? The Year of the Pen?
> Pen, I mean, not roller-ball. Come on, gang—
> you guys—applied to girls—those teenagers,
> they seem to have disappeared, behind
> a fit of the giggles, or a hot flush.

Tranter's brokenly conversational, stuttering lines here represent the
broken-up, gossipy, transitory conversation of its teen communities:

> One minute they're practicing the drawback,
> confusing innocence with ignorance, then
> you look into the glass, and they're gone.
> Did they just fade out, bathed in the glow
> from a fifties movie? Did the girls all wear
> plaid? And pony-tails? Hey Butch,
> let's have a pillow fight . . . outside,
> a snowfall blankets the small town.

(*UNDER*, 33)

As the teens, innocent or ignorant, recede from the poem (by growing up), they "just fade out"; no similarly vivid language, no other bodies can replace theirs, and the poem describes their absence along with the specially demarcated cultural space they create. That space for Tranter creates an occasion for lyric, because it also marks loss, as in another poem named after a B-movie, "The Creature from the Black Lagoon":

> The crew-cuts, the red and green
> checkered shirts adorn Dad's jalopy
> bumping away from the zone of focus
> like insignia stenciling a boundary
> around their tribe and epoch.
>
> (*UNDER*, 31)

"Tribe" here means both teenagers and Australians. The ethnographer Gaile McGregor finds in modern Australian culture an "obsession with 'coming-of-age' metaphors" and an unusual interest in intermediary or transitional zones such as beaches and suburbs (*Eccentric Visions*, 278, 219–21). If the adolescent "zone of focus" in Tranter represents a replacement for lost hopes about art, it can also represent Australia: a young country that wants to deem itself independent, too optimistic or naïve to see how its hectic transitions reflect international trends.

Even the most elegiac, most apparently personal parts of Tranter's writings remain awkwardly labile, unsure of themselves, tonally "immature.": "My parents of all people refused to permit / the sort of pleasure you need when it's night," he wrote in "Curriculum Vitae," and his later poems still seem to search for it (*Studio*, 94). The same poem cuts from a teen idyll to a memory of school; Tranter remembers "wanting to move away, to grow up, the big city," and then envisions his "muddled past" as

> a landscape
> seen from above, a film of a tiny town
> unrolling far below—you could have
> made it all up, knowing
> the teacher will always provide
> the answer you need, to save yourself
> from the shadow who follows you
> at the end of that delicate thread.
>
> (*STUDIO*, 95)

We want to believe (these lines suggest) in a greater Romantic ode, as in a model of adolescent self-discovery; we now know that such discoveries are at best mediated, at worst controlled or faked. Tranter represents himself, his stand-ins, and his poetry as both nostalgic for an adolescence always in part imaginary and as themselves in some ways adolescent—helplessly modern, excitable, liable to change.

"Tranter's poetry never believes in natural innocence," Rowe confirms; rather than the mythic childhood or the unspoiled landscapes favored by previous Australian poets, "it features cars, movies and adolescents" even when its setting is clearly rural (*Modern Australian Poets*, 42). No wonder, then, that Tranter's chief rival in Australian poetry, the antimodernist, anti-urban, fiercely agrarian and devoutly Catholic Les Murray, attacks the 1960s and all that they stand for in poems that also attack, explicitly, the idea and experience of adolescence. Murray's "Burning Want" describes his teen years as the worst in his life: "From just on puberty, I lived in funeral." He will have no truck with idealizations of adolescence, and his only interest in teen culture is to condemn it:

> But all my names were fat-names, at my new town school.
> Between classes, kids did erocide: destruction of sexual morale.
> Mass refusal of unasked love: that works. Boys cheered as seventeen-
> year-old girls came on to me, then ran back whinnying ridicule.
>
> (COLLECTED POEMS, 446)

"Burning Want" concludes by excoriating "what my school did to the world"; few poems (though Lowell's "St. Mark's" comes to mind) have looked so unflinchingly at the most humiliating segments of teen life.

In the context of Australian letters, "Burning Want" represents not just a catharsis but a quarrel between Murray's antimodernist, anti-1960s populism, on the one hand, and the Generation of '68 on the other; Murray condemns and dismisses, while Tranter investigates or emulates, whatever seems characteristic of modern teens. The two poets' antagonistic views of adolescence reflect, as well, two versions of pastoral. Pastoral in an Australian context can mean what I have denoted by it thus far: a literary mode that depicts self-consciously artificial, secluded, poetic Green Worlds. In this sense Tranter adapts—and at the same time mocks or scrambles—a teenage pastoral that replaces a discredited version of youth as revolution. Often, however, in Australian letters, "pastoral" means just "poetry about the countryside," about the rural Australia that has given that country its still-dominant self-image. Tranter himself grew up in very rural circumstances, to which his poetry rarely alludes; I might also say that he makes the altered or compromised "pastoral" of youth his replacement for the traditional "pastoral" (more properly, ruralist) poetry of earlier and rival schools.

In particular, it replaces or rivals the rural Australia that Les Murray views as the source of his strength; Murray, as David McCooey writes, has made "the pastoral" (in the sense of rural settings) "central to [his] development of [what he considers] an authentic Australian tradition" ("Contemporary Poetry," 171). Tranter retreats from adolescence as revolution into a renovated and ironized version of adolescence as pastoral; he does so partly in order to make his art adequate to a broader cultural uncertainty that he (and his critics) identify with an urban, secular postmodernism.

That uncertainty is for Murray something to loathe. We have seen, for most of this book, poets who find in adolescent states of mind, adolescent experience, or teen culture something to recommend, if not indeed something superior to adult life. These poets have been the ones who made, from twentieth-century adolescence, most of the distinctive poems about it. Adolescence is for many real people not their best, most interesting, or even riskiest time of life but simply their worst, most frustrating, least free. Yet poets who associated adolescence mostly with cruelty and misery have been understandably less inclined to derive their poetic forms from it.

Murray may therefore be one of the first poets in English to make such misery the dominant note not just of one poem (such as Lowell's "St. Mark's") but of a group on the subject; Murray's language, often flatfooted in its declarations, never showy, never evasive or "cool," matches his attitude toward adolescence, as Tranter's slippery language matches his. Reacting against the idea of innovation in literature as in social life, Murray identifies wholly both with his own adult "ancestors, / axemen, dairymen, horsebreakers" (note that each group has one occupation, which defines them) and with the awkward, quiet victims of school bullying, the least sociable members of any class (*Collected Poems*, 5). Take the victimized boy in "A Torturer's Apprenticeship": "be friends with him and you will never / be shaved or uplifted, cool or chic": "He must be suppressed, for modernity, / for youth, for speed, for sexual fun" (345). Student movements and their demonstrations ("demos") are simply extensions of teen bullying: "The first demos I saw, / before placards, were against me, / alone, for two years, with chants" (461).

Murray's poem "Rock Music" goes so far as to call popular, stylish teenagers "beautiful Nazis . . . who never leave school" (410). In context, this is not a claim about the fascinating aesthetics of fascism but a grim condemnation of sex appeal: "Sex is a Nazi. . . . To it, everyone's subhuman" (410). These lines appeared in a volume whose title, *Subhuman Redneck Poems*, announced Murray's role as spokesman for the rejected, the ugly, and the uncool. Murray's longest poem about a teenaged person lands as far as possible from any appreciation of teen culture. The segmented, self-isolating lines of "It Allows a Portrait in Line Scan at Age Fifteen" describe Murray's autistic son: *"Don't say word!* when he was eight forbade the word 'autistic' in his presence. / Battering questions about girlfriends cause a terrified look and blocked ears" (430–31).

Like Tranter (and like William Carlos Williams), Murray accepts both the equation of modern adolescent peer groups with modernity and the idea that a poetics that admires those peer groups will be some kind of modernism (or some sequel to it). For the "Boeotian" Murray, though, this equation means that modern adolescence, secular urban modernity, and modernism in poetry are all elitist, shallow, immoral and bad.[14] Murray's commitments to rural Australia (as opposed to the cities and suburbs where most Australians now live), to a national rather than cosmopolitan culture, to Catholic doctrine (with its notion of fixed authority), and to a style or antistyle that claims to resist all trends, indeed to resist historical change as such, let Murray write a poetry that goes out of its way to attack youth culture. Prominent poets not discussed in this book (Elizabeth Bishop, for example) largely ignore the developing idea of adolescence, and plenty of comic poets (Ciardi, for example), have mocked it. Murray may be the only prominent and aesthetically original twentieth-century poet who takes sustained notice of modern adolescence in order to attack it seriously and to repudiate all it represents.

6

Midair

T HINKERS OF THE 1950s, as I described in chapter 3, warned adults about the supposedly vanishing adolescent; social critics of recent years instead describe the vanishing adult. Richard Rodriguez (born in 1944) writes that his own "baby-boom generation made "youth . . . into a lifestyle, a politics, an aesthetic, a religion. . . . We do not know how to mark the end of adolescence" ("Invention of Adolescence," 125–26). Lawrence Grossberg calls American "baby-boomers . . . a generation that was never taught to be adults or even to value that identity" ("Political Status," 42).[1] These social changes, too, have prompted poems. We have seen already the formation and dissolution of the hopeful, even revolutionary mode in which poets of the 1960s celebrated the new, the young, and the incomplete; we have seen newer modes devoted to uncertainty, hesitancy, even indeterminacy, and to an adolescence defined by those qualities, in Robert Lowell, John Tranter, and Paul Muldoon. We have seen, too, how Laura Kasischke, Jorie Graham, and other female poets have organized poems and books around a female adolescence experienced as exhilaration and danger, around the risky new visibility of teen girls' bodies, and around the lost security of a homosocial girlhood.

That feminist project is not the only one going. The male poets of the American Baby Boom (roughly, those born between 1944 and 1962), discussed for part of this chapter, often treat adolescence with a far less ambivalent nostalgia; its end is the end of the 1960s, the end of hope, and the end of the poem. The youngest American poets, by contrast, sometimes write as if adolescence had no end. Many of them treat adolescence as a set of subcultures and signifiers which they have not yet left (and may never leave) behind. For these poets—as for the young Muldoon—maturity, authority, and stability do not offer stances or ways of speaking worth choosing or even worth trying to imagine; adolescence, and the subcultures that it harbors, offer a locus of present selfhood, a source of language, and a trope for the contemporary poem.

❖ ❖ ❖ ❖ ❖

Patricia Meyer Spacks in 1980 described "a movement toward increasingly intense identification with the young on the part of novelists who evoke them. More and more now, as social organization provides less satisfaction, *everyone* wants to be an outsider. The adolescent can appear heroic in not belonging; the novelist can express through adolescent characters a wistful longing to share their condition" (*The Adolescent Idea*, 294). Such speculations have not been confined to America; Julia Kristeva writes that the adolescent in Freudian and post-Freudian psychoanalysis—with his (or her) open-ended quest for self-definition—corresponds to the normal adult of our time, when "changes in the contemporary family, the blurring of sex roles and parental roles, and the lifting of moral and religious taboos" mean that "subjects are no longer structured according to rigorous prohibitions or laws" (*New Maladies*, 136). The end or weakening of such inherited "laws" has gone hand in hand, for many poets, with a rejection of inherited forms or of any form that implies that lives conform to stories—what Lyn Hejinian names "the rejection of closure" (*Language of Inquiry*). In Hejinian's own *My Life* (1980, 1987), "the person posits itself elsewhere, adolescent-like, as a figure in the distance escaping, while awaiting the advent of its more glorious self" (44).

Poets writing after the 1960s often find "glorious selves" in adolescence; often they explain that glory or lyricism or freedom may be found *only* there. The Canadian poet George Bowering's *Kerrisdale Elegies* (1984) are, in part, a rewriting of Rillke's *Duino Elegies* to fit contemporary urban conditions. One of Bowering's elegies reconfigures Rilke's yearnings so that they suggest pop songs and teens. Where Rilke has "Wer, wenn ich schriee, hörte mich denn aus der Engel / Ordnungen? [Who, if I cried out, would hear me among the angels'/ hierarchies?]" (*Selected Poetry*, 150–51) Bowering begins, "If I did complain, who among my friends / would hear?" ("Kerrisdale" 32). Bowering goes on:

> When your heart hungers,
>   sing a song of six-
> teen, remember your own maidenly love

and the girls that aroused it,

                                     make them famous.

Remember their plain friends who danced so well

because they never got into a back seat.

Bring them all back, become a lyric poet again.

Identify with heroes who die for love

and a terrific image,

                            you'll live forever

in your anguished exalted metaphors.

                            Oh yeah.

(34)

To "become a lyric poet again" is to become adolescent, not even a nine-teenth-century scholar-gypsy but a modern, dance-frequenting, backseat-necking teen; to use the high language of odes now is to say "Oh yeah." If Bowering pokes fun at the language of rock-star celebrity, in which exalta-tion implies fame (and vice versa), he offers nothing better with which to replace it; the language that for Rilke fit an adult's communion with non-human nature now (Bowering implies) fits (and, perhaps, fits *only*) teenag-ers in love.

Teen years mean sexual energy and secret, powerful language, too, in C. D. Wright's "Autographs" (1997), a poem that suggests that the vividness it depicts may not outlast high school. Each of Wright's forty-four lines tropes the self-descriptions, "senior superlatives," and intimate signatures found in American high school yearbooks. Where yearbooks convention-ally celebrate officially sanctioned attributes and aspirations ("most popu-lar," for example, or "most likely to succeed"), Wright's sometimes comic, sometimes breathlessly excited fragments celebrate sex:

Site of their desire: against a long high wall under vapor light
Most likely to succeed: the perpetual starting over
Inside his mouth: night after night after night
Directive: by any means necessary
Song: "Anarchy in the UK"
Sign: hibiscus falls off the ledge
Nightmare: actual horse seated on your ribs
Sonic relations: silent, breathy, ululant.

(*TREMBLE*, 13)

Sexual undertones turn into dominant notes: "Rambone: I need it I need it now / Back of her throat: slit light / Wish: compassion . . . Other sites: corridor, phone booth, shower, elevator, locker, filling station, boat dock, drive-in, cafeteria line" (14). The poem ends: "PS: have a wonderful summer and a wonderful life" (15). Will these imaginative, sexually hungry personae have wonderful lives? Perhaps, but perhaps not: the high school language here can produce celebratory fireworks because it does not have to tell us what came next.[2]

These individual poems by Wright and Bowering (born, respectively, in 1949 and 1935) continue the line of alert homages to and self-conscious modernist emulations of adolescence, the line that began with Williams. Larry Levis (1946–1996) offers instead the concentrated nostalgia in which male Baby Boom poets of adolescence have specialized; he made that nostalgia the cornerstone of his art. "The Poet at Seventeen" (its title perhaps a play on Rimbaud's "Poètes du Sept Ans") recalls

The trees, wearing their mysterious yellow sullenness
Like party dresses. And parties I didn't attend . . .
And inside, the adults with their cocktails before dinner,
The way they always seemed afraid of something,
And sat so rigidly, although the land was theirs.

(SELECTED, 82)

For all their disorienting solitudes, the poet's teen years allowed him a kind of freedom incompatible with adult social life. At that time Levis was closer to nature (for this poet a relatively untroubled concept) than he can be now. Adults owned the land (both housing and farmland), but only the young could possess it.

Levis has said that during his own teen years, poetry "gave voice to a kind of adolescent loneliness or alienation I felt. And it made sense of things" (Kelen, "After the Obsession," 33). He would come to see his later poetry both as a way to revivify those feelings, and as a way to return to the landscape and life-world that produced them, a life-world that included not only the agricultural landscapes of the Central Valley but also Levis's high school disappointments and friends (in particular, his friend Zamoi, who died in Vietnam). "I wanted poetry that would establish contact with . . . the world I knew in high school," he explained (Bargen, "Levis and Bargen," 115–16).[3] Levis uses the word *adolescence* as a modern name for Romantic power, for everything inimical to reason, practicality, and compromise: "if death is an adolescent, closing his eyes to the music / On the radio of that passing car, / I think he does not know his own strength" (*Selected*, 84). A poem entitled "Adolescence" remembers a romance, at fifteen, with a girl who would die of spinal meningitis; he wished then, and may wish now, "to disappear wholly into someone / Else, as into a wish on a birthday, the candles trembling" (*Selected*, 84). A poem called "Whitman" (whose speaker is Walt Whitman himself) implies that the power of fluid self-creation embodied in *Leaves of Grass* has passed, in 1980s America, to teens, who do not understand what they inherit: "Now that I'm required reading in your high schools, / Teenagers call me a fool" (*Selected*, 105).

In the long lines and detailed, almost novelistic settings of Levis's final book, *Elegy* (1997), adulthood means failure even more strongly than adolescence means hope. "In 1967" remembers Levis's grueling summer job:

> Some people spent their lives then, having visions.
> But in my case, the morning after I dropped mescaline
> I had to spray Johnson grass in a vineyard of Thompson Seedless
> My father owned—& so, still feeling the holiness of all things
> Living, holding the spray gun in one hand & driving with the other,
> The tractor pulling the spray rig & its sputtering motor—
> Row after row, I sprayed each weed I found
> That looked enough like Johnson grass, a thing alive that's good
> For nothing at all, with a mixture of malathion & diesel fuel,
> And said to each tall weed, as I coated it with a lethal mist,
> *Dominus vobiscum*, &, sometimes, *mea culpa*.
>
> (*ELEGY*, 5)

Levis's paid employment during the Summer of Love involved killing things that would otherwise grow up to be useless. As Levis accomplished this depressing, practical task, he experienced quasi-Shelleyan, drug-induced sympathies with a songbird, "part of me taking wing," as if to flee his own too practical future. The poem concludes not in Levis's father's vineyard but with a wide-angle shot of the Baby Boom's fate:

> As the summer went on, some were drafted, some enlisted
> In a generation that would not stop falling, a generation
> Of leaves sticking to body bags, & when they turned them
> Over, they floated back to us on television, even then,
> In the Summer of Love, in 1967,
> When riot police waited beyond the doors of perception,
> And the best thing one could do was get arrested.
>
> (6)

"Arrested" may include the sense "arrested development": it is as if the poet says *stop me before I grow up*. The falling leaves are Shelleyan ("Ode to the

West Wind"), as is the sense that a dramatic death might be better than ordinary life; what is not Shelleyan is the association of that sense with the
particular experience of a generation, of all those who were teens at that
time.

This view persists through Levis's other late poems: in "Elegy with an
Angel at Its Gate," the 1960s are "an age / Of revolutions that will . . . Free
everyone, put all of us to one side / To be part of another, larger thing that
ends / By becoming a movie about it" (*Elegy*, 60). For Levis (as to many of
his coevals) the decade called "the sixties" is to America what each adult's
teen years are to that adult: a promise that, of its nature, must partly fail. In
"Elegy for Whatever Had a Pattern in It" (note "Had," not "Has"), "the
Summer of Love has become the moss of tunnels" (*Elegy*, 33). The poem
concludes, "As if we're put on the earth to forget the ending" (38). Another
of Levis's elegies declares, "Poverty is what happens at the end of any story,
including this one, / When there are too many stories," "When one condition is as good as any other" (*Elegy*, 51). That poem then retells the myth of
Daphne, whom Levis envisions as an attempted suicide, "the only widow in
her high school, // After she has decided to turn herself // Into a tree" (*Elegy* 51). ("Turn herself into" means both "metamorphose" and "swerve her
vehicle so that she collides with.") Levis's long lines imagine the spaces occupied by lives that should have been full, lives hungry for experience, all of
which have already and inevitably fallen short.

We can find these patterns of nostalgia—of youth as energy already
wasted, potential already misspent—expressed in different geographical
and cultural spaces by Yusef Komunyakaa. In Komunyakaa's poems about
playground and high school sports, innocent energies are at once the motive for a poem and the representative of powers (either in American history or in the life course) that now seem lost. In "Slam, Dunk & Hook," the
"hang time" involved in a basketball shot (the time during which a player
appears suspended in midair) and the arc of the released basketball represent the empowered interval between childhood and adult life. The boys in
Komunyakaa's remembered pickup game

> could almost
> Last forever, poised in midair
> Like storybook seamonsters.
> A high note hung there
> A long second. Off
> The rim. We'd corkscrew
> Up & dunk balls that exploded
> The skullcap of hope & good

Intention. Lanky, all hands
& feet.

(*PLEASURE DOME*, 300-301)

The young athletes who dunk look neither innocent nor harmless but rather inexperienced and powerful. Their aestheticized and rule-governed competition presses back against impending adulthood and death:

When Sonny Boy's mama died
He played nonstop all day, so hard
Our backboard splintered. . . .

We had moves we didn't know
We had. Our bodies spun
On swivels of bone & faith,
Through a lyric slipknot
Of joy, & we knew we were
Beautiful & dangerous.

(301)

Sonny Boy's name is no accident; by encapsulating himself in a young man's game that makes him the aggressor, he avoids the larger world of mothers, and of mortality.

In his study of poems about sports, Don Johnson finds that "basketball poems celebrate the creation of ephemeral identities dependent upon the ebb and flow of a particular competition"; "poem after poem stresses getting into 'the zone,' rising above physical or sociological limitations—transcendence" (*The Sporting Muse*, 90). Such transcendence is always temporary, and perhaps unrepeatable. "Love of the game," writes John Edgar Wideman, "rises like the ball from a shooter's hand, rising"; "as sure as you're up, you're also coming down" (*Hoop Roots*, 18). For Komunyakaa, the arc of the ball is the arc of youth, the time between inchoate innocence and hardened experience, even between the start of a sentence and its sudden (unpredictable, syncopated) end. Spinning temporarily around and above the reality principle, the basketball players act out a power that—older, apart—none of them will have.

A similar pattern governs Komunyakaa's "White Port & Lemon Juice," in which illicit drinking, sexual exploration, early rock'n'roll, and high school football are all of a piece and belong to a pleasurable, now lost world. Johnson notes that football poems (unlike other sports poems) usually focus on physical pain and bodily failure. Troped or simulated destruction in sports is far preferable to the real danger that may overtake Komunyakaa or his teammates later on. Yet the erotic and alcoholic idyll of boys, girls, and homemade wine coolers at the "school dance" (after the football game) involves its own experience of defeat:

> We'd doo-wop song after song
> & hold the girls in rough arms,
> Not knowing they didn't want to be
> Embraced with the strength
> We used against fullbacks
> & tight ends on the fifty.
> Sometimes they rub against us,
> Preludes to failed flesh,
> Trying to kiss defeat
> From our eyes.
>
> (*PLEASURE DOME*, 326-37)

Poets of Komunyakaa's generation less attuned than he to autobiographical anecdote can also see their own adolescence as promise, their maturity as comedown and conundrum. The disappointments inherent in any passage from potentiality to actuality, from hope to realization, from adolescence to adulthood—one of Ashbery's many subjects—become for John Koethe perhaps the chief subject. Indeed, what Koethe adds to Stevens and Ashbery (who together account for almost all his verse techniques) is a greater concentration on the stages of the modern life course. In Koethe's "Sunday Evening"—an almost parodically Stevensian poem which features "intricate evasions" and "ambiguous undulation"—the time of reconciliation to disillusion is not the time when pigeons flock downward to darkness, but the time when "the adolescent / Boys that used to hang around the parking lot are gone" (*North*, 141). Koethe's "Secret Amplitude" begins by proposing that "the hardest feeling is the one / Of unrealized possibility"; "the proof, / If there is one, is by analogy / With the kind of adolescent 'knowledge'" Koethe "had on those afternoons in college / When I'd go to New York, and the evening / Deepened, and then the lights came on" (*North*, 211, 214). Such "knowledge" fades to black; nothing replaces it.

Koethe, as Willard Spiegelman has written, "accepts liminality, thresholds, our in-between status, as the major mark of identity"; his "reconsideration of nostalgia" finds both its most heartening examples of in-betweenness and the chief object of its belated nostalgia in his own

generation's adolescence ("Walllace Stevens," 183, 179). Middle age, belated-
ness, and the late-Romantic Stevensian point of view out of which Koethe
writes all consist for Koethe (as they had not for Stevens) of an understanding that the promise of youth, of his teens, will always remain beyond
his grasp. "A Parking Lot with Trees" asks, "Where is that person whom I
took myself to be? / Why has my life been mostly puzzlement, and hope,
and inexperience?" How did he feel, or think, about his future, when he was
far younger than he is now?

> I thought that there was time for me to start all over,
> To embark upon a program of interior definition
> That eventually might yield a quietly spectacular conclusion
> (But a private one) against the gradually emerging background of late
> Adolescent melodies that hadn't quite begun and
> That would soon be over. Cold midwinter sunlight
> Slanted through my dormitory window
> And each year I looked and felt no older.
>
> (NORTH, 188)

Koethe no longer feels he has that kind of time—his project now is not to
become the person he wants to be but to understand the person he was
back then. This project—less Stevensian than it is Wordsworthian—differs
from Wordsworth's in that what Koethe wants to understand is not a childhood innocence nor a connection to nature but a sense of choice, threshold,
and intellectual exploration that he associates with student life and even
with dormitory settings and pop songs: "I wish the songs that moved me
once might come to me again / And help me understand the person that
I've gradually become" (*North*, 190–91).

The nostalgia that for Koethe empowers lyric poetry points not only to
youth in general but to adolescence in the mid-1960s, when Koethe's generation attended college. "When There Was Time" begins by telling us
what Koethe studied there:

> Physics and—what?—existentialism?
> Guitar heroes and singer songwriters
> And death? You were supposed to write poems
> Breath by breath, movies were as serious
>
> As novels, and tomorrow was the name
> Of a different kind of life, a life

> Beyond imagining, hiding in the
> Darkness behind the adolescent sun.
> (*SALLY'S*, 51)

"You" supposed yourself then to be "preparing for a place . . . Where adolescence was supposed to end"; "Who'd want to go there now?" Koethe muses, deciding, instead, "I want the darkness back" (*Sally's*, 51–52). Koethe's nostalgia exceeds Ashbery's, as his flatter, clearer language differs from Ashbery's not only in the directness of its statements but in the ways by which Koethe links that nostalgia to a particular generation and its cultural markers. His consistent focus on his own life course and his attention to the connections between that life course and publicly available cultural history link him not to Ashbery and Stevens but to Larkin and Lowell. In his latest book, *Sally's Hair*, Koethe likens himself to the Larkin of "Sad Steps" / "Groping through the dark at 4 am to piss," "growing old / Without ever growing up" (*Sally's*, 43). The concluding poem in that book asks how "That adolescent image of myself dissolved, to be replaced by— / By *what?*" (*Sally's*, 83) Larkin's Katharine and the narrators in Kasischke's novels asked the same question; Koethe's answer—that "agency itself" vanishes in adulthood—resembles theirs (*Sally's*, 83).

Koethe's poems thus define his own adulthood—much as Levis's and Komunyakaa's do—by its distance from the remembered promises of his own and his generation's youth. Koethe's long, almost languid, indefinitely extensible sentences measure the distance from past to present self. "Falling Water," the long title poem from his 1997 volume, imagines

> The quaint ideas of perfection swept away like
> Adolescent fictions as the real forms of life
> Deteriorate with manically increasing speed. . . .
>
> Why can't the more expansive ecstasies come true?
> I met you more than thirty years ago, in 1958,
> In Mrs. Wolford's eighth grade history class. . . .
> (*NORTH*, 240)

That classroom (a sunlit, social, open interior, as the house of Koethe's previous stanza seems a private and closed one) exemplifies adolescence itself, a "half-completed / Structure made of years and willed with images / And gestures emblematic of the past." He relates that past in pop-cultural shorthand:

I can see us steaming off the cover of the Beatles'
Baby-butcher album at your house in Mission Bay;
And three years later listening to the Velvet
Underground performing in a roller skating rink.
Years aren't texts, or anything *like* texts;
And yet I often think of 1968 that way, as though
That single year contained the rhythms of the rest,
As what began in hope and eagerness concluded in
Intractable confusion, as the wedding turned into a
Puzzling fiasco over poor John Godfrey's hair.

(*NORTH,* 242)

The Beatles album in question is the original cover for *Yesterday and Today* (1966), which showed the Fab Four as butchers slicing the heads off dolls. Recalled after protests, the album became valuable to collectors, though the first fans who bought it could not have known that—just as the value of this moment in Mission Bay may not have struck Koethe until much later.[4] Koethe uses rock and roll (both the Beatles' and the Velvets') as a signifier of adolescence *and* as a sign that its naïve glories are no more.

So do many poets of his generation. Rock's ties to youth are as old as the music itself; Keir Keightley writes that Bill Haley's "Rock Around the Clock" (1955) "represents the final step in the mainstream recognition of separate, age-graded taste cultures for teens and adults" ("Reconsidering Rock," 112–13). While a few rockers sought "poetic" grandeur (a story I will not tell here), Baby Boomers who published books of poems after the 1960s used rock to invoke youth, rawness, energy, spontaneity, sex—all the supposedly adolescent qualities they could not claim for poetry itself. They wrote about rock when they wanted to think about the youth they felt they had lost, about its lost innocence or its failed revolutions.

Jim Elledge's anthology *Sweet Nothings* (1994), devoted to "Rock and Roll in American Poetry," compiles such poems. Elledge's volume focuses on Baby Boomers, for whom, Elledge writes, "the elements of rock and roll incorporated into their poetry . . . almost always represent . . . a time of innocence—or an era of innocence turned sour" (xix). Ronald Wallace's near-sonnet "Sound System," for example, remembers "necking / to 'Little Darlin'" and other 1950s hits "as my father from his wheelchair in his study / calls out to keep it down, and Buddy Holly, / The Big Bopper, and Richie Valens leave the ground" (Elledge, *Sweet Nothings*, 87). To Wallace, rock means youth, innocence, sex, rebellion, hope, and immediacy. Poetry, *by contrast*, frames those qualities and compares them to a disappointing present; poetry, unlike rock, makes us notice loss—the father's lost legs, or the loss of Holly, Valens, and the Bopper in their plane crash.[5] Similarly nostalgic examples occur throughout Elledge's volume; Nancy Schoenberger, for example, writes that when "Van Morrison sang *brown-eyed girl* . . . those songs were always me in my green time" (Elledge, *Sweet Nothings*, 207).

Reviewing *Sweet Nothings*, Thomas Swiss complained that "most [of the poems] embed their rock-related references in stories about adolescence" ("Poetry and Pop," 8). Poems about rock—until quite recently—have turned on such reflections: the reasons lie not only in the history of rock but also in the history of poetry. Rock music brings with it a far stronger claim to signify adolescence and to convey immediate, authentic feeling than any claims that literary poetry can now make. In asking readers to compare poems about rock songs to the songs that these poems describe, poems about rock admit their own failure to find or to keep the inner autonomy that we often hope poems can give—and that we associate with youth.

Remember, here, Thom Gunn's "Elvis Presley," published in 1957 and discussed in chapter four; remember that Gunn's admiring poem never sounds like the singer it praises—in fact, it never tries. Instead Gunn shows virtues (self-control, logic, reflection) that Elvis's singles seem to lack. Gunn, though, keeps his rock and roll poem impersonal, without reference to his own remembered youth. American Baby Boomers make such references the core of their rock and roll poems, many of which might fit under the not entirely ironized title Dave Smith gives to one poem in his sequence *Fate's Kite*: "The Endless Days of Sixties Sunshine" remembers how Smith and his then-girlfriend would "ride through valleys of years, Little Richard" and "Sam Cooke rocking between her half-opened knees" (37)

Smith's poem—and Wallace's, Koethe's and Schoenberger's—thus sound—when they bring up rock and roll—"sentimental" (or "reflective," *sentimentalisch*), in Friedrich Schiller's special sense. Modern poets, Schiller wrote in 1795, "will either *be* nature or they will *look for* lost nature"; the first are naïve and need only "feel" to create, the second, *sentimentalisch* and self-conscious (*On the Naïve*, 35, 68). Poets who put rock music into their poems cast rock as "naïve," natural, authentic, youthful, and their own poetry as "sentimental," reflective, artificial, grown-up. Baby Boomers write such poems almost whenever they write about rock at all. James Seay's poem on Chuck Berry and "Johnny B. Goode" relies on the changes Seay brings to Berry's familiar lyrics:

What a wonderful dumb story of America: country boy
who never learned to read or write too well, but could play

a guitar just like ringing a bell and his mother
told him he would be a man, the leader
of a big old band, maybe someday his name in lights.
(ELLEDGE, *SWEET NOTHINGS*, 43)

Seay's lines end up deliberately less euphonious and much less regular than the line breaks we would hear in the lyrics themselves. The poem comes off secondary, belated, dependent; Seay's poem, unlike Berry's song, *sounds* older and less hopeful than the "country boy" it describes.

Such contrasts also dominate David Wojahn's *Mystery Train* (1990), a history of rock in thirty-five poems, most of them off-rhymed and highly colloquial sonnets. In sonnet number 6, "Jerry Lee Lewis' Secret Marriage to Thirteen-Year Old First Cousin Revealed During British Isles Tour, 1959: His Manager Speaks," the Killer's songs convey the sublime, youthful energy his own grotesque career cannot preserve. "Go ahead and play piano with your nose," Wojahn admonishes Lewis, "And tear your shirt off singing 'High School Confidential,' / But the Feds'll take the Cadillac and clothes" (30). Wojahn's sonnets assume, as Kevin Stein writes, that "speaker and audience" have a "common cultural knowledge" that includes "the Baby Boom's generational myth" (*Private Poets*, 141). That myth describes the promise of 1960s youth, casting that generation as uniquely important, its teens as promising, its adulthood as failure, and its poets' goal as nostalgic or disillusioned reflection on adolescence, that is, on a hope already lost.[6]

❖ ❖ ❖ ❖ ❖

About adolescence in contemporary America and the modes it inspires in contemporary American poetry, we need not let the Baby Boom have the last word. Steven Mintz finds that now even more than in decades past, "we have institutionalized youth as a separate stage of life"; "the young are told to grow up [i.e. leave presexual, family-dominated childhood] fast, but also that they needn't grow up [i.e. assume adult responsibilities] at all" (*Huck's Raft*, 347, 381). Writing in the *New York Times Magazine*, Daniel Zalewski identified "infantilized adults," "teenagers trapped inside the bodies of grown-ups," in film and television: "What united all these stories from 2001," he wrote, "is the idea that adolescent angst often dominates people's lives well past adolescence. Or at least it does in contemporary America," where "so many Americans sail into their 30's without getting married or having kids" ("Infantilized Adults"). Three years later, also in the *Times*,

Christopher Noxon described "kidults" or "rejuveniles," "from childless fans of kiddie music to the grown-up readers of 'Harry Potter'"; he quotes the sociologist Frank Furendi calling this "deeply troubling trend" evidence that "adulthood has got nothing attractive about it anymore" (Noxon, "I Don't Want to Grow Up!").

The psychologist Jeffrey Arnett argues that developed nations in general, and the United States in particular, now harbor a new stage of life, "from the time [when young people] leave high school to the time they reach full adulthood" (*Emerging*, vi). Arnett calls this stage "emerging adulthood," though its subjective and emotional components sound very much like adolescence as older psychologists and social critics defined it. Emerging adulthood is "a highly self-reflective time of life," when emerging adults "struggle with uncertainty even as they revel in being freer than they ever were in childhood or ever will be once they take on the full weight of adult responsibilities" (viii, 3). Arnett sounds at times just like Friedenberg and just like Erikson: emerging adulthood "is the age of identity explorations," of "instability," "the most self-focused age of life," "the age of feeling in-between," and "the age of possibilities" (8).

Arnett's subjects "associate becoming an adult with stagnation"; "in their late teens and early twenties, marriage, home, and children are seen . . . as perils to be avoided" (218, 6). "In some respects," says one interviewee, "I feel like an adult, and in some respects I kind of hope I never become an adult" (219). "Emerging adults like these," Arnett adds, "idealize childhood"; they even appear to idealize high school (220).[7] Arnett's subjects rarely call themselves adolescents (14). And yet from the perspectives we have seen in this book—in which both poets and other sorts of writers define adolescence by its peer culture, shared tastes, instability, in-betweenness, self-exploration, and self-consciousness—this cohort represents (what less systematic social critics described or feared) the broader-than-ever, widely sanctioned, and even celebrated persistence of adolescence through the lives of people much older than high school age—old enough to have published books of verse.

The phase of life after presexual childhood and before adult responsibility no longer carries the promise of the 1960s that an emerging youth culture could transform a nation or repair its flaws. Poets born in the 1960s or 1970s likely associate such a promise not with their own youth but with that of their parents. On the other hand, that phase of life lasts longer than ever; some writers suggest that it never ends. And these changes in adolescence as idea and as lived experience inform the most recent poets' attempts to depict it. First and second books by recent poets can find exhilarated or puzzled antinarrative forms, neither pastoral nor revolutionary but satu-rated with argot, devoted to uncertainty, less given to closure than those before. They, too, see adolescence as preferable to a hollow adulthood, but they remain identified *with* adolescence, which they see first and last as an in-group, a set of subcultural signifiers. They write about adolescence or something like it—its volatility, antipathy to authority, distinctive argot, and visibly dissident tastes—as it were from within; they are less often nos-talgic or dejected than they are exhilarated and secretive.

Pamela Lu's *Pamela: A Novel* (1998)—a novella-length text that may be categorized as fiction, an essay, or simply "poet's prose"—makes this atti-tude unmistakable: the undecidabilities of contemporary poststructuralist theories represent, for the narrator and her friends (known only by initials), the inconclusiveness of postcollegiate life. Lu writes that

> Every generation preoccupied itself with the struggle to produce some-thing new—a defining moment, action or style that would mark it as unique and constitute an answer to the question of "Who are you?" or more often "Who were you?" Now we too were faced with the very same question and wondering if we were destined to be remembered for our refusal to answer the question.
>
> (43)

Lu's generation faces interminable membership in a notional subculture based on an aporia:

> My mother had gone to school to believe more and more with each passing year until finally she believed in all that was right and fitting to believe in and became more or less a convinced, educated person. I on the other hand had gone to school with the objective of doubting everything so that in the end I could not bring myself to believe in anything and was unable to graduate. My mother had graduated and become a graduate student, while I remained an undergraduate and undergraduated myself in every mode of thinking even after I had attained my degree.
>
> (72)

Lu may be remembering John Ashbery, with whose lines on the subject my book began: "None of us ever graduates from college / And perhaps think-ing not to grow up / Is the right kind of maturity for us" (88). The undecid-abilities and uncertainties that poets of Lu's generation found in Ashbery (among others) now fit the undecidabilities of the life course, undecidabilities whose shareable nature makes Lu's art possible. "For latecomers like R and me, it seemed as though the examination had been postponed indefinitely, and the question of our admission to the living suspended like aircraft over the interminable stretch of ocean between continents" (96). Lu's poem or novel therefore ends as her trans-Pacific flight crosses the International Date Line; the poet is stuck between times and suspended in midair.

Other poets identify with decidedly nonacademic, and racier, youth. Mark Bibbins populates *Sky Lounge* (2004) with club kids, runaways, would-be rock stars, and groupies' slang. "Arrival with Dark Circles and Premonition" depicts the poet's alter ego (the poet as virile youth, Stevens might say) as a drugged-out runaway, a neo-Rimbaud whom the adult world treats as a spectacle:

Say his name   is Jared or Zak

bumper-sticker vandal   T-shirt philosopher

tracking a god that's nothing

more than sleep   with schnapps and dregs

of opium   scraped from foil.   When he wakes up

in a park at dawn where armored cars   sail the sky

say all the statues have moved

have turned   to look at him.
(10)

An earlier poet (the Stevens of "Owl's Clover," or the Lowell of "For the Union Dead") would place a public leader on that public monument; here, instead, monuments gaze on the young man, whose narcissism—if we choose to call it that—seems preferable to adult disregard.

Brenda Shaughnessy's "Arachnolescence" (from *Interior with Sudden Joy*, 1999) embraces the ambiguities of teen years and teen personae in an indefinitely extensible present tense. Shaughnessy's title, like her fast-talking persona, is neither wholly one thing nor the other, and it attracts attention for being in between. Shaughnessy's rapid, percussive lines insist that the bodily changes she describes (menarche, apparently, among them: "I've

bullied you / into a few cramps myself") are sources of individuality, attention, usable creative power:

> Love me in my strict empire of phantom pain,
> in my wiliest contempt for all that is mere fever
> and sweat, strain and maculate, florid and maternal,
> decent and plain. I want theater, the domain
> of intoxicated grief. And spifflicated louts are we,
> absolute gourmands of the ugliest meal.
>
> (49)

Adult women are "florid and maternal"; Shaughnessy's theatrical spider
girl is risky, sexy, liberating instead: "Give me liberty / or give me everything you've ever loved" (50). The *Oxford English Dictionary* defines "to spif-
flicate" as "to deal with in such a way as to confound or overcome completely; to treat or handle roughly or severely; to crush, destroy."
Shaughnessy's apparently indestructible, yet "spifflicated" gang may derive
their adjective instead from "spiffy" (stylish), or from smoking spliffs (marijuana), which would make them hungry indeed ("gourmands").

Over and over the talented or promising new poets of recent years organize their effects and their tones around some sort of adolescent persona,
some avowedly immature voice, whose unpredictable language gives the
poems their characteristic, contemporary, effects. Jane Yeh in *Marabou*
(2005) portrays herself among "Teen Spies": "I'm the smallest. Elijah is our
control. / Our mission? That's undercover for now . . . *I am / past seventeen
and have never been kissed*" (23). Matt Hart in *Who's Who Vivid* (2006),
though he tells us that he is "thirty years old," associates his yearnings with
anyone's teens: "I don't know whether I'm talking / or if I'm nineteen. I do
know I need a haircut. / And the world opens its lips and spits . . . a fountain of youthful exuberance" (55, 39).

Such effects can dominate a volume. Shanna Compton's first book,
Downspooky (2005) opens by announcing that "we"—the audience the poet
imagines and also the group of people she represents—have no adult identity worth the name: "We refer intermittently to teenagers, / mercurial
freshmen. We who lead / do not need audible traffic signals" (1). Compton
wants to establish her identity as that of a generation and her generation as
especially unfixed, uninterested in, or else unable to achieve stability of
voice and point of view. In "Thank Y'All for Appreciating My Animals,"
"Her teens were actually twenties; / they were matter-of-factly male"; "The
teens shimmy / out of their shirts if you let them" (15). Life stories, continu-

ous causal narratives in which people grow or learn, are always for Compton unreliable and unsatisfying quotations from books she did not write: "He'd determined over the last few weeks that *We should have married before the baby was born* had been lifted from a book with a corner turned down on a page beginning with the word *disappointment*" (13). Compton's poems are less stories than they are puzzles and teases; one entitled "Clues Down" compares itself to a crossword.

We have seen something like this point of view—in which teen culture represents flux and uncertainty and the poem itself is a kind of puzzle—in Tranter and Muldoon; Compton and her contemporaries share that outlook but embed subcultural signals more deeply in their poems, often forsaking older structures of reference and torquing or rejecting prose syntax in order to do so. The code of Compton's poems is frankly teenage and subcultural (as well as Southern): its loci are drive-ins, garages, vague hangouts, malls, sidewalks, even sports fields. Compton even makes a mock-nostalgic poem out of school mascots:

I'll see your panther
and raise you wildcat,
so how you like that?
Skateboard the pristine paths
of the swank stripmall before
Grand Opening.

Grand indeed.

(32)

Compton calls the poem "Those Days of Pomp and Vigor"; after the first stanza (quoted above) comes another about high school football games and another about "totem animals" and a yearbook's senior picture. Her point is not only that poetry is its own subculture, with its own idiom, much like "jock" or "skater" subcultures in schools, but also that these terms call into being an energetic community more worthwhile than any substitutes from a recognizable adulthood—though "more worthwhile" may be faint praise, like "Grand indeed."

Rock and roll enters this new and antinostalgic poetry of adolescence in (among other books) Ange Mlinko's *Matinées* (1999), which imagines the adventures and misgivings of educated young people in Boston and Providence. Where Baby Boom rock and roll poems usually invoke chart hits to describe a lost youth, Mlinko names (and models some poems around)

obscure, sometimes local, rock songs and bands, implying that her own poetics and her favorite rock songs occupy common ground. Her poem "'No
one shone there'" recalls trips through New England:

> the blind men & in wheelchairs down by the winged memorial
> wash hands in the bathroom, sit cemetery cadillac
> baby Old Glory over gravesite, lawn toy of snuffling hamlet
> town center to town center
>
>   O Secret Stars stay secret.

(31)

The Secret Stars are also a Boston rock band whose contemplative, hushed
songs earned them devoted, if never numerous fans. The poet shares with
the band she names a "secret" world of peregrinations and distances to
which the flag, the Cadillac, and the older men cannot belong.[8]

Reviewing Jennifer Moxley's first book, *Imagination Verses* (1996),
Mlinko found "a pride of identity, parallel to the indie rock world's, that
thrives on belonging to and chafing against one's comrades" ("Fighting
Words"). She has also written about her own use of rock music: "The im-
brication of *Matinees* with Boston, indie rock, etc. is almost too overwhelming for me to summarize. . . . But most importantly, I was at the same time
involved in an alternative poetry scene in Boston and Providence that
seemed a direct parallel to indie rock," in which "DIY" (do-it-yourself)
publications such as "photocopied zines" represent "a communal identity
outside the 'mainstream'" (private communication).[9] Mlinko can think of
rock in this fluidly personal way because she can think about youth in that
way too, as a realm of conspiratorial, virtuous circles where "the whole
group is in lyrical motion," rather than as a self-enclosed idyll or a utopian
promise she must leave behind (*Matinées*, 41). "Three Representations of
Peacetime" describes a social set (by name: Matt, Courtney, Dan, Naoko),
to which the poet belongs: "They are striving to be Fellini's Juliet, seeing visions each time they close their eyes, / build a treasure of images, teenagers
putting on English accents for strangers / pretending to have just met. The
feeling the universe is conspiring to charm them" (41). That "charm" belongs
to a repertory of attitudes which the poems both associate with youth, and
try to produce in us.

Thomas Sayers Ellis's debut collection, *The Maverick Room* (2005), goes
even further than Mlinko and Compton in linking its own aesthetic to a
youth subculture and to a musical subgenre, which the poet insists that he
has not outgrown. Though Ellis's book refers to many sorts of music, from

George Clinton and Bootsy Collins of P-Funk to the "Baptist Beat" of gospel, a plurality of its musical references (starting with the title) point to go-go, a 1980s and 1990s style combining elements of funk and rap, played almost exclusively in Ellis's hometown of Washington, D.C. The music's relative obscurity and its association with one locale make it *more like* poetry, and more like adolescence as Ellis envisions it, than the better-known African American musical subgenres that many of Ellis's peers invoke instead.[10]

Go-go events and the kids who frequent them have their own, D.C.-specific code, which the poems incorporate just as they try to mimic go-go's polyrhythms: "Sugar Bear is the Abominable Snowman of Go-Go, / Laying stone-cold sheets of bottom / Over forgotten junk farms and Indian deathbeds" (53) "Bottom" here means both the bass line in a song and the low-lying ground on which much of Washington rests. "Take Me Out to the Go-Go" depicts another youthful crew and their temporary superstar:

> Nikita zips across stage
> Trailed by a troop of white-gloved
> One-wheelers: Killer Joes,
> The 12 & Under Crew
> In disguise. . . .
>
> Mere call & response
> Never knocked socks this way.
>
> (55)

Such a performance looks, to Ellis, more impressive (even) than a good gospel performance, more powerful (because more limited, semisecret) than older notions of community, but also more transient, more tied to the youthful body.[11] In Ellis, we might say, even more than in T. S. Eliot, we are the music while the music lasts.

If Ellis's poems do not seem especially haunted by the chance of outgrowing the subculture from which they speak, that may be because they are haunted by far worse losses. During the peak years of go-go, D.C. led the nation in murders per capita. Some of the freewheeling kids in Ellis's poetry are now incarcerated men, as his "Barracuda" makes clear, comparing the "tank" (pool) of a former high school swimmer to the "tank" (prison) that confines him now (*Maverick*, 28). Ellis's own remembered attempts to play music amount only to "Practice" in "A dank, dark basement":

The first thing you heard was feedback and sometimes
Anthony Ross, our manager's kid brother,

Snare- and pedal-less, pretending to kick.

(99)

This band, like their equipment, seems incomplete, unready, and yet it co-alesces into a temporary apotheosis: "timbales and rototoms, side-by-side, were / Like a finish of chrome," "a horn's valved prose / Asked for, asked for, asked for" (100). As so often in *The Maverick Room*, Ellis' in-groups, bands, and audiences—"My peeps. / My poetics. / My feet," he punningly calls them—can find their groove, get the life and the language they want, but may not be able to keep it (119).

Most comprehensive, and at times most baffling, among the contemporary poets who forge a new style from characteristics of adolescence—from encodedness, secretiveness, emotional volatility, extreme energies, in-group signals, and above all incompletion—is Liz Waldner, whose readers may feel as if they were eavesdropping or intercepting lines from cryptic diaries. Her works can sound at once "experimental," intellectually resistant to prose sense, and enthusiastically naïve. The range of reference in Waldner's first volume, *Homing Devices* (1997), takes in the New Wave music of her youth along with the modern and ancient poets she admires; Waldner calls her punctuation-studded, ellipsis-dotted prose-poems

> attempts to speak the language of loss and be/long/ing. . . . (and as it is in Sappho (whose poems got palimpsested [hello HD, everybody loves you now] got holes being used for wrapping up vases): I "The moon has set and the Pleiades. . . . See also The Talking Heads' "Fear of Music" for Elvis and Mimphis (as it is sayed in the South) and other hopes of post-industrial, post-toasties home and roam and you are so far away, and all I have are letters.
>
> (11; [*SIC*])

Attempts to grasp a renewable energy—one inseparable from the open secret of lesbian desire—originate in the pacts of Waldner's teens: "What am / I doing here where did I go where should I be? We / were all, perhaps, nineteen" (*Homing*, 20). Ancient Greek texts (especially Sappho's) appear in *Homing Devices* as parallels to the emotion-laden discoveries of adolescence, which return to adults (as Greek texts do to modern readers) in powerful, mysterious, frustrating fragments.

To say that Waldner grounds her poetry in the unstable codes of adolescence is not to say that she found her teen years delightful. Her prose poem "The Franklin's Tale" proves otherwise, at least if we take its sentences as memoir:

When I was fifteen I could have said with Mr. Berryman: *It's not a good position I'm in.* I melted drugs in spoons and shot them into my veins by the railroad tracks when the train came by with a roar. The captain of the football team called me a commie yankee nigger-lover in front of everybody when he and his friends wouldn't let me swim in the pool.

(*HOMING*, 55)

"The Franklin's Tale" names, in its title, Chaucer's story of faithful love, but its emotional (and erotic) burden updates Sappho instead. The poet remembers "voices at night. the sky. full of 'triangles and the names of girls'. instauration. she digs, shovel like a hat, like a snout pushes her head between legs and comes out. * *They read like love.* . . . She remembers how it is to be with me. / She remembers how it is to be. And wants. To be" (*Homing*, 45). Waldner's fear that her adolescent promise has abandoned her along with this early lover comes hand in hand with a fear that she has abandoned her distinctive region (in this case, Mississippi) for failed aspirations to metropolitan adulthood: "All these 20 years, I have lived out of that morning after, driving on the road through the gravel pit as if I were the field every disturbance was a blessing in, tuned, retu(r)ned to you" (*Homing*, 46).

How does Waldner's poetry, grounded as it is in memories of her own teens, differ from (say) Levis's lyric nostalgia or Bunting's look back at lost love? All these poets valorize (and find a basis for lyric in) adolescence as they understand it, but those understandings are as different as the forms the poets find. Waldner's own poems imitate the codes, the manner as well as the matter, of the covertly or secretly shared speech that she associates with that time, and Waldner refuses to adopt any point of view associated with maturity, distance, stability, age. She can sound nostalgic, in isolated passages, but more often she rails against nostalgia in the name of a vivid presence, a state of mind in which everything seems possible at once: "What's the point of Long Long Long and yearn and / Name That Tomb?" "Let them stay, these days. or make going go away" (*Dark*, 49, 11).

Many of the stylistic adaptations to modern adolescence that we have seen throughout this book involve diction—words, phrases, references, and common and proper nouns that suggest in-groups, new subcultures, teen tastes. Waldner uses such words (she even misspells them). Her most remarkable adaptations, though, involve a notionally adolescent syntax, in which incompleteness and shared secrets show up as stuttering, incomplete, or idiosyncratically assembled sentences. What Hejinian named "the rejection of closure" in contemporary style becomes for Waldner a way to reject the certainties, authoritative tones, even sexual behavior (monogamous, heterosexual, penetrative) she identifies with adulthood. This uncontrolledness permits, for Waldner, a combination (for her they are interdependent) of semantic and sexual abandon: "Dance a bee dance // in mind how good I smell"; "I would like to do it with you so the look of you is like the breeze" (*Dark*, 71, 77) A confident poem called "Ho, the Isle of Lesbos" even incorporates the distractable shorthand of instant messaging among its "secret signs": "A fish is / a secret sign for a secret meeting: / dear sexy thing, meet me @ the catacombs / with goldfish crackersnacks" (*Dark*, 24).[12]

Adult identities presuppose consistent conclusions, a life course as a story that can be told. Waldner's "Shrimpy Girl Talk" instead offers "the feel of Now (and now and now and now)," condensing into her verse and prose poems the upheavals, excesses, deprivations, and sexual adventures of her (real or reimagined) youth: "I am not allowed to sing has come to out I mean our house to say I mean stay, or am I?" (*Dark*, 33, *Homing*, 65) "So she set herself to win Omnity / From Nullity in her sublunary estate-and-sleeping-bag" (*Self*, 37). Declaring Waldner both perpetually adaptable and adaptably present, her poem "A Genitive Case (*Desiderus*)" alludes both to a youth subculture's style of dress (hip-hop, perhaps—or a butch look favored by certain young lesbians) and to a now-discredited biological theory by which organisms can pass on their acquired characteristics, as if nothing inherited—nothing associated with adulthood, procreation, the succession of generations—was therefore fixed:

> I wish there were a photograph of my hands when they were
>   younger . . .
>
> My fingers look like people, now in baggy clothes, the kind I favor.
>   Is this causal?
>
> "Micro-Lamarckian" could be my tribe, my life's title,
>   an address label.
>
> (SELF, 47)

We can see Waldner's writings as continuing not only the project described in this chapter, writing contemporary adolescence from within it, but also as continuing the feminist projects we saw in chapter 4, and the (queer) projects we saw in chapter 2. Waldner's poetry offers forms at once fluid and insistent, tropes for generation or creativity that is not procreation, and kinds of power marked as other than adult. Some of her flirtatious disguises emphasize at once extremes of excitement, contemporary trappings of youth, and a notion of gender as changeable performance: "O O O, waling around in my flippy new sundress I'm in drag. . . . Hello I'm in disguise as a girl, I have on a bra, a thing not donned since junior high and you don't know it's weird, you I don't know think it's me!" (*Dark*, 6) Representations of immaturity, of adolescent and hence unfixed yearnings and bodies, speak—for Waldner and for others of her generation—to the contradictions in earlier attempts to develop a feminist poetics from notionally stable, securely gendered, bodies and selves. Writing in *How(ever)*, a self-proclaimed journal of experimental feminist poetics, Kerry Edwards speaks of her "immense difficulties in—and desire to—create and live within a (feminist) politic that would be adequate to . . . instability," "a desire to speak from . . . a place whose borders haven't been tested," "to create a politics that will continually move toward the unfamiliar, uncomfortable, not-yet-understood" ("Listening"). That journal's successor, *How2* would later publish Waldner's own work.

Waldner's most recent book, *Saving the Appearances* (2005), returns explicitly to her teenage experience, implying that in some sense it is not over. Everything that happened to Waldner in her teens in Mississippi, good or bad, comic or painful, seems in her poems to be happening to her still. "It may have been hope that drove me to pinch my own neck one weekend so that in the 8th grade Mississippi Monday someone would tease me about making out"; the fake neck marks here in "Homing In" stand for poems and for the "appearances" that provide the volume with its title (*Saving*, 72). Teen shames and aspirations remain alive indefinitely in Waldner's fauxnaif, insistent "Winter Solstice":

I just got new glasses;
I guess I need remedial classes
because I still don't get the message,
I still don't believe I'm allowed to be:
the years turn and turn away
yet shames stay the same.

Let a voice come out of the heavens
saying Lo, or Yo,
I go before and prepare the way.
(*SAVING*, 46)

"Ways, Truth, Lights: Leaves of Glass" describes

the Mississippi and eventually
its creeks when seen from a plane.
I first flew when I was seventeen

but then I cared more to look at the clouds.
Water might sparkle a sign like speech
and a puddle could give you a shape or a face.
The sky, however, will always be far

enough and empty
a way on through.
(*SAVING*, 5)

"Give you a shape or a face" means both "yield an image for your contem-plation" and "reflect a self previously unknown or unformed." Like Lu, Waldner uses an airplane journey to suggest the in-between, adolescent state, though she also uses its aerial view to suggest memory. Like Lu's prose work, Waldner's lyric poem ends in midair.

❖ ❖ ❖ ❖ ❖

For all these poets, the association of poetry itself with adolescent subcul-tures (musical and otherwise) becomes both a way of depicting energetic flux and a response to all the cultural changes (chronicled by Spacks, Ar-nett, and others) that have made youth seem more valuable, maturity less so. That association also becomes a way of responding to poetry's own ap-parent loss of social power and status in the larger, "adult" world. Like the Secret Stars and like Sugar Bear—and unlike the Rolling Stones—young poets such as Ellis and Waldner acknowledge a necessarily limited audi-ence.[13] Their acknowledgments reflect both the postponement of—or resis-tance to—adulthood that seems to characterize this generation's life course, and the "rejection of closure" that much of this generation's poetry adopts as a formal goal.[14]

If social and cultural history and bits of the history of popular music can tell us where some young poets get their verbal resources, can these poets' attitudes and inventions, in turn, tell us anything about the life course? In America now, writes the social theorist Liah Greenfeld, "identity can no longer be a reflection of . . . social position, which one simply derives from the environment"; instead "it . . . has to be constructed . . . by the individual" ("When the Sky," 331). As a result, she argues, adults now experience and even seek out the flux and dislocation ascribed to adolescence. "In today's America, and in particular among the more materially comfortable strata, one, for the most part, does not know who one is. . . . What if one has chosen wrongly? What if being a mother or a college professor is not the real me? What if I am, as a matter of fact, an alpinist and a 'child-free' lesbian?" (331) Greenfeld writes that such "characteristic American self-searching is more common among the young . . . but it occurs often enough among other age groups to consider it a general problem" (332). "The 'life script'—our expectations of what we will do, and do next, and next after that in life—has been greatly scrambled," agrees the education researcher Nancy Lesko; "As a result, the sense of what youth or adulthood is comes into question" (quoted in Levine, *Harmful to Minors*, 87).

It is only a slight exaggeration to say that for a social thinker like Greenfeld, "adulthood" (maturity, authority, stability of identity, in her sense and in Erikson's) is no longer a possibility; adults are not what we imagine ourselves to be. In contemporary America, the social researcher Judith Levine concludes, "people do not grow up at sixteen, eighteen, or twenty-one, if they ever do" (*Harmful to Minors*, 88).[15] One does not have to agree with all such claims in order to see how some poets might find them sympathetic, nor to see how those poets might take not only subjects but also perspectives from the ways in which we imagine youth. From adults, we expect impossible certainties. From the young, we expect energy and novelty, but we do not expect "right choices," authoritative claims, or even stable beliefs. As much as they revel in its symbols, adolescence is no longer, for these newest poets, primarily a symbol of potential, of the chance that we might become something better than we are. Nor is it a pastoral, self-enclosed world; it is, simply, the state that we are in. Yet it might not be quite right to say that these poets never imagine an adulthood. Perhaps, instead, maturity, practicality, psychological fixity in one household and in one point of view, seems to them all too easy to imagine; adulthood is the state in and for which poetry—that now-subcultural, long-impractical, supposedly outmoded, style-conscious preoccupation—seems to have no value any more, so that the "poetry of a grown man" (in James Wright's famous phrase) would simply be no poetry at all (*Above the River*, 212).

I have been examining American—and British and Irish and Australian—poetry as it reacts to and takes its form from a social fact that is also a theme: the changing experiences and meanings of adolescence. Angus Fletcher warns that "thematic approaches to poetic effect are always bound to mislead, or else lead us away from the poetics of the poem in question" (*New Theory*, 154). Mindful of such warnings, I have tried to show how this theme finds its way into form, for the individual poets I have discussed and for the wider patterns those poets make. One such pattern involves changing perspectives; poets move from writing about youth in others, to writing about their own youth as they remember it, to writing about youth subcultures that their styles assert that they have not outgrown. A complementary pattern—much like the one Spacks discovered in modern novels—involves a progressive disidentification with adulthood, an ever "lessening faith in the possibilities of adult life" (*Adolescent Idea*, 226). A third pattern sets adolescence as pastoral (self-enclosed, notionally innocent, replicated in each generation) against adolescence as revolution (brand-new, able to change the adult world). Poets up through the 1960s pursue one or the other, if not both; poets afterward may modify or reject both in favor of adolescence as uncertainty.

Besides the conflict between pastoral and revolution, we have seen in these poems about adolescence a conflict between completion and incompletion, between closure and resistance to closure, in the forms of poems as in the adolescent life course. Barbara Herrnstein Smith has noted that poets can achieve strong closure by ending on words or topics that "signify termination or stability" (*Poetic Closure*, 172). One such topic is death, but another might be adulthood. Poets ambivalent about adulthood may be ambivalent about closure as well. Fletcher describes the tension in all poetry between the "play of perpetual metamorphosis" and the "odd inevitability in well-formed art" (*New Theory*, 177). Adolescence as a subject for modern poetry has allowed us to see that tension at work. Perpetual metamorphosis, aspirational or unending adolescence as a model for the modern, in poets from Williams forward, has accompanied resistance to closure, to anything obviously complete or well formed. In Marianne Moore, strong but unconventional closure, the closure of logical arguments and syllabic stanzas, suggests the unusual and valuable limits of the studious environments she cherished. In early Auden the closures are ironized, as adolescence must end, but nothing useful can replace it; Larkin's closures were sign-offs, resignations, that distanced him from the meanings he gave to the young. McGinley's poems of reassurance featured strong, uncomplicated closure; so did Gunn's poems of strong subcultures and strong men, in command of the attitudes (and the bodies) their subcultures produced.

As the meanings of adolescence have changed, so have the uses of closure among thoughtful poets who depicted it. Oppen's poems of optimistic uncertainty about the young (so promising, so unlike him) were poems of exceedingly tentative closure. In Brooks' late-1960s poems, violent hyperclosure and sharp and irregular (often rhymed) lines opened a new world as they shut off the old. Lowell's hyperclosure—in which every line could be the last—denied the progress his contemporaries associated with the young. Kasischke, Moss, and Graham invent disconcerting styles that move sideways rather than forward, backward rather than onward as they explore girls' resistance to the teleologies of heterosexual womanhood—a resistance Waldner's tactics celebrate. Ironic or merely formal closure returned in Muldoon and in Tranter, for whom few young people succeed in becoming anything: nostalgic, strong closure returned in Komunyakaa and in Levis, to whom adolescence usually meant the past. Resistance to closure and to narrative shape animates the recent writers with whom this study concludes; they favor, instead, an allusive language of in-groups, an aesthetic of frequent interruption, and a sense of immediate secrets shared.

Adolescence means selfhood and sociability; energy and volatility; peer culture, subculture, and distance from culture; the development of an inner core of being; and the exploration of becoming. It has meant all these things at once, and with vastly increased visibility, since the turn of the twentieth century. If, as Fletcher argues, contemporary poems imagine especially fluid environments, where "forms are troped into an ontological game of their becoming," then adolescence—a state of being which also connotes becoming—will remain one way to represent what poems can do (*New Theory*, 185). Ideas of the life course, of lyric poems as versions of the self, and of adolescence as the phase of life in which the self is formed help explain why so many modern poets have made adolescence a figure for poetry as such. The same ideas suggest that adolescence—whatever else it comes to mean—will remain a compelling figure for the twenty-first century poem.

Notes

Introduction

1. "So much of 20th-century culture," explained Allen Metcalf, "has been influenced by the notion of the teenager, of teenagers and the teens being a separate age, a time that you revel in, that music and movies are made for" (Cornwell, "The Words of the Decade," ii).

2. Ariés's claims about the absence of childhood in medieval and early modern Europe are no longer taken at face value by historians, though they retain their importance in the historiography of childhood and youth; see, for example, Ben-Amos, *Adolescence and Youth in Early Modern England*, and Bruce Smith, *Homosexual Desire in Shakespeare's England*.

3. For such recognitions, see Brumberg, *The Body Project*; Chudacoff, *How Old Are You?*; Esman, *Adolescence in Culture*; Hunter, *How Young Ladies Became Girls*; and Kett, *Rites of Passage*. The historian Ilana Ben-Amos concludes that "few, if any, of the features we . . . associate with a cohesive [youth] subculture can be attributed to young people in early modern English society" (*Adolescence and Youth in Early Modern England*, 205). Another historian, Barbara Hanawalt, writes that "the absence of a fully developed youth culture for both males and females . . . is perhaps the chief difference between adolescence [in medieval England] and [adolescence] now" (*Growing Up in Medieval London*, 127–28).

4. Books and articles on all these topics abound. See especially, for education and youth, 1870–1930: Chudacoff, *How Old Are You?*; Hunter, *How Young Ladies Became Girls*; and Kett, *Rites of Passage*; on 1920s youth: Bailey, *From Front Porch to Back Seat*; and Fass, *The Damned and Beautiful*; on teenagers after 1945: Bailey, *From Front Porch to Back Seat*; and Palladino, *Teenagers*. On feminist readings of girls' adolescence: Driscoll, *Girls*; Gilligan, *In a Different Voice*; McRobbie, *Feminism and Youth Culture*; and Emily White, *Fast Girls*.

5. The poem has occasioned much admiring commentary. John Shoptaw describes its "fantasy of passive resistance," quoting Ashbery's remark that it describes his own "youth . . . but also anyone else's" (*On the Outside*, 107, 105); David Herd praises its "sense of self equal to its [historical] moment" (*Ashbery and American*, 119). John Hollander writes that Ashbery's lines differentiate "between 'thinking not to grow up'

and pretending not to have done so," adding that "American visions of maturity— particular during the nineteen-sixties and seventies—should drive the good man screaming to the cradle" ("Soonest Mended," 211).

6. LeTendre found that "Japanese teachers had no clear idea what adolescence was . . . and failed to recognize the English loan word"; American middle school teachers "not only knew the word 'adolescence' but also had very specific ideas about what it meant" (*Learning to Be Adolescent*, 1).

7. Spacks's study informs this book throughout; subsequent work on adolescence in literature has confined itself almost exclusively to prose life-writing and to the novel. On twentieth-century novels, see Dalsimer, *Female Adolescence*; Pifer, *Demon or Doll*; Saxton, introduction to *The Girl*; Barbara White, *Growing Up Female*; and Kiell, *The Adolescent Through Fiction*. On continental prose fiction, see especially Steedman, *Strange Dislocations*; and Neubauer, *The Fin-de-Siècle Culture of Adolescence*. On nineteenth-century American fiction, see Tanner, *The Reign of Wonder*, chaps. 9–10.

8. For more recent historically oriented studies, see especially Neubauer, *Fin-de-Siècle Culture of Adolescence*; Palladino, *Teenagers*; West, *Growing Up in Twentieth-Century America*; and Kevin White, *The First Sexual Revolution*.

9. Palinode, in "Maye," celebrates "the merry moneth of May, / When loue lads masked in fresh aray" and "Yougthes folke now flocken in." Piers responds by telling a fable about the perils of youth; his example, a "very foolish and vnwise" "Kidde" (young goat), appears to be going through goat puberty (Spenser, *Complete Poetical Works*, 23, 25).

10. An anonymous poem published in 1593 described "The brainsick race that wanton youth ensues / Without regard to grounded wisdom's lore" (Jones, *Sixteenth Century Verse*, 605). Thomas, Lord Vaux expressed a similar sentiment in a poem of 1576: "When I look back and in myself behold / The wand'ring ways that youth could not descry. . . . My knees I bow and from my heart I call, / O Lord forget youth's faults and follies all" (Jones, *Sixteenth Century Verse*, 130).

11. On early modern apprentices and their riots, and on Oxford and Cambridge students' cliques, see Bruce Smith, *Homosexual Desire in Shakespeare's England*; and Steven R. Smith, "The London Apprentices as Seventeenth-Century Adolescents."

12. The historian and social theorist John Gillis writes that "many of the traditions of youth that we treat as contemporary—student radicalism, bohemianism, gang behavior, delinquency—can be traced back" to late-eighteenth- and early-nineteenth-century England and Wales (*Youth and History*, ix, 32–33). No major poets, however, found in these traditions a language suited to lyric purpose and form, not even when Blake, Wordsworth, and other Romantics discovered powerful models for lyric in the separate (and newly interesting) category of children's speech. On Romantic views of childhood in many fields, including later literature and medicine, see especially Steedman, *Strange Dislocations*, and Coveney, *Poor Monkey*. For Romantic children in modern poetry, see especially Flynn, "'Infant Sight,'" and Travisano, *Mid-Century Quartet*, chap. 3.

13. "The paradox of imitated authenticity," writes David Wellbery, "still today a prominent feature of youth culture . . . found in the 'Werther-fashion,'" with its blue coat and yellow vest, "one of its earliest manifestations" (*New History of German Literature*, 387).

14. Another sonnet of Arnold's invokes "Youth like a star; and what to youth belong— / Gay raiment, sparkling gauds, elation strong." The sonnet adds, however, that the

Muse wears, under such gauds, "sackcloth" and sad thoughts; its title is "Austerity of Poetry" (*Poetical Works*, 166).

15. Joseph Kett writes that in early-nineteenth-century America, "No one symbolized the poetic undisciplined nature of youth better than Byron," through his life and reputation as much as through his poems (*Rites of Passage*, 103).

16. Byron appears to take these sentiments in part from Rousseau, in whose Swiss locales—as Byron puts in—"air is the young breath of passionate thought" (*Major Works*, 133).

17. The confrontation that Huck Finn creates between innocence and experience, between—as Tanner puts it—a naive "principle of youngness" and ineffective or hypocritical adult society, requires no third term, no adolescence, only a boy who is able to talk and act; in fact, it makes impossible any such term, leaving only the corrupt adult world and an asocial, "unattainable paradise" (*The Reign of Wonder*, 181, 172).

18. Frost gave the first edition of *A Boy's Will* a series of subtitles that identify the poet with earlier pastoral youth, even with Spenser's Colin Clout, e.g., "The youth is persuaded that he will be rather more than less himself for having forsworn the world" (Frost, *Collected*, 969). I thank Bonnie Costello for calling them to my attention.

19. Rimbaud even connects unstable artistic yearnings not only to drugs and drink but to the hormonal changes of the early teens, though he does so most clearly in a poem intended as satire of another poet, François Coppée: "Why did puberty come so late and why such suffering / At the hands of overactive glands? [Pourquoi la puberté tardive et le malheur / Du gland tenace et trop consulté?]" (*Rimbaud Complete*, 152, 464)

20. Auden's sonnet "Rimbaud" treats him almost dismissively: "Verse was a special illness of the ear; / Integrity was not enough; that seemed / The hell of childhood; he must try again" (*EA* 237) Auden's 1939 review of Enid Starkie's biography makes no mention of the poet's youth, nor of youth as a theme (*Prose Volume II*, 39).

21. Such analogies find an apotheosis in Henry Miller's *Time of the Assassins: A Study of Rimbaud* (1956): "Like Lucifer, Rimbaud succeeds in getting himself ejected from Heaven, the Heaven of Youth"; "I like to think of him as the Columbus of Youth" (77, 151).

22. On young people as writers, see Damon, who argues that teens in South Boston "redefine poetry and the creative process in the context of their own community" (*Dark End*, 97). On major poets' youthful works, see instead Vendler, *Coming of Age*: "to find a personal style," Vendler asserts, "is, for a writer, to become adult" (2).

1. Modernist Poetics of Adolescence

1. By the 1920s, Mintz continues, "as a result of cars, telephones, and the movies, the young had broken away from the world of adults and established their own customs, such as dating. . . . Girls' growing freedom evoked alarm" (*Huck's Raft*, 214–15). Twenties social critics such as the Lynds attributed the rise in dating to the automobile; John Modell points out that movie theaters and telephones, emerging slightly earlier, played at least as large a role (*Into One's Own*, 88–89).

2. Catherine Driscoll quotes a 1916 "guidance manual" by Mary Moxcey that explains that "the recognition of adolescence as a period of human life separate from childhood and from maturity has been a slow achievement of civilization" (quoted in Driscoll, *Girls*, 56). Even in 1920, Macleod points out, "only one child in six gradu-

ated from high school"—regular schooling in the later teen years had become normal only for "students from families of white-collar workers," the families from which most modernist poets came (*Age of the Child*, 149).

3. Fass describes the debate about this new youth in American periodicals: "Journals of the twenties"—from mass-market weeklies to *The New Republic*—"were filled with an image of youth out of control, of energy released from social restraints, and of raw forces unleashed" (*The Damned and Beautiful*, 20). "Mass-market publications" Chudacoff finds, "directed particular attention to young adulthood, in part because of the emergence of a youth culture" (*How Old Are You?* 120).

4. Spacks examines Hall's work, and its consequences for prose fiction, at length; see especially *The Adolescent Idea*, 228–337.

5. Bourne added an age range: "If we get few ideas after twenty-five," he wrote, "we get few ideals after we are twenty" (*Youth and Life*, 13).

6. Readers today remember Bourne as an opponent of U.S. entry into the Great War, or as an inventor (with Horace Kallen) of the set of ideas now termed multiculturalism. His friends remembered him as an apostle of youth. Gorham Munson devotes an entire chapter in his memoirs to Bourne's accomplishment. Paul Rosenfeld's memorial calls Bourne "the youth of a beautiful, unrealized ever-imminent plane of existence sprung from a society banked against that plane" ("Randolph Bourne," 549). Rosenfeld's tribute reappeared in *Port of New York* (1924), one of the first studies of American modernism; other chapters covered Marsden Hartley, Alfred Steiglitz, and William Carlos Williams.

7. "The most precious moment in human development," Jane Addams rhapsodized, "is the young creature's assertion that he is unlike any other human being. . . . Is it only the artists who really see these young creatures as they are—the artists who themselves are endowed with immortal youth?" (*Spirit of Youth*, 8–9)

8. John Gould Fletcher's summary of recent British poetry in issue 1 of *Youth* notes that "most of the younger men are writing about the war"; "when one considers that most of the younger poets here are actually in immediate danger of getting killed, one can excuse them for dwelling on this topic" (*Youth*, 1:12). A later issue discovers "the impulse of the people to sing themselves" in the collaboratively-written pageants of towns and colleges in North Dakota: one 1917 pageant extols "the spirit of youth—of invincible Youth" (*Youth*, 10:1).

9. The *Little Review* also showed a sporadic interest in poems by children: W.L. Comfort's 1915 article described an eleven-year-old who spontaneously utters "a Japanese poem": she belonged, Comfort wrote, to "our new generation, the elect of which seems to know innately that an expression of truth in itself is a master-stroke" ("Education," 5). The next issue ran a five-page spread of poems by seven- through twelve-year-olds (all in vers libre, of course) (*Little Review* 2, no. 5, 38–42). Other journals and publishers during these years attended to very young poets as well: surveying American poetry and its recent history in 1926, Marianne Moore remembered that "various child poets received, in 1920, the respectful attention of the public" (*Complete Prose*, 123). Moore likely had in mind Hilda Conkling (daughter of the established poet Grace Conkling), who at ten published *Poems of a Little Girl*.

10. Louis Gilmore's poem described an adolescent monkey with romantic human yearnings: "If only our tails were a little longer / We might touch each other" (54).

11. Published in a 1918 *Little Review*, R. Reiss's "Sixteen" reads like a parody of Loy: "all around arose the ovoviparous neophytes / with monomania. . . . Youths of sixteen are mollusks" (59).

12. William Carlos Williams's poem "The Ogre" (1917) ("little girl with well-shaped legs, / you cannot touch the thoughts / I put over and under and around you") invites us to condemn Williams for his lecherous feelings or (following Kerry Anne Driscoll) to praise his surprising frankness (*CPW* 95; 151). *Others* coeditor Alfred Kreymborg in "Hemstitches" (1916) promises to console "lasses . . . when you are lonesome / and no boy gives you a thought" (41). Nor was the subgenre of love poems to underage girls limited to *Others*: consider James Weldon Johnson's "Girl of Fifteen": "I see you each morning from my window / As you pass on your way to school. . . . And my heart leaps through my eyes" (*Complete*, 73).

13. Stevens's sonnet 2 begins "Come, said the world, thy youth is not all play"; sonnet 5 hopes for "eyes undimmed and youth both pure and strong" (*Souvenirs*, 29, 31). The very Keatsian sonnet 8 begins, "The soul of happy youth is never lost / In fancy on a page"; in sonnet 10, "youth is better than weak, wrinkled age . . . and no disturbing gleam . . . Mars the high pleasure of youth's pilgrimage" (*Souvenirs* 32, 33).

14. On Crane's reception and his dealings with his closest contemporaries (Josephson, Munson, Tate, Toomer, Winters), see, in particular, Hammer, *Janus-Faced*.

15. In Loy's play *The Pamperers* (1915–16), in part a satire of futurists, Diana (who more or less speaks for Loy) declares, "I am the elusion that cooed to your adolescent isolation, crystallized in the experience of your manhood" ("Two Plays," 13). Carnevali's salon devoted to "youth" involved him in explicating Italian futurist poetry, Papini's included (*Autobiography*, 125–28).

16. Geoff Gilbert has argued otherwise, finding "modernism as youth and more specifically as adolescence" in British novels and in the Vorticist periodical *Blast* (*Before Modernism Was*, 52).

17. Eby's psychoanalytic reading considers Williams's choice to publish this poem in the Rutherford High School magazine solely as an act of exhibitionism, "exposing his sexual desires before the . . . schoolgirls." Yet Williams also published in the same magazine poems connected to school but not to sex. In "Peter Kip to the High School," the eponymous landowner, speaking from beyond the grave, addresses New Jersey's expanding public schools, now being built on his former property: "You are the new generation. I have had / my time" (*CPW* 566).

18. A good survey of recent approaches is Steinman, "William Carlos Williams," who finds in Williams's sequence "places where . . . social history and aesthetics are related" (409).

19. At least one reviewer thought Williams's work imitated adolescence all too well: writing in *Poetry* magazine in 1923, Marion Strobel decided that [Williams] "is like an adolescent boy, who while loving something of soft-petalled beauty, scoffs at it, so that he will be considered a He-Man; yet again and again approaches the same beauty" ("Middle-Aged Adolescence," 75–76). Williams courted just such comparisons, both in his explicit references to adolescence and in the post-Keatsian ambivalence Strobel finds so hard to take.

20. Some of those qualities provoked from Moore not praise but dissent; Celeste Goodridge has described Moore's "ambivalence" toward Williams's "defiant posture" and her growing discomfort with his subjects (*Hints and Disguises*, 85).

21. Moore's *Dial* also reviewed *Men, Women, and Colleges; Poems for Youth: An American Anthology* (edited by her onetime neighbor William Rose Benét) and *Why Do They Like It?* whose "author—about fifteen years old—protests" the English public school, displaying "verisimilitude and charm as exhibiting masculine juvenile psychology" (*Complete Prose*, 248, 254, 239, 253).

22. When the final issue of the *Little Review* in 1929 sent questionnaires to modernist writers and artists, it asked each respondent to send a photograph; the photo Moore sent shows the poet on a Gothic quad, and may date from her Bryn Mawr days (Moore, [Answers], 64).

23. Moore's late poems return to her affections for educational institutions. "Values in Use" (1956) begins: "I attended school and I liked the place" (*PMM* 249). A sententious 1967 tribute to "Katharine Elizabeth McBride, President of Bryn Mawr College" (unpublished during Moore's lifetime) likens the college to a church, quoting St. Paul (*PMM* 306). "In Lieu of the Lyre" (1965), addressed to and first printed in the Harvard *Advocate*, makes a gracious, almost flattering tribute to that student magazine while acknowledging Harvard's single-sex policy (Moore herself being "debarred from enrollment") (*PMM* 302). "Dream" defends the idea of "academic appointments for artists" by imagining "master-classes" taught by Bach, where "students craved a teacher and each student worked" (*PMM* 301).

24. Robin Schulze confirms that Moore "revised and arranged her poems" herself in *Observations* (*Becoming Marianne Moore*, 34).

25. David Bromwich writes that "the Baconian essay or prose-ramble may be the least misleading analogy" for Moore's poems ("Emphatic Reticence," 116); "A Jelly-fish," Margaret Holley records, began among Moore's class notes on just such prose (*Poetry*, 3).

26. Darlene Erickson's extended reading sees the poem as directed against New York Dada and Marcel Duchamp (*Illusion*, 59–68).

27. Moore has arranged quotations about the prophets so that they describe the oceans as well: her concluding lines incorporate quotations from G.A. Smith, *Expositor's Bible* and W.R. Gordon, *The Poets of the Old Testament* (*PMM* 331).

28. "The Steeple-Jack" came first in all the volumes of Moore's verse in which it appeared: though that decision was initially Eliot's (since he arranged her 1935 *Selected*) Moore's later decisions suggest that he was right in viewing that poem as one key to the whole.

29. Costello emphasizes the poem's admiration for Dürer, who also noticed "minute particulars"; Ambrose, too, "can see the flaws and compromises in this town which seems so prim" (*Marianne Moore*, 196).

30. When Moore cut Ambrose from "The Steeple-Jack" for her 1951 *Collected*, "the student" remained in the poem, though the only antecedent noun that suggested a student's presence was "school-house" (*PMM* 142). Moore restored Ambrose, along with several stanzas describing animals, for the 1967 *Complete*.

31. Dorothy Ross, *G. Stanley Hall*, describes Hall's role in these debates; for arguments in favor of "tracking"—associated, at the time, with Deweyan liberalism—see Lewis, *Democracy's High School*.

2. From Schools to Subcultures

1. Public school "'youths,'" Springhall adds, "passed as schoolboys at an age when most of their less privileged contemporaries had already been in employment for some years" (*Coming of Age*, 26). Only in 1918 did England extend compulsory school attendance to age fourteen, and not until 1947 to fifteen (Springhall, *Coming of Age*, 48; Gillis, *Youth and History*, 134). By contrast, thirty-one U.S. states by 1918 required attendance to age sixteen, and seven more to fifteen; "legal coercion was almost certainly not the primary cause of rising school attendance," however, and even in 1920

most "children still got most of their education in the elementary grades" (Macleod, *Age of the Child*, 74–75).

2. Reviewing Connolly's *Enemies of Promise*, Auden described "one great psychological class division in English society, the division between those who have been educated at a public school . . . and those who have not" (*Prose Volume II*, 19).

3. I follow Bozorth in using "homosexual," rather than the anachronistic "gay," for the sex in Auden's poems and for his life before 1935 but "queer" where the more inclusive term is warranted as a description of the writing.

4. The same match inspired a poem in *The Orators*:

Look down to the river when the rain is over,
See him turn in the river, hearing our last
Of Captain Ferguson.

It is seen how excellent hands have turned to commonness.
One, staring too long, went blind in a tower;
One sold all his manors to fight, broke through, and faltered.
(AUDEN, *JUVENILIA*, 240)

The "excellent hands" have failed to fulfill their promise; perhaps they wrongly sought help from "Captain Ferguson," "a temporary master at Sedbergh who was looked down on by the other members of the staff," and who courted Carritt (Auden, *Juvenilia*, 241).

5. Mendelson suggests that only Auden did any work for the planned three-volume study; the surviving notebook for this abortive project contains letters about Marlborough and Sedbergh along with clips from the St. Edmund's school magazine, including one "which describes Auden's participation in the drill of the school's Rifle Club" (*PTB* 693, 734). During 1932 he wrote (with a younger coauthor) "an article about public schools"; submitted to *Life and Letters*, it never appeared (Carpenter, *Auden*, 132).

6. Carpenter suggests that Gresham's contributed to Auden's guilt about his sexuality; "in many public schools, where mild homosexual intrigues and scandals were part of daily life, such feelings would probably not have seemed very serious. But the Gresham's Honour System was designed to suppress exactly this sort of thing" (*Auden*, 27).

7. John Bayley wrote that this "apparently denunciatory poem about industry and politics . . . makes its impact . . . by a use—how conscious a use one cannot say—of the attitudes and imagery of adolescence" ("W. H. Auden," 62, 64).

8. Auden "experimented with communal drama" when he taught at the Downs, producing "a revue whose cast included everyone at the school" (*Plays*, xxi).

9. Fuller finds in "Adolescence" "the half-hidden message of the whole work: that the introverted adolescent is obsessed and motivated by mother love" (*Auden*, 88).

10. Compare the Old Boys of the school in *Stalky & Co.*, whose fates Kipling summarizes thus: "Young blood who had stumbled into an entanglement with a pastrycook's daughter at Plymouth; experience who had come into a small legacy but mistrusted lawyers; ambition halting at cross-roads, anxious to take the one that would lead him farthest; extravagance pursued by the money-lender; arrogance in the thick of a regimental row—each carried his trouble to the head" (207). Critics recognize other models in the *Exeter Book* (Fuller, *Auden*, 96).

11. Auden told Naomi Mitchison that *The Orators* was "my memorial to Lawrence" (quoted in Carpenter, *Auden*, 122). But Lawrence's theories, as expressed in *Fantasia*

of the Unconscious, had little to do with elite education as such; he attacked universal schooling and modern family life in the name of instinct and sexual health. "Let all schools be closed at once. Keep only a few technical training establishments, nothing more" (77, 65).

12. Auden later remarked that "the ideas behind *Les Faux-Monnayeurs* are exciting but badly executed" (Ansen, *Table Talk*, 24); Davenport-Hines suggests an earlier enthusiasm for its "energetic youth" (*Auden*, 97).

13. "At school," Auden remembered in 1965, "my total lack of interest and aptitude for games of any kind did not make me despise athletics; on the contrary, I greatly admired them . . . but I did not envy them, because I knew that their skill could never be mine" (*Forewords*, 508).

14. Larchfield and the Downs were "prep" schools, for boys under thirteen. Though Auden at Larchfield told Anne Fremantle, "I enjoy teaching. And I like teaching small boys best," he soon pursued teaching jobs in public schools (Sedbergh and later Bryanston) (Spender, *Tribute*, 59, 79).

15. The original, two-part version of the poem made its school setting more visible. Part 1, a sort of dream-vision of England and its politics, began with Auden (like a medieval poem's dreamer) set in a place appropriate to his vision, the Larchfield school: "Into a windless morning I stepped and passed / Outside the windows of untidy rooms / Where boys were puzzled by exams" (*EA* 444).

16. Decades later, Francois Duchêne saw in *Poems* (1930) "the radical manifesto of a youth," its "adolescent sense of awakening" designed to create the "myth of the budding poet's ambition," which other young writers recognized (*The Case of the Helmeted Airman*, 37, 45–46).

17. A 1939 lecture, "The Future of English Poetic Drama," apparently explained to its French audience that "that the world does not belong to the young"; "never has there been a time when, on the one hand, it has been more difficult to attain maturity, and, on the other hand, when maturity was more necessary" (*PTB* 717) Years later, Auden retained enough interest in boarding schools, teachers, and students not only to visit Richard Eberhart's class at St. Mark's School but to contribute an end-of-term "Ode" whose jokey style resembles his later light verse ("School Writings," 44–47).

18. David Herd has noticed how Ashbery, Koch, and Schuyler, like Auden and Isherwood, used coterie markers and collaborative techniques "to heighten . . . ordinary lives" (*Ashbery and American*, 65). John Shoptaw has elicited in Ashbery's poems a "homotextual" code: Shoptaw also calls "And We Know" "a parody of . . . *Goodbye, Mr. Chipps,*" contrasting it unfavorably to another classroom poem, James Schuyler's "Current Events" (*On the Outside*, 4–5, 40)

19. Like Larkin, John cannot remember much joy in his own youth: bombed-out Coventry reveals to him "a kind of annulling of his childhood. The thought excited him. It was as if he had been told: all the past is cancelled: all the suffering connected with that town, all your childhood, is wiped out" (*Trouble*, 219).

20. Larkin wrote to Amis, for example: "I am glad you liked Brunette's poems: I think all wrong-thinking people ought to like them. I used to write them whenever I'd seen some particularly ripe schoolgirls, or when I felt sentimental: 'Fam Damnay' was written for fun . . . writing about grown women is less perverse and therefore less satisfying" (*Selected Letters*, 70).

21. In 1972, Larkin reviewed, for the leftish *Guardian* "a book . . . which enthusiastically compared 'the young' to Negroes—in revolt, seeking their identity" (*Selected Letter*s, 468). What Larkin reviewed was Richard Middleton's *Pop Music and the Blues*: his

review quotes the book as declaring that "[the white adolescent] has created a new community—a classless international community, which is as real as any traditional group or class" (Larkin, "Negroes," 21; brackets in original). Larkin comments: "Like the Negro, adolescents are trying to be free and so form a conscious group seeking its own identity; their morality is 'specific, momentary and circumstantial.' Mr. Middleton's obvious respect for these characteristics tempts one to add that neither group is very bright." Yet Larkin treats Middleton's argument, if not its protagonists, with some respect: "One can't say this book is true or false, any more than one could of [Denis] de Rougemont's *Passion and Society*; it interprets a set of circumstances" (21).

22. Larkin also contributed a verse epigram to his Hull colleague C.B. (Brian) Cox's anti-modernizing *Black Papers on Education* (1968–69), which warned that "the teacher is no longer regarded as the exponent of the great achievement of past civilization; his job is to 'decode' the 'radical critique of the young'" (Cox and Dyson, *Fight for Education*, 3, 1). A book that Cox lent Larkin (Christopher Booker's *Neophiliacs*, a hostile neo-Catholic account of the 1960s) "made [Larkin] realize how little in touch I have been with the world since 1945 . . . I have registered the Beatles and the miniskirt, but that's about all" (*Selected Letters*, 426).

23. Larkin told J.B. Sutton in 1947 that Lawrence "is so great that it is silly to start saying where he was wrong," though he also wrote the following year that "if we had known as many women as we have read books by DHL we should have a clearer idea" of romance and courtship (Motion, *A Writer's Life*, 173, 185).

24. Unsurprisingly, some older critics demurred: Kenneth Allott in 1962 attacked Gunn's "uncritical sympathy for nihilistic young tearaways in black leather jackets" (quoted in Bold, *Gunn and Hughes*, 26).

25. Gunn returned to Elvis decades afterward in a disillusioned memorial poem, one cast not in solid quatrains but in halting, short-lined free verse. The "disobedience" and "revolt" Elvis's first singles celebrate (that poem argued) grew from a "pain" that dissolved when its causes (immaturity, uncertainty, exclusion) did: the late-model Vegas Elvis, "the puffy King," instead "needed to kill . . . the ultimate pain // of feeling no pain" (*CPG* 362).

26. This searcher, Gunn continues, "is the subject of [Duncan's] *Moly* poems of 1971," which Duncan based on Gunn's own volume *Moly*; in these poems, Gunn continues, Duncan "is haunted by the ghost of himself at fifteen" (*Occasions*, 129).

3. Soldiers, Babysitters, Delinquents, and Mutants

1. On adolescence in Jarrell, see Burt, *Randall Jarrell and His Age*, chap. 5.

2. "Women especially were struck by the anomaly of teenagers turned soldiers," writes Fussell (*The Great War*, 52).

3. Langdon Hammer argues that Sylvia "Plath's late work develops a protest against the culture of the school" ("Plath's Lives," 67).

4. McGinley complained in the *Ladies' Home Journal*: "At seven, little girls ought to start casting warm looks on their favorite cub scout. . . . At thirteen or fourteen, they should have turned into accomplished sirens" (*Sixpence*, 235). Writing in 1956 for *Mademoiselle*, Jarrell put forth a similar protest: "O future, here around me now in which junior-high-school girls go steady with junior-high-school boys, marry in high school and repent at college! Or rather do not repent"; "the well-counseled Montagues, the well-worked-over Capulets ship the children off to the University of

Padua, where, with part-time jobs, allowances from both families, and a freezer full of TV Dinners, they live in bliss with their babies" (*Kipling*, 251).

5. Allen Ginsberg (echoing, as Ginsberg may have known, the young Auden) dreamt that John Clellon Holmes wrote him a letter which read: "'The social organization which is most true of itself to the artist is the boy gang'" (*Howl*, 47).

6. The July 1965 *Esquire*, as Braunstein notes, proclaimed a "'total take-over by youth of the entire United States market'... 'that vague no-man's land of adolescence'" had "'suddenly turned into a way of life'" ("Forever Young," 245).

7. On American poetry and the Vietnam War, see especially Chattarji, *Memories of a Lost War*.

8. My thanks to Helen Vendler, who spotted these lines' reference to Yeats.

9. Claudia Tate writes that that the introverted Annie "forfeits the possibility of independence and continues to spin bits of an imaginary life" ("Anger So Flat," 145).

10. "Girls still in high school, and ... women graduated from high school," Drake and Cayton write, would "form cliques and social clubs that discriminated against" dropouts (*Black Metropolis*, 516). Parents worried about the "thousands of lower-class young men who were never arrested as delinquents but who skirted the borderline of crime," "'cats' who, clad in 'zoot-suits,' stood around and 'jived' the women" (589).

11. In 1969 the U.S. Senate investigated the Rangers' alleged misuse of federal funds; one Vice Lord remembered that during the investigations, "the Rangers were made out to be the worse [*sic*] cats in the world" (quoted in Dawley, *Nation of Lords*, 167). Brooks would later dissociate herself from the Rangers, telling *Essence* in 1971: "The Blackstone Rangers are a teenage gang in Chicago of immense size and not all of the things they do are nice. I'm not sure just what to say about what they're doing now, because I'm not close to them" (*Report from Part One*, 168).

12. Though "Riot" and "Boy Breaking Glass" describe violence in Chicago's black communities, the riots downtown at the Democratic Convention in August 1968 must have attracted some notice from Brooks as well; one historian writes that the demonstrating Yippies "attempted to use the energy and playfulness of youth culture to wildly redefine radical politics" (and got beaten bloody instead) (Farber, *Chicago '68*, xvi).

13. I take *Notebook* (1970) as my preferred source, rather than the earlier *Notebook, 1967–68* (1969) (which omits many poems included in *Notebook*), the later triptych *History, For Lizzie and Harriet*, and *The Dolphin* (1973–1974), or the 1976 *Selected Poems*; when, as is often the case, poems exist in several versions, *Notebook* (1970) is the one I cite unless my text gives reasons otherwise.

14. In February 1968, for example, the *New York Review of Books* treated readers to the Berkeley Free Speech Movement partisan Michael Rossman's "Notes from the County Jail." Irving Howe complained that the journal had "done the New Left a considerable service by providing it with a link of intellectual responsibility" ("Intellectuals," 51). Another issue, to Howe's dismay, "printed on its cover a diagram explaining how to make a Molotov cocktail" (*Margin*, 316).

15. Lowell told Elizabeth Bishop in June 1967 that he had written "not a poem for a year and a half" (*Letters*, 486). By August he was writing to Adrienne Rich that he had "been poeticizing ... furiously, and now have three poems, all *momento moris* [*sic*] about summer and being fifty," one of them "long, about a hundred lines" (*Letters*, 486).

16. "After the demonstrators had been removed from one building," the Ehrenreichs

averred, observers "could see through a window cops ripping up a room, throwing furniture, and books around, breaking chairs, etc." (*Long March*, 145).

17. The rubbish heaps may also reflect the New York City garbage collectors' strike, which, as Spender notes, "took place at almost the same time as the Columbia riots"; "food, and God knows what else, rotted uncollected" (*Year of the Young*, 8).

18. Other remarks from the same years strike the same note: if "our students have more generosity, idealism and freshness than any other group, . . . they are only us, younger, and the violence that has betrayed our desires will also betray theirs if they trust to it" (*Letters*, 513). To Donald Davie in April 1970, Lowell wrote, "I have no faith in idealist violence or in revolution." And yet, he added, "I don't like the drear safe / unsafe iron frame of what's established" (*Letters*, 533).

19. Examining hippie and New Left manifestos, Braunstein describes the counterculture's "deep ambivalence about teleology per se—the notion that ideas, phenomena, people should be tending *toward* something, heading in some direction" ("Forever Young," 258). If (as I contend) Lowell's suspicion of progress reacts to utopian youth culture as it erupted and flourished between 1966 and 1973, his antiteleological orientation, his rejection of plan, structure, stepwise progress, itself duplicates a topos of radical youth.

4. Are You One of Those Girls?

1. Barbara White contends that in twentieth-century fiction, female adolescence differs from male adolescence in that the former "portends a future of continued secondary status" (*Growing Up Female*, 19).

2. For other especially salient examples, see Alison Joseph, "Adolescence," *Spoon River Poetry Review* 18, no. 1 (1993): 108; Rebecca Gordon, "Adolescence," *Calyx* 8 (1983): 9; Laura Shovan, "Adolescence Prepared Me For This," *Paterson Literary Review* 29 (2000): 150.

3. In "Two Girls," Kasischke depicts herself as Persephone again and adolescence as a fall, a danger; she and a friend "stroll together down the path / of woe," picking up "that scattered candy in the grass—those / were the hardest brightest flowers / of spring" (*Gardening*, 59). For other contemporary poets' retellings of the Persephone myth, see Dove, *Mother Love*, and Zucker, *Eating in the Underworld*.

4. She may have in mind David Bowie's 1971 hit "Life on Mars" (on *Hunky Dory*), a song whose descriptions of an anomic "girl with . . . mousy hair" makes a similar point.

5. The exception, Randall Jarrell, described such dilemmas almost exclusively when writing in the voices of women and girls: the middle-aged homemaker of "Next Day," for example, reflects: "For so many years / I was good enough to eat: the world looked at me / And its mouth watered" (*Complete Poems*, 279).

6. In her memoir *Tale of a Sky-Blue Dress*, Moss remembers thinking, in ninth grade, "*Now I must begin to separate from my parents. . . . As an adolescent, I don't see the collective experience well; only the personal and solitary. I don't like it much*" (181; italics in original).

7. Laurence Goldstein's earlier discussion—likely the first extended reading of this poem—also pursues these analogies but reaches far more optimistic conclusions: for him, "the poet's revenge" on these cultural systems "is to create a secondary world of enduring power" (perhaps analogous to the medium of film itself) (*The American Poet at the Movies*, 235).

8. Hostile film critics singled out Lyon's "well-built" Lolita as too developed or too old; the *New York Times* thought her "a good seventeen" (Hughes, *The Complete Kubrick*, 99).

9. On feminist resistance to being seen and its consequences for visual art, see also Phelan, *Unmarked*, chaps. 1 and 3; my thanks to Laura Engel for the reference.

10. Sharon Cameron has suggested that lyric poetry as a genre works to remove particular moments from time: "the contradiction between social and personal time," she writes, "is the lyric's generating impulse" (*Lyric Time*, 206).

11. "The way the sentence operates," Graham told Thomas Gardner, "became connected, for me, with notions like ending-dependence and eschatological thinking," with "manifest destiny, westward expansion" (*Regions of Unlikeness*, 218).

5. An Excess of Dreamy Possibilities

1. According to Erica Carter, "The word teenager first entered the German language in the 1950s, imported like chewing gum and Coca-Cola from the USA" ("Alice," 199).

2. Ortega y Gasset wrote that "modern art begins to appear comprehensible and in a way great when it is interpreted as an attempt to instill youthfulness into an ancient world. . . . Europe is entering upon an era of youthfulness. . . . For a while women and old people will have to cede the rule over life to boys" (*Dehumanization*, 50–52).

3. Kendall has said that the poem "evokes, but never explains or even confirms . . . mutilation" (*Paul Muldoon*, 35).

4. As a boy, Muldoon tried to purchase a bow from Richard Greene (ITV's Robin Hood) "when [Greene/Robin Hood was] done with it" ("Getting Round," 113).

5. One such entry seems to take place in "Mules," whose hybrid foal "should have the best of both worlds" but cannot, since its innocence is a condition it has lost by the time it has hit the ground. (*PMP* 67).

6. Muldoon wrote in the unpublished essay "Chez Moy": "Though my student days coincided with a period of extreme political unrest in Northern Ireland, I myself never took any direct part in political activity. . . . I've often considered how easily, though, I might have been caught up in the kinds of activity in which a number of my neighbors found themselves involved. As it was I preferred to come to terms with the political instability of Northern Ireland through poetry, often in an oblique, encoded way" (quoted in Kendall, *Paul Muldoon*, 16–17).

7. Heaney used the metaphor of a "lever" to describe Muldoon's poetry in the 1980s; Muldoon's "lever for the Troubles has never been less than the proverbial forty-foot pole" (Heaney, "Pre-Natal Mountain," 479).

8. For example: in the memoir, Gypsy moves from vaudeville to burlesque in Chicago, and it is her egregious mother (rather than Gypsy herself) who keeps the cow head packed for "the moment vaudeville comes back" (Lee, *Gypsy*, 255). For more of Muldoon's sources, see pp. 253 (horse dung), 257 (Nudina), 296–97 (the Eve costume), and 307 (the *Daily Worker*).

9. The persistence of legal censorship in Australia—where Donald Allen's *New American Poetry* "was banned for several years" as obscene (one could not legally bring it into the country)—gives the sense of rebellion particular force (Tranter, *New Australian Poets*, xvii).

10. David McCooey writes that the Generation of '68's "revolutionary rhetoric and commitment to alternative forms of publication (and poetic culture generally) . . . equated formal freedom with political freedom"; late-1960s "rock music briefly gave poetry new cultural capital" ("Contemporary Poetry," 160–61).

11. Kate Lilley describes the "incapacitating welter of perception" in this characteristic passage: "the faster we drive the younger we grow until the fuel boils, / clearing the sky completely" ("Tranter's Plots").

12. Tranter's 1977 essay "Four Notes on the Practice of Revolution" complains that the Generation of '68's program had run its course: "Rebellion for its own sake belongs to the selfish rhetoric of adolescence, and once the opposition has been badly damaged enough, it's time to stop" (quoted in McCooey, "Contemporary Poetry," 163).

13. A note says that these phrases come "alternately from the writings of Arthur Rimbaud and an article in the *Sydney Sun-Herald*" in 1992 (*Studio*, 109).

14. On "Boeotia"—a catchword in Murray's own prose—see, for example, Leer ("This Country," 27): "Boeotian traditional wisdom makes [Australia] habitable as a culture by centering it and containing it in a place"; the inherited farm is "more than a place from which to criticize the metropolis," because "farming and writing are chiastically connected."

6. Midair

1. A longer statement of similar claims deserves notice: in 1978 the essayist George W. S. Trow argued that American "culture . . . did not make available any but the grimmest, most false-seeming adulthood." Instead, "childhood was provided. . . . An adolescence had to be improvised, and it was. That it *was* improvised—mostly out of rock-and-roll music—so astounded the people who pulled it off that they quite rightly considered it the important historical event of their time, and have circled around it ever since" (*Within the Context*, 86). The demographer John Modell backs up such assertions with data: "The late 1960s and early 1970s," he writes, "saw . . . the ability of young people to craft their own life courses virtually *ad lib . . . as long as they did not seek to support full adult establishments*," i.e. a home with children, a fixed career, and a dependent spouse (*Into One's Own*, 322–23; italics his).

2. Wright is not the only American writer to organize a poem around yearbook inscriptions; see Mel Glenn's "Stuart Rieger" (Anderson and Hassler, *Learning*, 146).

3. "By the age of sixteen" in 1964 and 1965, Levis wrote, "I was already a kind of teenage failure, an unathletic, acne-riddled virgin who owned the slowest car in town"; "the self-pity of adolescence . . . made me feel, for a moment anyway, at once posthumous and deliciously alive" (Levis, "Levine," 105). Levis's Baby Boom coevals, he said in another interview, "were all violated by a little bit of history, by the Vietnam era" (Michael White, "Interview," 280).

4. For the so-called "butcher cover" and its lore, see, for example, http://www.eskimo.com/~bpentium/butcher.html and http://www.eskimo.com/~bpentium/whobutch.html (both viewed April 16, 2006).

5. Poems from Elledge's compilation that describe later, harsher rock music nevertheless repeat the associations of rock with the immediacy of youth and of poetry with belated adult reflection. Robert Long's "What's So Funny 'bout Peace, Love, and Understanding" uses Elvis Costello's cover of Nick Lowe's song to describe all Long's teenage years:

I remember adolescence.
It went by in a blur of hallucinogens,
Peace signs, and speechlessness: days,
Hot beach, then the beach at night:
That perfect sleep sound,

And the stars,
Like push pins in really lovely material.
(ELLEDGE, *SWEET NOTHINGS*, 155)

6. On rock and roll in literary poetry, see also Wojahn, *Strange*, chap. 12, which focuses
on Bob Dylan as an influence. "Contemporary poetry has received more of a benefit
from rock than rock has gained from contemporary poetry," Wojahn writes, because
"rock has been the soundtrack for the baby-boomer generation and the generations
that have followed it"; "most boomer and post-boomer poets have a greater familiar-
ity with rock lyrics than with the poems they profess to revere" (198).

7. "To my surprise," Arnett writes, "most of them (58%) said their high school years
were *less* stressful and difficult" than their current lives; "only 24% said high school
was more stressful and difficult" (*Emerging*, 220).

8. The Secret Stars—Geoff Farina and Jodi Buannano—released two full-length al-
bums and several singles on indie-rock labels during the 1990s; for more information, see http://outersound.com/band/secret/bio.htm, viewed April 6, 2007.

9. Other poets of Mlinko's generation note the same analogy. Ben Friedlander, for example, remembers that when he entered the social world of Bay Area experimental
writing in the late 1980s, "punk became for me a model of artistic ferment" (*Simulcast*, 11). "I came to see language writing as a 'subculture' in Dick Hebdige's sense," he
adds; "popular music provided a model for understanding poetry as both aesthetic
artifact and social phenomenon" (12).

10. His prose definition of "go-go" emphasizes, first, the music's ability to call into being
a community and, second, its association with youth: "1. A vernacular dance music
unique to Washington, D.C.; a non-stop, live party music . . . 2. a music/dance event
featuring Go-Go bands . . . frequented by teens and young teens 'hooked up' in the
latest casual wear" (*Maverick*, 49).

11. The title "12 & Under Crew" puns on age and locale: the unicyclists may hail from
west of 12th St NE or SE, or from east of 12th St NW, in Washington's directional
street address system.

12. Such language, new to American poetry during the 1990s, parallels the subcultural
talk—at once girlish, aggressive, and "out," or at least queer-positive—that entered
American popular music in those years, with the much-publicized movement called
Riot Grrrl. One writer of Riot Grrrl fanzines labeled herself "not a girl," but "not a
woman because of the pre-pubescent dresses, the messy bedrooms, & the toys"
(quoted in Leonard, "Rebel Girl," 232).

13. Here see, in particular, Beach, who argues that recent American poetry relies less
than its precursors did on "institutions" and more on "communities"; the latter involve "poets with shared interests," reliant on informal local "scenes" and transnational "networks" (*Poetic Cultures*, 5–6).

14. Tony Hoagland describes the most recent poetry, in a very ambivalent essay, with
terms that practically brand it as adolescent, though he does not notice the association; this poetry seeks "to break rules, to turn against its obligation, to be irresponsi-
ble, to recast conventions" ("Fear of Narrative," 517).

15. Levine cites a "three-decade study of thirty thousand adolescents and adults" that
concluded that "cognitively and emotionally, both groups operated at an average de-
velopmental age of sixteen" (*Harmful to Minors*, 88).

Works Cited

Abbreviations

CPB	Basil Bunting, *Complete Poems*, ed. Richard Caddel
CPG	Thom Gunn, *Collected Poems*
CPL	Philip Larkin, *Collected Poems*, ed. Anthony Thwaite
CPRL	Robert Lowell, *Collected Poems*, ed. Frank Bidart and David Gewanter
CPW	William Carlos Williams, *Collected Poems*, volume 1
EA	W.H. Auden, *The English Auden*, ed. Edward Mendelson
I	William Carlos Williams, *Imaginations*
N	Robert Lowell, *Notebook*
ONCP	George Oppen, *New Collected Poems*, ed. Michael Davidson
PMM	Marianne Moore, *Poems of Marianne Moore*, ed. Grace Schulman
PMP	Paul Muldoon, *Poems, 1968–1998.*
PTB	Auden and Isherwood, *Prose and Travel Books*, ed. Edward Mendelson
R	Jorie Graham, *Region of Unlikeness*

❖ ❖ ❖ ❖ ❖

Acland, Charles. "Fresh Contacts: Global Culture and the Concept of Generation." In *The Radiant Hour: Versions of Youth in American Culture*, ed. Neil Campbell, 31–52. Exeter: University of Exeter Press, 2000.

Addams, Jane. *The Spirit of Youth and the City Streets.* 1909. Intro. Allen F. Davis. Urbana: University of Illinois Press, 1972.

"A.E.D." "Sophomoric Epigrams." *Little Review* 2, no. 6 (1915): 37–38.

Alldritt, Keith. *The Poet as Spy: The Life and Wild Times of Basil Bunting.* London: Aurum, 1998.

Allen, Donald, ed. *The New American Poetry.* 1960. Berkeley: University of California Press, 2000.

American Poetry: The Twentieth Century. 2 vols. New York: Library of America, 2000.

Amit-Talai, Vered. "The 'Multi' Cultural of Youth." In *Youth Cultures: A Cross-Cultural Perspective*, ed. Vered Amit-Talai and Helena Wulff, 223–33. New York: Routledge, 1995.

Anderson, Alan, and George Pickering. *Confronting the Color Line: The Broken Promise of the Civil Rights Movement in Chicago*. Athens: University of Georgia Press, 1986.

Anderson, Maggie, and David Hassler, eds. *Learning By Heart: Contemporary American Poetry About School*. Iowa City: University of Iowa Press, 1999.

Anderson, Margaret. "Announcement." *Little Review* 1, no. 1 (1914): 1–2.

———. "The Germ." *Little Review*, 1, no. 2 (1914): 1–2.

———. "Reveals." *Little Review* 2, no. 6 (1915): 1–3.

Andrews, Nin. "Adolescence." *The Prose Poem: An International Journal* 6 (1997): 7.

Ansen, Alan. *The Table Talk of W. H. Auden*. Ed. Nicholas Jenkins. Intro. Richard Howard. London: Faber and Faber, 1991.

Apollonio, Umbro, ed. *Futurist Manifestos*. New York: Viking, 1973.

Ariés, Phillipe. *Centuries of Childhood*. Trans. Robert Baldick. New York: Knopf, 1962.

Arnett, Jeffrey Jensen. *Emerging Adulthood*. New York: Oxford University Press, 2004.

Arnold, Matthew. *Poetical Works*. Ed. C.B. Tinker and H.F. Lowry. New York: Oxford University Press, 1950.

Ashbery, John. *April Galleons*. New York: Farrar, Straus and Giroux, 1984.

———. *Selected Poems*. New York: Penguin, 1985.

———. *Some Trees*. Intro. W.H. Auden. New Haven, Conn.: Yale University Press, 1956.

Auden, W.H. *Collected Poems*. Ed. Edward Mendelson. New York: Vintage, 1976.

———. *The Dyer's Hand*. 1962. New York: Vintage, 1989.

———. *The English Auden: Poems, Essays, and Dramatic Writings, 1927–1939*. Ed. Edward Mendelson. London: Faber and Faber, 1977.

———. *Juvenilia: Poems, 1922–1928*. Ed. Katherine Bucknell. Princeton, N.J.: Princeton University Press, 1994.

———. *Forewords and Afterwords*. New York: Random House, 1973.

———. *The Orators: An English Study*. Third ed. London: Faber and Faber, 1966.

———. *Prose Volume I: Prose and Travel Books in Prose and Verse, 1926–1938*. Ed. Edward Mendelson. Princeton, N.J.: Princeton University Press, 1996.

———. *Prose Volume II: 1939–1948*. Ed. Edward Mendelson. Princeton, N.J.: Princeton University Press, 2002.

———. "School Writings." Ed. and intro. Richard Davenport-Hines. In *"The Language of Learning and the Language of Love": Auden Studies 2*, ed. Katherine Bucknell and Nicholas Jenkins, 1–48. Oxford: Clarendon, 1994.

———. *Selected Poems*. Ed. and intro. Edward Mendelson. New York: Vintage, 1979.

Auden, W. H., and Christopher Isherwood. *Plays and Other Dramatic Writings, 1928-1938*. Ed. Edward Mendelson. Princeton, N.J.: Princeton University Press, 1988.

Avorn, Jerry, and the staff of the *Columbia Daily Spectator*. *Up Against the Ivy Wall: A History of the Columbia Crisis*. New York: Atheneum, 1969.

Bailey, Beth. *From Front Porch to Back Seat: Courtship in Twentieth-Century America*. Baltimore: Johns Hopkins University Press, 1988.

Bargen, Walter. "Larry Levis and Walter Bargen: A Conversation." In *A Condition of the Spirit: The Life and Work of Larry Levis*, ed. Christopher Buckley and Alexander Long, 113–32. Spokane: Eastern Washington University Press, 2004.

Bate, Walter Jackson. *The Burden of the Past and the English Poet*. Cambridge, Mass.: Harvard University Press, 1970.

Batten, Guinn. "'He Could Barely Tell One From the Other': The Borderline Disorders of Paul Muldoon." *South Atlantic Quarterly* 95, no. 1 (winter 1996): 171–204.

Bayley, John. "W. H. Auden." 1957. In *W. H. Auden: A Collection of Critical Essays*, ed. Monroe K. Spears, 60–80. Englewood Cliffs, N.J.: Prentice-Hall, 1964.

Beach, Christopher. *Poetic Cultures: From Institution to Community.* Tuscaloosa: University of Alabama Press, 1999.

Beauvoir, Simone de. *The Second Sex.* Trans. H. Parshley. New York: Knopf, 1953.

Bedient, Calvin. "The Crabbed Genius of Belfast." *Parnassus* 16, no. 1(1990): 195–216.

Bell, Vereen. *Robert Lowell: Nihilist as Hero.* Cambridge, Mass.: Harvard University Press, 1983.

Ben-Amos, Ilana. *Adolescence and Youth in Early Modern England.* New Haven, Conn.: Yale University Press, 1994.

Bennett, Alan. "Instead of a Present." In *Larkin at Sixty*, ed. Anthony Thwaite, 69–74. London: Faber and Faber, 1982.

Berger, Harry. *Revisionary Play.* Berkeley: University of California Press, 1988.

——. *Second World and Green World: Studies in Renaissance Fiction-Making.* Berkeley: University of California Press, 1988.

Berman, Marshall. "Sympathy for the Devil: Faust, the 60s, and the Tragedy of Development." *American Review* 19 (1974): 23–75.

Bernstein, Charles. *My Way.* Chicago: University of Chicago Press, 1999.

Berryman, John. *The Freedom of the Poet.* New York: Farrar, Straus and Giroux, 1976.

Bibbins, Mark. *Sky Lounge.* St. Paul: Graywolf, 2004.

Bloom, Harold, ed. *Rimbaud: Modern Critical Views.* New York: Chelsea House, 1988.

——. "Introduction." In *Rimbaud*, ed. Bloom, 1–6.

Blos, Peter. *On Adolescence.* New York: Free Press of Glencoe/Macmillan, 1962.

Blum, W. G. "Some Remarks on Rimbaud as Magician." *The Dial* 68 (1920): 719–32.

Bogan, Louise. *Achievement in American Poetry, 1900–1950.* Chicago: Regnery, 1951.

Bold, Alan. *Thom Gunn and Ted Hughes.* New York: Barnes and Noble, 1976.

Booth, James, ed. *New Larkins for Old: Critical Essays.* New York: St. Martin's, 2000.

Bourne, Randolph. *Youth and Life.* 1913. Freeport, N.Y.: Books for Libraries, 1967.

Bowering, George. "Kerrisdale Elegies." In *Open Field: Thirty Canadian Poets*, ed. Sina Queyras, 32–37. New York: Persea, 2005.

Bowie, David. *Hunky Dory.* Virgin, 1971.

Bozorth, Richard. *Auden's Games of Knowledge: Poetry and the Meanings of Homosexuality.* New York: Columbia University Press, 2001.

Braunstein, Peter. "Forever Young: Insurgent Youth and the Sixties Culture of Rejuvenation." In *Imagine Nation: The American Counterculture of the 1960s and 70s*, ed. Peter Braunstein and Michael William Doyle, 243–76. New York: Routledge, 2002.

Bromwich, David. "Emphatic Reticence." *Poetry* 139, no. 6 (March 1982). Reprint, in *Marianne Moore: Modern Critical Views*, ed. Harold Bloom, 107–18. New Haven, Conn.: Chelsea House, 1987.

Brooks, David. "Feral Symbolists: Robert Adamson, John Tranter, and the Response to Rimbaud." *Australian Literary Studies* 16, no. 3 (1994): 280–88.

Brooks, Gwendolyn. *Blacks.* 1987. Chicago: Third World Press, 1992.

——. *In Montgomery.* Chicago: Third World Press, 2003.

——. *Report from Part One.* Detroit: Broadside Press, 1972.

——. *Report from Part Two.* Chicago: Third World Press, 1996.

Brooks, Van Wyck. *America's Coming of Age.* Garden City, N.Y.: Doubleday, 1958.

Brumberg, Joan Jacobs. *The Body Project: An Intimate History of American Girls*. New York: Random House, 1997.

Brunner, Edward. *Cold War Poetry*. Urbana: University of Illinois Press, 2001.

Buckley, Christopher, and Alexander Long, eds. *A Condition of the Spirit: The Life and Work of Larry Levis*. Spokane: Eastern Washington University Press, 2004.

Bunting, Basil. *Collected Poems*, ed. Richard Caddel. New York: New Directions, 2003.

Burke, Kenneth. "The Armor of Jules Laforge" [*sic*]. *Contact* 3 (1992): 9–10.

Burt, Stephen. *Randall Jarrell and His Age*. New York: Columbia University Press, 2002.

Bynner, Witter. "Youth Sings to the Sea." *Youth* (1918): 10.

Byron, Lord (George Gordon). *The Major Works*. Ed. Jerome McGann. New York: Oxford University Press, 2000.

Caddel, Richard, and Anthony Flowers. *Basil Bunting: A Northern Life*. Newcastle-upon-Tyne and Durham: Newcastle Libraries Information Service/ Basil Bunting Poetry Centre, 1997.

Cairns, Ed. *Caught in Crossfire: Children and the Northern Ireland Conflict*. Belfast: Appletree Press, 1987.

Cameron, Sharon. *Lyric Time: Dickinson and the Limits of Genre*. Baltimore, Md.: Johns Hopkins University Press, 1979.

Cannell, Skipwith. "Ikons." *Others* 2, no. 2 (1916): 156–66.

Carnevali, Emanuel. "Arthur Rimbaud." *Others* 5, no. 3 (1919): 20–24.

———. *The Autobiography of Emanuel Carnevali*. Ed. Kay Boyle. New York: Horizon, 1969.

Carpenter, Humphrey. *W. H. Auden: A Biography*. Boston: Houghton Mifflin, 1981.

Carroll, Peter N. *It Seemed Like Nothing Happened: The Tragedy and Promise of America in the 1970s*. New York: Holt, Rinehart and Winston, 1982.

Carter, Erica. "Alice in the Consumer Wonderland." In *Gender and Generation*, ed. Angela McRobbie and Mica Nava, 185–214. Houndmills: Macmillan, 1984.

Casper, Robert. "About Jorie Graham: A Profile." *Ploughshares* 27, no. 4 (Winter 2001–02). http://www.pshares.org/issues/article.cfm?prmarticleID=7400. Viewed October 30, 2003.

Cendrars, Blaise. *Poésies complètes*. 1947. Ed. Claude Leroy. Paris: Editions Denoel, 2001.

Charters, Ann, ed. *The Portable Sixties Reader*. New York: Penguin, 2002.

Chattarji, Subarno. *Memories of a Lost War*. New York: Oxford University Press, 2001.

Chudacoff, Howard. *How Old Are You? Age Consciousness in American Culture*. Princeton, N.J.: Princeton University Press, 1989.

Ciardi, John. *The Little That Is All*. New Brunswick, N.J.: Rutgers University Press, 1974.

Clampitt, Amy. *Collected Poems*. London: Faber and Faber, 1998.

Clarke, Cheryl. *"After Mecca": Women Poets and the Black Arts Movement*. New Brunswick, N.J.: Rutgers University Press, 2005.

Coates, Jennifer. "Changing Femininities: The Talk of Teenage Girls." In *Reinventing Identities: The Gendered Self in Discourse*, ed. Mary Bucholtz, A.C. Liang, and Laurel A. Sutton, 123–44. Oxford: Oxford University Press, 1999.

Comfort, W.L. "Education by Children." *Little Review* 2, no. 4 (1915): 5–7.

Compton, Shanna. *Downspooky*. Austin, Tex.: Winnow , 2005.

Connolly, Cyril. *The Condemned Playground*. New York: Macmillan, 1946.

———. *Enemies of Promise*. Boston: Little, Brown, 1939.

———. *The Evening Colonnade*. 1973. New York: Harcourt Brace Jovanovich, 1975.

Cornwell, Tim. "The Words of the Decade, the Century, and the Millennium." *Times Higher Education Supplement*, December 17, 1999, ii.

Corso, Gregory. *Mindfield*. New York: Thunder's Mouth, 1989.

Costello, Bonnie. *Marianne Moore: Imaginary Possessions.* Cambridge, Mass.: Harvard University Press, 1981.

Coveney, Peter. *Poor Monkey: The Child in Literature.* London: Rockliff, 1957.

Cox, C. B., and A. E. Dyson, eds. *Fight for Education: A Black Paper. Critical Survey* 4, no. 1 (1969).

Crane, Hart. *Complete Poems.* Ed. Marc Simon. New York: Liveright, 1986.

Creeley, Robert. *The Collected Poems of Robert Creeley, 1945–75.* Berkeley: University of California Press, 1982.

Cummings, E. E. *Collected Poems, 1913–1962.* New York: Harcourt Brace Jovanovich, 1972.

Cushman, Stephen. *William Carlos Williams and the Meanings of Measure.* New Haven, Conn.: Yale University Press, 1985.

Dalsimer, Katherine. *Female Adolescence: Psychoanalytic Reflections on Works of Literature.* New Haven, Conn.: Yale University Press, 1986.

Damon, Maria. *The Dark End of the Street.* Minneapolis: University of Minnesota Press, 1993.

Davenport-Hines, Richard. *Auden.* New York: Pantheon, 1995.

Davidson, Michael. *Guys Like Us: Citing Masculinity in Cold War Poetics.* Chicago: University of Chicago Press, 2004.

Davie, Donald. "One Way to Misread *Briggflatts.*" In *Basil Bunting: Man and Poet,* ed. Carroll F. Terrell, 161–68. Orono, Maine: National Poetry Foundation, 1981.

———. *Two Ways Out of Whitman: American Essays.* Ed. Doreen Davie. Manchester: Carcanet, 2000.

Davis, Mary Carolyn. "Song of a Girl." *Others* 1, no. 1 (1915): 3–5.

Dawley, David. *A Nation of Lords: The Autobiography of the Vice Lords.* 1973. Prospect Heights, Ill.: Waveland, 1992.

Diski, Jenny. "Damp-Lipped Hillary." *London Review of Books,* May 23, 2002. http://www .lrb.co.uk/v24/n10/disk01_.html.http://books.guardian.co.uk/lrb/articles/0,6109, 716769,00.html. Viewed April 26, 2006.

Dobrez, Livio. *Parnassus Mad Ward: Michael Dransfield and the New Australian Poetry.* St. Lucia: University of Queensland Press, 1990.

Donaghy, Michael. "A Conversation with Paul Muldoon." *Chicago Review* 35, no. 1 (1985): 76–85.

Donne, John. *Complete Poetry.* Ed. John Shawcross. New York: New York University Press, 1968.

Douglas, Keith. *The Complete Poems.* 1978. Ed. Desmond Graham. Intro. Ted Hughes. London: Faber and Faber, 2000.

Dove, Rita. *Mother Love.* New York: Norton, 1995.

———. *Selected Poems.* New York: Pantheon, 1993.

Drake, St. Clair, and Horace R. Cayton. *Black Metropolis: A Study of Negro Life in a Northern City.* 1945. Chicago: University of Chicago Press, 1993.

Driscoll, Catherine. *Girls: Feminine Adolescence in Popular Culture and Cultural Theory.* New York: Columbia University Press, 2002.

Duchêne, Francois. *The Case of the Helmeted Airman.* London: Chatto and Windus, 1972.

Dupee, F. W. "The Uprising at Columbia." *New York Review of Books,* September 26, 1968, 20–38.

Duwell, Martin. *A Possible Contemporary Poetry.* St. Lucia: Makar, 1982.

Eberhart, Richard. "West Coast Rhythms." *New York Times Book Review,* September 2, 1956. Reprint, in *The Beats: a Literary Reference,* ed. Matt Theado, 70–71. New York: Carroll & Graf, 2001.

Eby, Carl. "'The Ogre' and the 'Beautiful Thing': Voyeurism, Exhibitionism, and the Image of 'Woman' in the Poetry of William Carlos Williams." *William Carlos Williams Review* 21, no. 1 (1996): 29–45.

Edwards, Kerry. "Listening to Feminism." *How(ever)* 5, no. 3 (1989). Reprint, http://www.how2journal.com/archive, viewed May 1, 2006.

Ehrenreich, Barbara, and John Ehrenreich. *Long March, Short Spring: The Student Uprising at Home and Abroad.* New York: Modern Reader/Monthly Review, 1969.

Eliot, T. S. *Collected Poems.* London: Faber and Faber, 1974.

——. "Marianne Moore." *Dial* 75 (December 1923): 594–597. Reprint, in *Marianne Moore: A Collection of Critical Essays,* ed. Charles Tomlinson, 48–51. Englewood Cliffs, N.J.: Prentice-Hall, 1969.

——. *Selected Prose.* Ed. Frank Kermode. New York: Harcourt, 1975.

——. *The Varieties of Metaphysical Poetry: The Clark Lectures at Trinity College Cambridge, 1926, and the Turnbull Lectures at Johns Hopkins University, 1933.* Ed. Ronald Schuchard. London: Faber & Faber, 1993.

Elledge, Jim, ed. *Sweet Nothings: An Anthology of Rock and Roll in American Poetry.* Bloomington: Indiana University Press, 1994.

Ellis, Thomas Sayers. *The Maverick Room.* St. Paul, Minn.: Graywolf, 2005.

Empson, William. *Seven Types of Ambiguity.* 1930. Norfolk, Conn.: New Directions, 1947.

Erickson, Darlene. *Illusion Is More Precise Than Precision: The Poetry of Marianne Moore.* Tuscaloosa: University of Alabama Press, 1992.

Erikson, Erik. *Childhood and Society.* 1950. Second ed. New York: Norton, 1963.

Esman, Aaron. *Adolescence in Culture.* New York: Columbia University Press, 1990.

"Etiemble." *Le mythe de Rimbaud.* 1954. Paris: Gallimard, 1968.

Everett, Barbara. "Philip Larkin: After Symbolism." *Essays in Criticism* 30 (1980): 227–42.

Ezard, John. "Poetic Justice for Bainbridge and Gunn." *Guardian,* March 28, 2003. http://books.guardian.co.uk/print/0,3858,4635196-99819,00.html. Viewed April 25, 2006.

Farber, David. *Chicago '68.* Chicago: University of Chicago Press, 1988.

Fass, Paula. *The Damned and Beautiful.* New York: Oxford University Press, 1977.

Fiedler, Leslie. "The New Mutants." *Partisan Review* 32 (1965): 505–25.

——. "On Being Busted at Fifty." *New York Review of Books,* July 13, 1967, 8–14.

Finkelstein, Norman. "The Dialectic of *This In Which.*" In *George Oppen: Man and Poet,* ed. Burton Hatlen, 361–73. Orono, Maine: National Poetry Foundation, 1981.

Firchow, Peter. *W. H. Auden: Contexts for Poetry.* Newark: University of Delaware Press, 2002.

Five Young American Poets. Vol. 3. Norfolk, Conn.: New Directions, 1944.

Fletcher, Angus. *A New Theory for American Poetry.* Cambridge, Mass.: Harvard University Press, 2004.

"Florizel Adolescent (A Sermon)." *The Double Dealer* 7 (1924): 54–55.

Flynn, Richard. "'Infant Sight.'" In *Literature and the Child,* ed. James McGavran, 105–29. Iowa City: University of Iowa Press, 1999.

Ford, Mark. "Out of the Blue." *London Review of Books,* December 10, 1987, 20–21.

Fowlie, Wallace. "Rimbaud in 1949." *Poetry* 75, no. 3 (1949): 166–69.

——. *Rimbaud: The Myth of Childhood.* London: Dennis Dobson, 1946.

Frank, Florence Kiper. "Psycho-Analysis." *Little Review* 3, no. 4 (1916): 15–17.

Fried, Michael. *Art and Objecthood.* Chicago: University of Chicago Press, 1998.

Friedan, Betty. *The Feminine Mystique.* New York: Norton, 1963.

Friedenberg, Edgar Z. *The Vanishing Adolescent.* New York: Dell, 1959.

Friedlander, Benjamin. *Simulcast: Four Experiments in Criticism.* Tuscaloosa: University of Alabama Press, 2004.

Frost, Robert. *Collected Poems, Prose, and Plays*. Ed. Richard Poirier and Mark Richardson. New York: Library of America, 1995.

Fuller, Hoyt. "Towards a Black Aesthetic." In *Within the Circle: An Anthology of African-American Literary Criticism*, ed. Angelyn Mitchell, 199–206. Durham: Duke University Press, 1994.

Fuller, John. *W. H. Auden: A Commentary*. Princeton, N.J.: Princeton University Press, 1998.

Fussell, Paul. *The Great War and Modern Memory*. New York: Oxford University Press, 1975.

Gardner, Thomas. *Regions of Unlikeness: Explaining Contemporary Poetry*. Lincoln: University of Nebraska Press, 1999.

Gass, William. *On Being Blue*. Boston: David R. Godine, 1976.

Gilbert, Geoff. *Before Modernism Was*. New York: Palgrave Macmillan, 2004.

Gil de Biedma, Jaime. *El Pie de la letra*. Barcelona: Crítica, 1994.

Gilligan, Carol. *In a Different Voice*. Cambridge, Mass.: Harvard University Press, 1982.

———. "Teaching Shakespeare's Sister: Notes from the Underground of Female Adolescence." In *Making Connections: The Relational Worlds of Adolescent Girls at Emma Willard School*, ed. Carol Gilligan et al., 6–29. Cambridge, Mass.: Harvard University Press, 1990.

Gillis, John. *Youth and History*. New York: Harcourt, Brace, Jovanovich, 1974.

Gilmore, Louis. "Florizel Adolescent (A Scenario)." *The Double Dealer* 7, no. 39 (1924): 54–55.

Ginsberg, Allen. *Howl*. 1956. Ed. Barry Miles. New York: HarperPerennial, 1995.

Glück, Louise. *The First Four Books of Poems*. Hopewell, N.J.: Ecco, 1995.

Golding, Douglas. "The Highbrowettes." *Others* 2, no. 1 (1916): 131.

Goldstein, Laurence. *The American Poet at the Movies*. Ann Arbor: University of Michigan Press, 1994.

Goodman, Paul. *Growing Up Absurd: Problems of Youth in the Organized System*. New York: Random House, 1960.

Goodridge, Celeste. *Hints and Disguises: Marianne Moore and Her Contemporaries*. Iowa City: University of Iowa Press, 1989.

Graham, Jorie. *The Dream of the Unified Field: Selected Poems, 1974–1994*. Manchester: Carcanet, 1996.

———. *Region of Unlikeness*. New York: Ecco, 1991.

Greenfeld, Liah. "When the Sky Is the Limit: Busyness in Contemporary American Society." *Social Research* 72, no. 2 (2005): 315–38.

Greif, Mark. "Afternoon of the Sex Children." *n + 1* 4 (2006): 169–88.

Grossberg, Lawrence. "The Political Status of Youth and Youth Culture." In *If It's Too Loud You're Too Old: Adolescents and Their Music*, ed. Jonathan Epstein, 25–46. New York: Garland, 1994.

Grossman, Allen, and Mark Halliday. *The Sighted Singer*. Baltimore, Md.: Johns Hopkins University Press, 1992.

Grosz, Elizabeth. *Volatile Bodies: Toward a Corporeal Feminism*. Bloomington: Indiana University Press, 1994.

Gunn, Thom. *Boss Cupid*. New York: Farrar, Straus and Giroux, 2000.

———. *Collected Poems*. New York: Farrar, Straus and Giroux, 1994.

———. *The Occasions of Poetry*. Berkeley, Calif.: North Point, 1982.

———. *Shelf Life*. Ann Arbor: University of Michigan Press, 1993.

Haffenden, John, ed. *W. H. Auden: The Critical Heritage*. London: Routledge and Kegan Paul, 1983.

Hall, G. Stanley. *Adolescence: Its Psychology and Its Relations to Physiology, Anthropology, Sociology, Sex, Crime, Religion, and Education*. 2 vols. 1904. New York: D. Appleton, 1921.

Hamilton, Ian. *Robert Lowell: A Biography*. New York: Vintage, 1983.

Hammer, Langdon. *Janus-Faced Modernism: Hart Crane and Allen Tate*. Princeton, N.J.: Princeton University Press, 1993.

———. "Plath's Lives." *Representations* 75 (2001): 61–88.

Hanawalt, Barbara. *Growing Up in Medieval London: The Experience of Childhood in History*. New York: Oxford University Press, 1993.

Hardwick, Elizabeth. *Bartleby in Manhattan*. New York: Random House, 1983.

———. "Chicago." *New York Review of Books*, September 26, 1968, 5–7.

Hart, Matt. *Who's Who Vivid*. Buffalo, N.Y.: Slope, 2006.

Hartman, Geoffrey. *Beyond Formalism*. New Haven, Conn.: Yale University Press, 1970.

Hausknecht, Gina. "Self-Possession, Dolls, Beatlemania, Loss." In *The Girl: Constructions of the Girl in Contemporary Fiction by Women*, ed. Ruth Saxton, 21–42. New York: St. Martin's, 1998.

Heaney, Seamus. "The Pre-Natal Mountain: Vision and Irony in Recent Irish Poetry." *Georgia Review* 42, no. 3 (1988): 465–80.

Hebdige, Dick. *Subculture: The Meaning of Style*. London: Routledge, 1979.

Hecht, Ben. "The American Family." *Little Review* 2, no. 5 (1915): 1–4.

Hejinian, Lyn. *The Language of Inquiry*. Berkeley: University of California Press, 2000.

———. *My Life*. 1980. 2nd expanded ed. Los Angeles: Sun and Moon, 1987.

Herd, David. *John Ashbery and American Poetry*. New York: Palgrave, 2000.

Hewison, Robert. *Too Much: Art and Society in the Sixties, 1960–75*. London: Methuen, 1986.

Hoagland, Tony. "Fear of Narrative and the Skittery Poem of Our Moment." *Poetry* (March 2006). http://www.poetrymagazine.org/magazine/0306/comment_177773.html. Viewed April 20, 2006.

Hoggart, Richard. *The Uses of Literacy*. 1957. New Brunswick, N.J.: Transaction, 1998.

Hollander, John, ed. *Poems of Our Moment*. New York: Pegasus, 1968.

———. "Soonest Mended." 1981. Reprint, in *John Ashbery: Modern Critical Views*, ed. Harold Bloom, 207–15. New York: Chelsea House, 1985.

Holley, Margaret. *The Poetry of Marianne Moore*. Cambridge: Cambridge University Press, 1989.

Hough, Graham. *Legends and Pastorals*. London: Gerald Duckworth, 1961.

Housman, A. E. *Collected Poems*. New York: Henry Holt, 1965.

Howe, Irving. *A Margin of Hope*. New York: Harcourt Brace Jovanovich, 1982.

———. "The New York Intellectuals." *Commentary* 46, no. 4 (October 1968): 29–51.

Hudson, Barbara. "Femininity and Adolescence." In *Gender and Generation*, ed. Angela McRobbie and Mica Nava, 31–53. Houndmills: Macmillan, 1984.

Hughes, David. *The Complete Kubrick*. London: Virgin, 2000.

Hunter, Jane. *How Young Ladies Became Girls*. New Haven, Conn.: Yale University Press, 2002.

Hutchens, John K., ed. *The American Twenties: A Literary Panorama*. Philadelphia: J.B. Lippincott, 1952.

Hynes, Samuel. *The Auden Generation: Literature and Politics in England in the 1930s*. Princeton, N.J.: Princeton University Press, 1976.

Innes, Sherrie A. *Intimate Communities: Representation and Social Transformation in Women's College Fiction, 1895–1910*. Bowling Green, Ohio: Bowling Green State University Press, 1995.

Isherwood, Christopher. *Exhumations*. New York: Simon and Schuster, 1966.
———. *Lions and Shadows*. 1938. Norfolk, Conn.: New Directions, 1948.
Izzo, David Garrett. "The Student and the Master: A Pupil's Recollections of the Poet W.H. Auden." In *W. H. Auden: A Legacy*, ed. David Garrett Izzo, 29–38. West Cornwall, Conn.: Locust Hill, 2002.
Jameson, Fredric. "Rimbaud and the Spatial Text." In *Rewriting Literary History*, ed. Tak-Wai Wong and M.A. Abbas, 66–93. Hong Kong: University Press of Hong Kong, 1984.
Jarrell, Randall. *The Complete Poems*. New York: Farrar, Straus & Giroux, 1969.
———. *Kipling, Auden, and Co.* New York: Farrar, Straus and Giroux, 1980.
———. *The Third Book of Criticism*. New York: Farrar, Straus and Giroux, 1969.
Johnson, Don. *The Sporting Muse*. Jefferson, N.C.: MacFarland, 2004.
Johnson, James Weldon. *Complete Poems*. New York: Penguin, 2000.
Johnston, Andrew. "Surviving Desire: The Poetry of John Tranter." *Landfall* 187 (1994). Reprint, http://andrewjohnston.org/tranter.htm. Viewed April 26, 2006.
Jones, Emrys, ed. *The New Oxford Book of Sixteenth-Century Verse*. New York: Oxford University Press, 1991.
Kalstone, David. *Five Temperaments*. New York: Oxford University Press, 1977.
Kasischke, Laura. *Boy Heaven*. New York: HarperCollins, 2006.
———. *Dance and Disappear*. Amherst: University of Massachusetts Press, 2002.
———. *Fire and Flower*. Farmington, Maine: Alice James, 1998.
———. *Gardening in the Dark*. Keene, N.Y.: Ausable, 2004.
———. *Housekeeping in a Dream*. Pittsburgh: Carnegie-Mellon University Press, 1995.
———. *What It Wasn't*. Pittsburgh: Carnegie-Mellon University Press, 2002.
———. *White Bird in a Blizzard*. New York: Hyperion, 1999.
———. *Wild Brides*. New York: New York University Press, 1992.
Keats, John. *The Major Works*. Ed. Elizabeth Cook. New York: Oxford University Press, 2001.
Keightley, Keir. "Reconsidering Rock." In *The Cambridge Companion to Pop and Rock*, ed. Simon Frith et al., 109–42. Cambridge: Cambridge University Press, 2001.
Kelen, Leslie. "After the Obsession with Some Beloved Figure: An Interview with Larry Levis." In *A Condition of the Spirit: The Life and Work of Larry Levis*, ed. Christopher Buckley and Alexander Long, 31–50. Spokane: Eastern Washington University Press, 2004.
Keller, Lynn. "An Interview with Paul Muldoon." *Contemporary Literature* 35, no. 1 (1994): 1–29.
Kendall, Tim. *Paul Muldoon*. Chester Springs, Penn.: Dufour, 1996.
Kent, George. *A Life of Gwendolyn Brooks*. Lexington: University of Kentucky Press, 1990.
Kermode, Frank. "The Young and Their Elders." *Partisan Review* 37 (1970): 184–98.
Kett, Joseph. *Rites of Passage: Adolescence in America, 1790 to the Present*. New York: Basic, 1977.
Kidd, Kenneth. *Making American Boys: Boyology and the Feral Tale*. Minneapolis: University of Minnesota Press, 2005.
Kiell, Norman. *The Adolescent Through Fiction*. New York: International Universities Press, 1959.
Kincaid, James R. "Resist Me, You Sweet Resistible You." *PMLA* 118, no. 5 (October 2003): 1325–33.
Kipling, Rudyard. *Stalky & Co.* Vol. 18 of *Works*. New York: Charles Scribner's Sons, 1920.
Koethe, John. *North Point North: New and Selected Poems*. New York: Harcourt, 2002.

———. *Sally's Hair*. New York: Harcourt, 2006.

Komunyakaa, Yusef. *Pleasure Dome: New and Collected Poems*. Middletown, Conn.: Wesleyan University Press, 2001.

Kreymborg, Alfred. "Hemstitches." *Others* 3, no. 4 (1916): 41.

Kristeva, Julia. *New Maladies of the Soul*. Trans. Ross Guberman. New York: Columbia University Press, 1995.

Kunitz, Stanley. *A Kind of Order, a Kind of Folly*. Boston: Atlantic Monthly, 1975.

Lane, Homer. *Talks to Parents and Teachers*. 1928. Intro. A.S. Neill. New York: Schocken, 1969.

Larkin, Philip. *All What Jazz*. London: Faber & Faber, 1970.

———. *The Collected Poems,* ed. Anthony Thwaite. London: Faber & Faber/The Marvell Press, 1988.

———. *Further Requirements*. London: Faber & Faber, 2001.

———. *A Girl in Winter*. Woodstock, N.Y.: Overlook Press, 1985 (1947).

———. *Jill*. 1946. Woodstock, N.Y.: The Overlook Press, 1976.

———. "Negroes of Europe." *Guardian*, November 30, 1973, 21.

———, ed. *The Oxford Book of Twentieth-Century English Verse*. Oxford: Clarendon, 1973.

———. *Selected Letters of Philip Larkin*. Ed. Anthony Thwaite. London: Faber and Faber, 1992.

———. *Trouble at Willow Gables and Other Fictions*. Ed. James Booth. London: Faber and Faber, 2002.

Lawrence, D.H. *Fantasia of the Unconscious and Psycho-analysis of the Unconscious*. 1923. London: Heinemann, 1971.

Lee, Gypsy Rose. *Gypsy: A Memoir*. New York: Harper and Brothers, 1957.

Leer, Martin. "'This Country Is My Mind': Les Murray's Poetics of Place." In *The Poetry of Les Murray: Critical Essays*, ed. Laurie Hergenhan and Bruce Clunies Ross, 15–42. St. Lucia: University Press of Queensland, 2001.

Leonard, Marion. "'Rebel Girl, You Are the Queen of My World': Feminism, 'Subculture' and Girl Power." In *Sexing the Groove: Popular Music and Gender*, ed. Sheila Whiteley, 230–55. London: Routledge, 1997.

LeTendre, Gerald K. *Learning to Be Adolescent: Growing Up in U.S. and Japanese Middle Schools*. New Haven, Conn.: Yale University Press, 2000.

Levertov, Denise. *The Poet in the World*. New York: New Directions, 1973.

———. *To Stay Alive*. New York: New Directions, 1971.

Levine, Judith. *Harmful to Minors: The Perils of Protecting Children from Sex*. 2002. New York: Thunder's Mouth, 2003.

Levis, Larry. *Elegy*. Pittsburgh: University of Pittsburgh Press, 1997.

———. "Philip Levine." In *A Condition of the Spirit: The Life and Work of Larry Levis*, ed. Christopher Buckley and Alexander Long, 105–12. Spokane: Eastern Washington University Press, 2004.

———. *The Selected Levis*. Rev. ed. Pittsburgh: University of Pittsburgh Press, 2003.

Lewis, William D. *Democracy's High School*. Intro. Theodore Roosevelt. Boston: Houghton Mifflin, 1914.

Lilley, Kate. "Tranter's Plots." *Australian Literary Studies* 14, no. 1 (1989). Reprint, http://www.austlit.com/a/lilley-k/1989-tranter-als.html. Viewed April 26, 2006.

Longenbach, James. *Modern Poetry After Modernism*. New York: Oxford University Press, 1997.

———. *The Resistance to Poetry*. Chicago: University of Chicago Press, 2004.

Longfellow, Henry Wadsworth. *Poems and Other Writings*. Ed. J.D. McClatchy. New York: Library of America, 2000.

Longley, Edna. "Larkin, Decadence, and the Lyric Poem." In *New Larkins for Old: Critical Essays*, ed. James Booth, 29–50. New York: St. Martin's, 2000.

Lowell, Amy. "Miss Columbia: An Old-Fashioned Girl." *Little Review* 1, no. 4 (1914): 36–37.

Lowell, Robert. *Collected Poems*. Ed. Frank Bidart and David Gewanter. New York: Farrar, Straus and Giroux, 2003.

———. *The Letters of Robert Lowell*. Ed. Saskia Hamilton. New York: Farrar, Straus and Giroux, 2005.

———. *Notebook*. New York: Farrar, Straus and Giroux, 1970.

———. *Prometheus Bound*. New York: Farrar, Straus and Giroux, 1967.

———. *Selected Poems*. New York: Farrar, Straus and Giroux, 1976.

Loy, Mina. "O Hell." *Contact* 1 (1920): 7.

———. "Perlun." *The Dial* 71 (1921): 141.

———. "Songs to Joannes." *Others* 3, no. 6 (1917): 6.

———. "Two Plays." Ed. Julie Schmid. *Performing Arts Journal* 52 (1996): 8–17.

Lu, Pamela. *Pamela: A Novel*. Berkeley, Calif.: Atelos, 1998.

Lund, Mary Graham. "Adolescence." *Poet Lore* 69, no. 2 (summer 1974): 185.

MacInnes, Colin. *England Half English*. 1961. London: Chatto and Windus, 1986.

Macleod, David I. *The Age of the Child: Children in America 1890–1920*. New York: Twayne, 1998.

Mailer, Norman. *The Armies of the Night*. New York: New American Library, 1968.

Makin, Peter. *Bunting: The Shaping of His Verse*. New York: Oxford University Press, 1991.

"Man of the Year: The Inheritor." *Time*, January 6, 1967, 18–23.

Martin, Robert K. *The Homosexual Tradition in American Poetry*. 2nd ed. 1979. Iowa City: University of Iowa Press, 1998.

Martin, Taffy. *Marianne Moore: Subversive Modernist*. Austin: University of Texas Press, 1986.

Masefield, John. *Poems*. New York: Macmillan, 1951.

Matthews, Steven. *Irish Poetry: Politics, History, Negotiation*. London: Macmillan, 1997.

McCooey, David. "Contemporary Poetry: Across Party Lines." In *The Cambridge Companion to Australian Literature*, ed. Elizabeth Webby, 158–82. Cambridge: Cambridge University Press, 2000.

McDonald, Peter. *Mistaken Identities: Poetry and Northern Ireland*. Oxford: Clarendon Press, 1997.

McGinley, Phyllis. *Sixpence in Her Shoe*. New York: Macmillan, 1964.

———. *Stones from a Glass House*. New York: Viking, 1946.

———. *Times Three: Selected Verse from Three Decades with Seventy New Poems*. New York: Viking, 1961.

McGrath, Charles. "Being 13." *New York Times Magazine*. May 17, 1998, 29.

McGregor, Gaile. *Eccentric Visions: Reconstructing Australia*. Waterloo, Ont.: Wilfrid Laurier University Press, 1994.

McRobbie, Angela. *Feminism and Youth Culture*. New York: Routledge, 2000.

Medovoi, Leerom. "Democracy, Capitalism, and American Literature: The Cold War Construction of J.D. Salinger's Paperback Hero." In *The Other Fifties*, ed. Joel Foreman, 255–87. Urbana: University of Illinois Press, 1997.

Melly, George. *Revolt Into Style*. New York: Anchor, 1971.

Melville, Herman. *Battle-Pieces*. Ed. Hennig Cohen. New York: Thomas Yoseloff, 1963.

Mendelson, Edward. *Early Auden*. 1981. Cambridge, Mass.: Harvard University Press, 1983.

Millay, Edna St. Vincent. *Collected Poems*. New York: Harper and Row, 1956.

Miller, Cristanne. *Marianne Moore: Questions of Authority*. Cambridge, Mass.: Harvard University Press, 1995.

Miller, Henry. *The Time of the Assassins: A Study of Rimbaud*. London: Neville Spearman, 1956.

Milton, John. *Poetical Works*. Ed. Helen Darbishire. New York: Oxford University Press, 1958.

Mintz, Steven. *Huck's Raft: A History of American Childhood*. Cambridge, Mass.: Harvard University Press, 2004.

Mitchell, Angelyn, ed. *Within the Circle: An Anthology of African-American Literary Criticism*. Durham, N.C.: Duke University Press, 1994.

Mlinko, Ange. "Fighting Words." Review of *Imagination Verses*, by Jennifer Moxley. *Arts-Media* (1997): n.p.

———. *Matinees*. Boston: Zoland, 1999.

Molesworth, Charles. *Marianne Moore: A Literary Life*. New York: Atheneum, 1990.

Modell, John. *Into One's Own: From Youth to Adulthood in the United States, 1920–1975*. Berkeley: University of California Press, 1989.

Moore, Marianne. [Answers to questionnaire.] *Little Review* 12 (1929): 64.

———. *Becoming Marianne Moore: The Early Poems, 1907–1924*. Ed. Robin G. Schulze. Berkeley: University of California Press, 2002.

———. *The Complete Prose of Marianne Moore*. New York: Viking, 1986.

———. *The Poems of Marianne Moore*. Ed. Grace Schulman. New York: Viking, 2003.

———. *Selected Letters*. Ed. Bonnie Costello with Celeste Goodridge and Cristanne Miller. New York: Penguin, 1997.

Moss, Thylias. *Last Chance for the Tarzan Holler*. New York: Persea, 1998.

———. *Small Congregations*. Hopewell, N.J.: Ecco, 1993.

———. *Tale of a Sky-Blue Dress*. New York: Bard-Avon, 1998.

Motion, Andrew. *A Writer's Life: Philip Larkin*. London: Faber & Faber, 1993.

Mottram, Eric. "The Political Responsibilities of the Poet: George Oppen." In *George Oppen: Man and Poet*, ed. Burton Hatlen, 149–67. Orono, Maine: National Poetry Foundation, 1981.

Muldoon, Paul. *The Annals of Chile*. London: Faber, 1994.

———. "Getting Round: Notes Towards an Ars Poetica." *Essays in Criticism* 48, no. 2 (1998): 107–28.

———. *Poems, 1968–1998*. New York: Farrar, Straus and Giroux, 2000.

———, ed. *The Scrake of Dawn*. Belfast: Blackstaff, 1979.

———. "Under Saturn." *Times Literary Supplement*, February 27, 1981, 219.

Mulvey, Laura. "Visual Pleasure and Narrative Cinema." 1975. Reprint, in *The Film Studies Reader*, ed. Joanne Holloway, Peter Hutchings, and Mark Jancovich, 238–48. London: Arnold, 2000.

Munson, Gorham. *The Awakening Twenties*. Baton Rouge: Louisiana State University Press, 1985.

Murray, Les. *Collected Poems*. Manchester: Carcanet, 1998.

Nash, Ilana. *American Sweethearts: Teenage Girls in Twentieth-Century Popular Culture*. Bloomington: Indiana University Press, 2006.

Naylor, Paul. "The Adolescent." *Chicago Review* 45, no. 1 (1999): 46.

Nethercot, Arthur H. "The Sophisticated Innocents of Modern Verse." *The Double Dealer* 5 (1923): 202–6.

Neubauer, John. *The Fin-de-Siècle Culture of Adolescence*. New Haven, Conn.: Yale University Press, 1992.

Noxon, Christopher. "I Don't Want to Grow Up!" *New York Times Magazine*, August 31, 2003, 1, 9.

Nuttall, Jeff. *Bomb Culture*. New York: Delacorte, 1968.

Oppen, George. *New Collected Poems*. Ed. Michael Davidson. Manchester: Carcanet, 2002.

———. *The Selected Letters of George Oppen*. Ed. Rachel Blau DuPlessis. Durham, N.C.: Duke University Press, 1990.

Oppen, Mary. *Meaning a Life*. Santa Barbara, Ca.: Black Sparrow, 1978.

Oppenheim, James. "Randolph Bourne." *The Dial* 67 (January 11, 1919): 7.

———. "The Young World." *The Dial* 64 (February 28, 1918): 175–80.

Ortega y Gasset, Jose. *The Dehumanization of Art*. Trans. Helene Weyl et al. Princeton, N.J.: Princeton University Press, 1968.

Osborn, Andrew. "Skirmishes on the Border: The Evolution and Function of Paul Muldoon's Fuzzy Rhyme." *Contemporary Literature* 41, no. 2 (2000): 323–58.

Palladino, Grace. *Teenagers: An American History*. New York: Basic Books, 1996.

Papini, Giovanni. *The Failure*. 1912. Trans. Virginia Pope. New York: Harcourt, Brace, 1924.

Parisi, Joseph, and Stephen Young, eds. *Dear Editor: A History of Poetry in Letters, The First Fifty Years, 1912–1962*. New York: Norton, 2002.

Peck, John. "Bardic 'Briggflatts.'" In *Basil Bunting: Man and Poet*, ed. Carroll F. Terrell, 169–85. Orono, Maine: National Poetry Foundation, 1981.

Perloff, Marjorie. *The Futurist Moment: Avant-Garde, Avant-Guerre, and the Language of Rupture*. Chicago: University of Chicago Press, 1986.

Phelan, Peggy. *Unmarked*. London: Routledge, 1993.

Pickard, Tom. *High on the Walls*. Preface by Basil Bunting. London: Fulcrum, 1968.

Pifer, Ellen. *Demon or Doll: Images of the Child in Contemporary Writing and Culture*. Charlottesville: University Press of Virginia, 2000.

Plath, Sylvia. *The Bell Jar*. 1963. New York: Bantam, 1972.

———. *Collected Poems*. Ed. Ted Hughes. London: Faber and Faber, 1981.

Podhoretz, Norman. "The Know-Nothing Bohemians." 1958. In *The Beats: A Literary Reference*, ed. Matt Theado, 74–81. New York: Carroll & Graf, 2001.

Poirier, Richard. *The Performing Self*. 1972. New Brunswick, N.J.: Rutgers University Press, 1992.

Pound, Ezra. "Others." *Little Review* 4, no. 11 (1918): 56–58.

Power, Kevin. "An Interview with George and Mary Oppen." *Montemora* 4 (1978): 187–203.

Price, Richard. "Basil Bunting and the Problem of Patronage." In *The Star You Steer By: Basil Bunting and British Modernism*, ed. James McGonigal and Richard Price, 89–108. Amsterdam: Rodopi, 2000.

Ransom, John Crowe. *The World's Body*. New York: Scribner, 1938.

Ransom, John Crowe, et al. *I'll Take My Stand*. New York: Harper's, 1930.

Redmond, John. "Interview with Paul Muldoon." *Thumbscrew* 4 (1996): 2–18.

Reiss, R. "Sixteen." *Little Review* 6, no. 2 (1998): 59.

Rexroth, Kenneth. "Disengagement: The Art of the Beat Generation." *New World Writing* 11 (1957): 29–41. Reprint, in Rexroth, *The World Outside the Window*, 41–57. New York: New Directions, 1987.

Rhino 39. "J. Alfred." On *American Youth Report*, by various artists. Bomp Records, 1982.

Rich, Adrienne. *Blood, Bread, and Poetry*. New York: Norton, 1986.

Rickard, John. *Australia: A Cultural History*. London: Longman, 1988.

Ricks, Christopher. *The Force of Poetry*. Oxford: Clarendon, 1984.

———. *Keats and Embarrassment*. Oxford: Clarendon, 1974.

Rilke, Ranier Maria. *Selected Poetry*. Trans. Stephen Mitchell. New York: Vintage, 1984.

Rimbaud, Arthur. *Rimbaud Complete*. Trans. and ed. Wyatt Mason. New York: Modern Library, 2002.

Rodriguez, Richard. "The Invention of Adolescence." Afterword to *Fast Forward: Growing Up in the Shadow of Hollywood*, by Lauren Greenfield, 124–26. New York, Knopf/Melcher, 1997.

Rosen, David. "The Lost Youth of Modern Poetry." *MLQ* 64, no. 4 (2003): 473–94.

Rosenfeld, Paul. *Port of New York*. 1924. Urbana, Ill.: University of Illinois Press, 1961.

———. "Randolph Bourne." *The Dial* 75 (1923): 545–60.

Rosenthal, M. L. "Streams of Tonality in Bunting's 'Briggflatts.'" In *Basil Bunting: Man and Poet*, ed. Carroll F. Terrell, 187–93. Orono, Maine: National Poetry Foundation, 1981.

Ross, Dorothy. *G. Stanley Hall: The Psychologist as Prophet*. Chicago: University of Chicago Press, 1972.

Ross, Kristin. *The Emergence of Social Space: Rimbaud and the Paris Commune*. Minneapolis: University of Minnesota Press, 1988.

———. "Rimbaud and the Resistance to Work." In *Rimbaud: Modern Critical Views*, ed. Harold Bloom, 195–223. New York: Chelsea House, 1988.

Rossen, Janice. *Philip Larkin*. Hempstead: Harvester Wheatsheaf, 1989.

Rossman, Michael. "Notes from the County Jail." *New York Review of Books*, February 15, 1968, 19–24.

Rowe. M.W. "Unreal Girls: Lesbian Fantasy in Early Larkin." In *New Larkins for Old: Critical Essays*, ed. James Booth, 79–96. New York: St. Martin's, 2000.

Rowe, Noel. *Modern Australian Poets*. Sydney: Sydney University Press, 1994.

Rukeyser, Muriel. *Collected Poems*. Ed. Janet E. Kaufman et al. Pittsburgh: University of Pittsburgh, 2005.

Saxton, Ruth O. Introduction to *The Girl: Constructions of the Girl in Contemporary Fiction by Women*, ed. Ruth Saxton, xi–xxix. New York: St. Martin's, 1998.

Schiller, Friedrich. *On the Naïve and Sentimental in Literature*. 1795. Trans. Helen Watanabe-O'Kelly. Manchester: Carcanet, 1981.

Schweik, Susan. *A Gulf So Deeply Cut: American Women Poets and the Second World War*. Madison: University of Wisconsin Press, 1991.

Seevak, Alison. "Adolescence." *Many Mountains Moving* 4, no. 3 (2001): 125.

Sexton, Anne. *Transformations*. 1971. Boston: Houghton Mifflin, 2001.

Shapiro, Karl. *The Bourgeois Poet*. New York: Random House, 1964.

———. *Collected Poems, 1940–1978*. New York: Random House, 1978.

———. *The Poetry Wreck: Selected Essays, 1950–1970*. New York: Random House, 1975.

Shaughnessy, Brenda. *Interior with Sudden Joy*. New York: Farrar, Straus and Giroux, 1999.

Shoptaw, John. *On the Outside Looking Out: John Ashbery's Poetry*. Cambridge, Mass.: Harvard University Press, 1994.

Smith, Barbara Herrnstein. *Poetic Closure*. Chicago: University of Chicago Press, 1968.

Smith, Bruce R. *Homosexual Desire in Shakespeare's England*. Chicago: University of Chicago Press, 1991.

Smith, Dave. *Fate's Kite*. Baton Rouge: Louisiana State University, 1995.

Smith, Steven R. "The London Apprentices as Seventeenth-Century Adolescents." *Past and Present* 61 (1973): 149–61.

Snodgrass, W.D. *Not for Specialists: New and Selected Poems*. Rochester, N.Y.: BOA, 2006.

Sorby, Angela. *Distance Learning*. Kalamazoo: New Issues/Western Michigan University Press, 1998.

———. *Schoolroom Poets: Childhood, Performance, and the Place of American Poetry, 1865–1917*. Portsmouth, N.H.: University of New Hampshire Press, 2005.

Southworth, James. *Sowing the Spring: Studies in British Poets from Hopkins to MacNeice.* 1940. Freeport, N.Y.: Books for Libraries, 1968.

Spacks, Patricia Meyer. *The Adolescent Idea: Myths of Youth and the Adult Imagination*. New York: Basic Books, 1981.

Spender, Stephen. *Letters to Christopher*. Ed. Lee Bartlett. Santa Barbara, Ca.: Black Sparrow, 1980.

———. *Poems*. New York: Random House, 1930.

———, ed. *W. H. Auden: A Tribute*. New York: Macmillan, 1975.

———. *The Year of the Young Rebels*. New York: Random House, 1969.

Spenser, Edmund. *Complete Poetical Works*. Ed. R. E. N. Dodge. Boston: Houghton Mifflin, 1908.

Spiegelman. Willard. "Walllace Stevens' 'Second Selves' and the Nostalgia of Discursiveness." *Wallace Stevens Journal* 24, no. 2 (2000): 176–86.

Springhall, John. *Coming of Age: Adolescence in Britain, 1860–1960*. Dublin: Gill and Macmillan, 1986.

Stabler, Jane. "Alive in the Midst of Questions: A Survey of the Poetry of Paul Muldoon." *Verse* 8, no. 2 (1991): 52–61.

Stafford, William. "Juke Joint." *Poetry* 75, no. 4 (1950): 259.

Steedman, Carolyn. *Strange Dislocations: Children and the Idea of Human Interiority, 1780–1930*. London: Virago, 1995.

Stein, Kevin. *Private Poets, Worldly Acts*. Athens: Ohio University Press, 1996.

Steinman, Lisa. "William Carlos Williams: *Spring and All*." In *A Companion to Twentieth-Century Poetry*, ed. Neil Roberts, 403–13. Oxford: Blackwell, 2001.

Stevens, Holly. *Souvenirs and Prophecies: The Young Wallace Stevens*. New York: Knopf, 1977.

Stevens, Wallace. *Collected Poetry and Prose*. Ed. Frank Kermode and Joan Richardson. New York: Library of America, 1997.

Strobel, Marion. "Middle-Aged Adolescence." *Poetry* 23, no. 2 (November 1923): 103–5. Reprint, in *William Carlos Williams: The Critical Heritage*, ed. Charles Doyle, 75–76. London: Routledge, 1980.

Swarbrick, Andrew. *Out of Reach: The Poetry of Philip Larkin*. London: Macmillan, 1995.

Swiss, Thomas. "Poetry and Pop." *Popular Music* 15, no. 2 (1994): 233–40. Reprint, at http://bailiwick.lib.uiowa.edu/swiss/poetry+pop/poetry+pop.html. Viewed January 8, 2007.

Tanner, Tony. *The Reign of Wonder*. Cambridge: Cambridge University Press, 1965.

Tate, Claudia. "Anger So Flat: Gwendolyn Brooks' *Annie Allen*." In *A Life Distilled: Gwendolyn Brooks, Her Poetry and Fiction*, ed. Maria K. Mootry and Gary Smith, 140–52. Urbana: University of Illinois Press, 1987.

Taylor, Andrew. "Resisting the Mad Professor: Narrative and Metaphor in the Poetry of John Tranter." *Journal of Narrative Technique* 21, no. 1 (1991): 14–23. Reprint, at http://johntranter.com/reviewed/1990taylor-a.php. Viewed January 8, 2007.

Taylor, Charles. *Sources of the Self*. Cambridge, Mass.: Harvard University Press, 1989.

Terrell, Carroll F., ed. *Basil Bunting: Man and Poet*. Orono, Maine: National Poetry Foundation, 1981.

Theado, Matt, ed. *The Beats: A Literary Reference*. New York: Carroll and Graf, 2001.

Thwaite, Anthony, ed. *Larkin at Sixty*. London: Faber and Faber, 1982.

Tranter, John, ed. *The New Australian Poetry*. Newcastle-upon-Tyne: Bloodaxe, 1979.

———. *Studio Moon*. Cambridge: Salt, 2003.

———. *Trio*. Cambridge: Salt, 2003.

———. *Under Berlin*. St. Lucia: University of Queensland Press, 1988.

Travisano, Thomas. *Mid-Century Quartet*. Charlottesville: University Press of Virginia, 1999.

Trow, George W.S. *Within the Context of No Context*. 1980. Boston: Atlantic Monthly Press, 1997.

Van Deburg, William L. *New Day in Babylon: The Black Power Movement and American Culture, 1965–1975*. Chicago: University of Chicago Press, 1992.

Van Doren, Carl. "Youth and Wings: Edna St. Vincent Millay, Singer." 1924. Reprint, in *Critical Essays on Edna St. Vincent Millay*, ed. William B. Thesing, 121–28. Boston: G.K. Hall, 1993.

Vendler, Helen. *Coming of Age as a Poet*. Cambridge, Mass.: Harvard University Press, 2003.

———. *The Given and the Made*. Cambridge, Mass.: Harvard University Press, 1995.

———. "Indigo, Cyan, Beryl." *London Review of Books*, January 23, 2003, 13–16.

———. "Lowell in the Classroom." *Harvard Advocate* 113 (November 1979): 22–29.

———. *Part of Nature, Part of Us*. Cambridge, Mass.: Harvard University Press, 1980.

Wagner, Linda Welshimer. *Phyllis McGinley*. New York: Twayne, 1971.

Waldner, Liz. *Dark Would (the missing person)*. Athens: University of Georgia Press, 2002.

———. *Homing Devices*. Oakland, Calif.: O Books, 1998.

———. *Saving the Appearances*. Boise, Idaho: Ahsahta, 2005.

———. *Self and Simulacra*. Farmington, Maine: Alice James, 2001.

[Walsh, Ernest.] "A Young Living Genius." *This Quarter* 1, no. 2 (1925): 322–39.

Wasley, Aidan. "The 'Gay Apprentice': Ashbery, Auden, and a Portrait of the Artist as a Young Critic." *Contemporary Literature* 43, no. 4 (2002): 667–708.

Weaver, Mike. *William Carlos Williams: The American Background*. Cambridge: Cambridge University Press, 1971.

Weinstein, Deena. "Rock: Youth and Its Music." In *If It's Too Loud You're Too Old: Adolescents and Their Music*, ed. Jonathan Epstein, 3–23. New York: Garland, 1994.

Wellbery, David. *A New History of German Literature*. Cambridge, Mass.: Harvard University Press, 2004.

West, Elliott. *Growing Up in Twentieth-Century America: A History and Reference Guide*. Westport, Conn.: Greenwood Press, 1996.

White, Barbara. *Growing Up Female: Adolescent Girlhood in American Fiction*. Westport, Conn.: Greenwood, 1985.

White, Emily. *Fast Girls: Teenage Tribes and the Myth of the Slut*. New York: Scribner, 2002.

White, Kevin. *The First Sexual Revolution: The Emergence of Male Heterosexuality in Modern America*. New York: New York University Press, 1993.

White, Michael. "An Interview with Larry Levis." In *A Condition of the Spirit: The Life and Work of Larry Levis*, ed. Christopher Buckley and Alexander Long, 265–83. Spokane: Eastern Washington University Press, 2004.

Whitman, Walt. "Walt Whitman and His Poems." In Francis Murphy, ed. *Walt Whitman: A Critical Anthology*. Harmondsworth, Middlesex: Penguin, 1969. 29–37.

Wideman, John Edgar. *Hoop Roots*. New York: Houghton Mifflin, 2001.

Widmer, Edward. *Young America: The Flowering of Democracy in New York City*. New York: Oxford University Press, 1999.

[Williams, William Carlos.] "Belly Music." *Others* 5, no. 6 (1919): 25–32.

Williams, William Carlos. *Collected Poems, Vol. I: 1909–1939*. 1986. Third ed. Ed. A. Walton Litz and Christopher MacGowan. New York: New Directions, 1995.

———. "Critical Note." *Contact* 5 (1923): n.p.

———. "Gloria!" *Others* 5, no. 6 (1919): 3–4.

———. *Imaginations*. New York: Norton, 1970.

———. "Yours, O Youth." *Contact* 3 (1922): 14–16.

Williamson, Alan. *Pity the Monsters: The Political Vision of Robert Lowell*. New Haven, Conn.: Yale University Press, 1974.

Wills, Clair. *Reading Paul Muldoon*. Newcastle-upon-Tyne: Bloodaxe, 1998.

Wilson, William A. "Paul Muldoon and the Poetics of Sexual Difference." *Contemporary Literature* 28, no. 3 (1997): 317–31.

Wiman, Christian. "Free of Our Humbug." *New Criterion* (April 2004): 38–42.

Wojahn, David. *Mystery Train*. Pittsburgh: University of Pittsburgh Press, 1990.

———. *Strange Good Fortune: Essays on Contemporary Poetry*. Fayetteville: University of Arkansas Press, 2001.

Woods, Gregory. *Articulate Flesh: Male Homoeroticism and Modern Poetry*. New Haven, Conn.: Yale University Press, 1987.

Wordsworth, William. *The Prelude: The Four Texts*. Ed. Jonathan Wordsworth. New York: Penguin, 1995.

Wright, C.D. *Tremble*. Hopewell, N.J.: Ecco, 1997.

Wright, James. *Above the River: The Complete Poems*. New York and Middletown, Conn.: Noonday and Wesleyan University Press, 1992.

Yeats, W.B. *The Poems: Collected Works*, Vol. 1. Rev. ed. Ed. Richard J. Finneran. New York: Macmillan, 1989.

Yeh, Jane. *Marabou*. Manchester: Carcanet, 2005.

Yenser, Stephen. *Circle to Circle: The Poetry of Robert Lowell*. Berkeley: University of California Press, 1975.

Zalewski, Daniel. "Infantilized Adults." *New York Times Magazine*, December 9, 2001, 79.

Zucker, Rachel. *Eating in the Underworld*. Middletown, Conn.: Wesleyan University Press, 2003.

Acknowledgments

All reasonable efforts have been made to ascertain the holders of rights in poems or parts thereof reprinted here at lengths which exceed fair use. Copyright holders whom we have failed to reach in a timely fashion should contact the Press at their earliest convenience so that appropriate arrangements can be made. We are happy to acknowledge the following:

Poems by Liz Waldner reprinted with permission from SAVING THE APPEARANCES by Liz Waldner, Ahsahta Press, 2004. Laura Kasischke, excerpts from "Impressions on Wax Tablets" and "Sacred Flower" from GARDENING IN THE DARK. Copyright © 2004 by Laura Kasischke. Reprinted with the permission of Ausable Press, www.ausablepress.org. Poems and parts thereof by Basil Bunting from COMPLETE POEMS (Bloodaxe Books, 2000) appear by permission of Bloodaxe Books. Lines from Gwendolyn Brooks: Reprinted by consent of Brooks Permissions. Poems by William Carlos Williams, George Oppen and Jorie Graham appear by kind permission of Carcanet Press. Poems and parts thereof by Marianne Moore, Philip Larkin, Thom Gunn, and Paul Muldoon appear by permission of Faber and Faber. "Because sap fell away" and "Summer quickens grass" Copyright © 1994 by the Estate of W. H. Auden (both poems). Reprinted by permission of Curtis Brown, Ltd. Poems by Laura Kasischke reprinted from HOUSEKEEPING IN A DREAM by permission of Carnegie Mellon University Press © 1995 by Laura Kasischke. Reprinted by permission of Farrar, Straus and Giroux, LLC. Excerpts from COLLECTED POEMS by Thom Gunn. Copyright © 1994 by Thom Gunn. Excerpts from COLLECTED POEMS by Philip Larkin. Copyright © 1988, 1989 by the Estate of Philip Larkin. Excerpts from COLLECTED POEMS by Robert Lowell. Copyright © 2003 by Harriet Lowell and Sheridan Lowell. Excerpts from NOTEBOOK: Revised and expanded edition by Robert Lowell. Copyright © 1967, 1968, 1969, 1970 by Robert Lowell, copyright renewed 1998 by Harriet Lowell. Selections from POEMS 1968–1998 by Paul Muldoon. Copyright © 2001 by Paul Muldoon. Thirty-one lines from "Fission," seventeen lines from "The Hiding Place" and nine lines from "Region" from REGION OF UNLIKENESS by JORIE GRAHAM. Copyright © 1991 by Jorie Graham. Reprinted by permission of HarperCollins Publishers. Eight lines from "A Parking Lot with Trees" and sixteen lines from "Falling Water," as specified, from NORTH

POINT NORTH: NEW AND SELECTED POEMS by John Koethe. Copyright © 2002 by John Koethe. Reprinted by permission of HarperCollins Publishers. Six lines from "When I Was Bout Ten We Didn't Play Baseball" from SMALL CONGREGATIONS: NEW AND SELECTED POEMS by THYLIAS MOSS. Copyright © 1983, 1990, 1991, 1993 by Thylias Moss. Reprinted by permission of HarperCollins Publishers. "Some San Francisco Poems," "Exodus": By George Oppen, from COLLECTED POEMS, copyright © 1972 by George Oppen. Reprinted by permission of New Directions Publishing Corp. "A Language of New York," "Pedestrian": By George Oppen, from COLLECTED POEMS, copyright © 1975 by George Oppen. Reprinted by permission of New Directions Publishing Corp. "The Students Gather," "A Modern Incident," "The New People": By George Oppen, from NEW COLLECTED POEMS, copyright © 1968 by George Oppen. Reprinted by permission of New Directions Publishing Corp. "Spring and All," "The Descent of Winter": By William Carlos Williams, from COLLECTED POEMS: 1909–1939, VOLUME I, copyright © 1938 by New Directions Publishing Corp. Reprinted by permission of New Directions Publishing Corp. Poems by Angela Sorby from DISTANCE LEARNING, copyright © 1998 by Angela Sorby. Reprinted by permission of New Issues Poetry and Prose. "Landscape Without Figures," "A Certain Age," copyright © 1956 by Phyllis McGinley, "Portrait of Girl with Comic Book," copyright 1952 by Phyllis McGinley, from TIMES THREE by Phyllis McGinley, copyright 1932–1960 by Phyllis McGinley; Copyright 1938–42, 1944, 1945, 1958, 1959 by The Curtis Publishing Co. Used by permission of Viking Penguin, a division of Penguin Group (USA) Inc. "Never Stronger," copyright 1934 and copyright renewed 1972 by W. H. Auden, from COLLECTED POEMS by W.H. Auden. Used by permission of Random House, Inc. "Adolescence" by Nin Andrews appears by permission of Rodger Moody and Silverfish Review Press. Lines from "The Steeple-Jack" and "The Hero" by Marianne Moore: Reprinted with the permission of Scribner, an imprint of Simon & Schuster Adult Publishing Group, from COLLECTED POEMS by Marianne Moore. Copyright © 1935 by Marianne Moore; copyright renewed © 1963 by Marianne Moore & T. S. Eliot. All rights reserved. Lines from "The Student": Reprinted with the permission of Scribner, an imprint of Simon & Schuster Adult Publishing Group, from COLLECTED POEMS by Marianne Moore. Copyright © 1941 by Marianne Moore, copyright renewed © 1969 by Marianne Moore. All rights reserved. Poems by John Tranter appear by kind permission of John Tranter. Fifteen lines reprinted by permission of The University of Massachusetts Press from DANCE & DISAPPEAR by Laura Kasischke copyright © 2002 by Laura Kasischke. Excerpts from "In 1967" from ELEGY, by Larry Levis, © 1997. Reprinted by permission of the University of Pittsburgh Press. Poems by Yusef Komunyakaa from PLEASURE DOME (Wesleyan University Press, 2001). © 2001 by Yusef Komunyakaa and reprinted by permission of Wesleyan University Press.

Index